Atlas
of the
Human
Heart

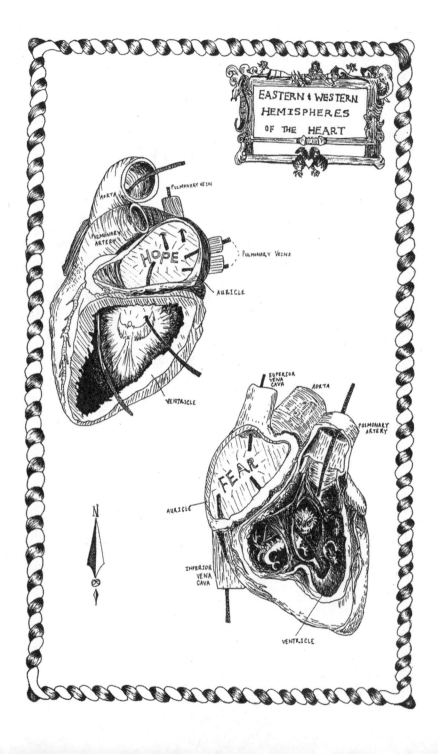

Atlas

of the

Human

Heart

ARIEL GORE

Seal Press

Atlas of the Human Heart
© 2003 by Ariel Gore
Published by
Seal Press
An Imprint of Avalon Publishing Group Incorporated
161 William St., 16th Floor
New York, NY 10038

Grateful acknowledgment is made to the following publishers for the right to excerpt material:

Farrar, Straus and Giroux, for the excerpt from *The Journey to the East* by Hermann Hesse, English translation by Hilda Rosner, copyright © 1956; Harcourt for the excerpt from *The Little Prince* by Antoine de Saint-Exupery, English translation by Katherine Woods, copyright © 1943, Harcourt, Brace, and Company, Inc. and the excerpt from *Invisible Cities* by Italo Calvino, English translation by William Weaver, copyright © 1974, Harcourt. Inc.

Library of Congress Cataloging-in-Publication Data

ISBN 1-58005-088-3

9 8 7 6 5 4 3 2 1

Map Illustrations by Maria Fabulosa
Designed by Paul Paddock
Printed in Canada
Distributed by Publishers Group West

CONTENTS

Prelude

They say that back back back, before I was born, people actually believed the stories they told themselves. This may be true, but no one can prove it.

I'll tell you where I came from: northern California. A peninsula surrounded by the sea. Water and more water. The second illegitimate daughter of intuition and paranoia. Tide pool hermit crab, fierce and private. Vulnerable belly. Destined for lifelong homelessness, squatting, outgrowing shells, searching for new ones, hitchhiking with anemones. Of the ocean, but terrestrial.

I was still an infant when my bio-dad realized he was cracking up. Maybe it was just the time, he told himself. He'd been trying to edit the Merry Pranksters' bus trip video, but there was nothing in it worth saving. My sister's birth had coincided neatly with the "hippie funeral" in Golden Gate Park. And now Hendrix and Joplin. The Manson trial just heating up. Genocide and rumors of genocide. Everything that wasn't dead seemed crazy. Or maybe it was the place. The Monterey Peninsula with its high levels of seismic activity and thick fog of memories. The time and the place. There's always hoping, anyway. So my bio-dad packed us up—two kids and common-law wife—and we spent long months chasing sanity from California to Devon, England; Devon, England, to central London; central London to Amsterdam; Amsterdam to Montparnasse; Montparnasse to the French countryside, where my bio-dad decided that my mother was an Iranian spy and locked us all in a little stone house until I learned to walk and talk and my sister learned to count in French and my bio-dad gave up on his runaway sanity and my mother gave up on him and we escaped—flew home to California.

That's what I'm told, anyway. And the pretty green and blue entrance and exit visas stamped in my baby passport would tend to substantiate the story.

Stories. Patterns from scraps.

This one's a work of fiction, meaning it's about 76 percent true.

Or it's a memoir, meaning it's about 76 percent false.

Maybe it should have been a Choose Your Own Adventure book: You're Little Red Riding-Hood. You can't see the forest through the trees (no one can). You have some cookies and you have some wine. You're wearing your red velvet cape. Of course you are. It's your favorite. You wear it everywhere you go. You're walking and you're singing and you're thinking of your grandmother when suddenly . . . What's it going to be? A wolf? A missed connection? An unexpected massacre? Maybe it'll be your own madness jumping out in front of you on that dusty trail. Or god. Maybe it'll be that damned old woman, sneaky-wise with her famous red apple—the one you know you should refuse. It's knowledge or it's poison. But you can't help it, can you? (You're still immortal at this point.) You reach for it. And what happens next? From here, it's all possibilities. . . .

Part I
Heartbeat

In an average lifetime, the heart beats
more than two and a half billion times.

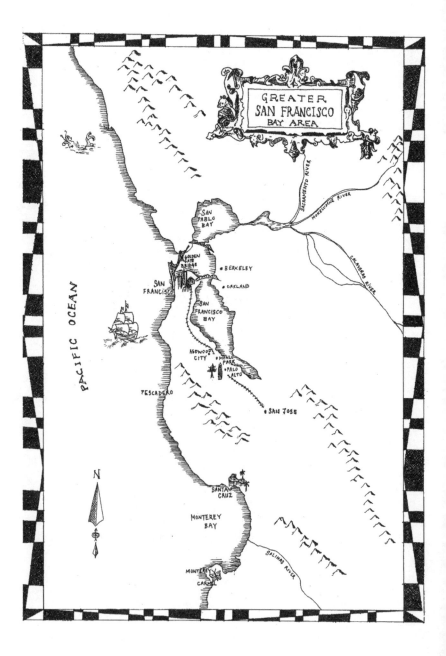

Palo Alto High School

We begin with a setting. Somewhere to run from.

The cool thing about Palo Alto High School: There really was a place for everyone. And finding your place was pretty simple once you understood the rules. You could get a map of the campus from the guidance office and start to plot your place by drawing three concentric circles radiating out from the quad to the streets and then calculating your family's annual income. If the figure was over one hundred thousand dollars, your starting point was in the center. Under twenty-five thousand dollars, the outskirts.

Once you found your starting point, you considered the other circumstances of your life. If you or either one of your parents were queer or crazy, or had AIDS, you moved one circle out from your starting point. If you'd ever been to juvie, or if you played in a punk band, you moved a circle out. If you came to school with visible bruises, or if you started smoking pot before the seventh grade, you moved a circle out. If everything in the world looked dead to you, or if Led Zeppelin lyrics were your main spiritual text, you moved a circle out. And if you were noticeably ugly, or pregnant, you moved two circles out. This was the way everyone eventually found their place. A handful of characters seemed to break the rules, of course, but a few carefully posed questions would reveal the justification for their transgression. Either they had a summer modeling contract in Tokyo (in one circle), their dad had just been convicted of rape (out one circle), or they were dealing coke (automatic central quad placement).

Once you determined your distance from the center, the only thing left to figure out was which direction you had to walk from the center in order to find your place. The further you went from the quad, the further you had to travel from the cafeteria every day with your hot dog and Fudgesicle, but the more possibilities there were in terms of who you were going to hang out with. If you were college-bound, even on scholarship, you went north. If you listened to heavy metal, you went south. Student government members and wannabe student government members went west. Those who'd rather overthrow the student government went east.

After all this plotting and walking you'd find your place, take a look around.

In the center you'd be surrounded by magazine-quality people with silicone tits and silicon dads, and you could buy coke without even standing up.

Midrange you'd find the thespians, the exchange students, the imperfect cheerleaders, the student council members, the future English majors, the chess club guys. The drug supply in the middle was never stable, but there you'd learn the difference between French and espresso roast and you might even get invited to a wine tasting in somebody's mother's basement.

On the outskirts there was plenty of room for the art geeks, the tortured poets, the sexually ambiguous, the punks, the goths, the skinheads, the smokers, the sweatshop workers, the Marxists, the pregnant girls, the rockers, the people of color who were neither wealthy nor sporty, and me. Any drug that was sold in five- and ten-dollar bags could be found out there. Freshman year, I sat just inside the northeastern rim of the outer circle, where "Do it so it feels real" had been stenciled on the curb and "Eat, Buy, Consume, Die" had been spray painted on the walkway. My place was between the punks and the tortured poets, both of whom had staked out coveted spots nearest the hole in the chainlink fence and the gravel path that led to the train tracks along the eastern edge of campus—just in case any one of us ever had to suicide during lunch hour.

Downtown Train

I fell for Guy in the heat of Indian summer, next to the train tracks a mile from campus, under the tallest tree. I fell soft and sudden, like night. We were lying on our stomachs, side by side, on a tiny patch of dry grass next to the rails, arms tight at our sides, heads turned to face each other.

"Close your eyes," Guy whispered. He was slightly hung-over.

I closed one eye, kept the other fixed on his soft, brown face.

"Pretend we're right on the tracks." He wrinkled his nose, listened at the ground. "I can already hear it. Where do you think it is?"

I pressed my ear to the dirt. "Redwood City? Menlo Park at the closest."

"Yeah, maybe Menlo Park."

I wanted to reach over and touch Guy's face, run my finger over the pimples where he'd shaved.

Shhh . . . a low rumbling sound deep in the earth like plates shifting underground. *Shhh* . . . The train sounded its somber, moaning horn.

"Just breathe," Guy said.

One.

Two.

Three.

"Now your last breath." His broad shoulders rose slightly as his lungs filled with the dusty air.

I inhaled like this was it. "For real," I whispered. And my whole body vibrated with the percussion of the train barreling toward us, toward the Southern Pacific station, over the San Francisquito creek bridge—*ch clack ch clack ch clack.*

Guy grimaced, arched his back in anticipation of the full speed full weight full impact of the iron wheels that would rip through his long body.

I closed both eyes tight now, a searing pain starting at the crown of my head as it sped through us, sped past us.

One.

Two.

Three.

Exhale.

Guy rolled over onto his back. "That's so intense." He gazed up the trunk of the giant twin redwood.

I wanted to stay there, just like that forever, watching Guy in the late-September light as he stared upward like some ancient bronze statue.

"Every time I do that it's like I start over," he said. "I get a whole new life."

My mother had the habit of taking in stray children, so that night I was sharing my room with a curly-haired blond girl named Feral.

"I cannot *believe* you didn't kiss him." She sat at the foot of my double bed, dumbfounded, placed her hand dramatically over her heart. Her wild ringlets gleamed like phosphorescent seaweed in the dim glow from the streetlight outside my open window.

It hadn't occurred to me to kiss him. I just wanted him to stay there, perfectly still. I wanted to watch him. I wanted to trace the line of his jaw with my index finger.

See, I'd had this crush on Guy since I'd first laid eyes on

him—leaning against a pillar outside my English class, wearing a black and red silk-screened Free Nelson Mandela T-shirt, daydreaming. The other boys buzzed around him, go-getters after girls, grades, goals. He was still as a Buddha, lanky and beautiful.

I was a sophomore now, fifteen years old, just getting back into the dull rhythm of high school after a long, slow summer in Botswana, where I'd visited an elementary school friend, Rosa. She'd moved after seventh grade when her mom took a job with the World Health Organization. The two of us wandered dusty shopping malls in Gaborone, talked about the way things were when we were little kids, prayed when her boyfriend took his Camero drag racing on the dirt roads, danced at Club X. With her mom, we visited Victoria Falls, traveled through southern Zimbabwe, moving only in the hot, clear light of day, seeking shelter as darkness fell so as to avoid being caught in the crossfire of a nighttime civil war we didn't understand.

I'd come home in early September to find my few friends freshly dispersed. Sid had moved to New York for art school. And Veda was off for a dad-year in Key West (she wanted to spend some time with the old man before he got too sick—it wasn't full-blown AIDS yet). My sister had moved out while I was gone, into a studio apartment filled with quartz crystals in San Francisco's Tenderloin. And my Chinese-language tutor— back to Suzhou. When I was alone, I put on my Walkman and listened to the Mandarin tapes he'd left me from the Beijing Language Institute. I paged through *National Geographic* picture books of communist China, vaguely dreamed of running away. Pretty watercolor letters arrived in the mail from Sid and Veda. I sucked the color from the pages, but the paint tasted like loneliness. I never went out.

When Feral's mother came to my stepdad for spiritual counseling on Labor Day and left without her daughter, the girl made herself at home in my room. She wanted to know *every-thing* about my love life. There wasn't anything to tell, so I described the tall boy to her.

"Is he black?"

"Yeah. I guess so. Or mixed."

"I know the one you mean. He plays bass for the Naked Eskimos. I think he's a junior."

So I'd asked around when school started: Who knew where the Naked Eskimos played? But no one knew. Maybe they didn't play anywhere—just one of those bands that practiced a lot.

But on a Saturday night at quarter to midnight the red telephone next to my bed rang and woke me. I answered it in my half-sleep.

"He's *here!*" Veda's friend Jack squealed into the phone.

"Who's where?" I rubbed my eyes, turned on my porcelain bedside lamp.

"The tall kid from the Naked Eskimos. Listen, we're at this party near the creek, he's drunk but you *have* to come. Ariel, do you understand? You *have* to come."

"Yeah. All right. I'll be over in a little bit." I pulled back my gray flannel sheets, crawled out of bed, wrestled on a pair of black Levi's from the floor. I realized they were Feral's when I had trouble buttoning them. *Whatever.* Feral wasn't home yet. I put a bra on under my sleep shirt, tied my hair back with a red rubber band, slipped silently out my bedroom window.

Two miles to the party house. I didn't know who lived there, but I could hear Tom Waits thundering out an upstairs window. I hid my blue one-speed in a cherry bush in the backyard.

Jack met me on the porch. "Oh my *god*, Ariel! I'm *totally* sorry. Guy is, like, *way* more out of it than I realized." Jack bounced up and down a little as he talked. "I shouldn't have *even* gotten you out of bed. I am *such* a loser. I just saw him and I was like, *That's him that's him that's him*! I *have* to call Ariel."

I rubbed my eyes. "It's OK. I'm here now anyway."

Jack led me into the old Victorian where Guy sat crouched at the dining room table, face in his hands. I pulled a chair up next to him. "Are you OK, man?" My throat felt hot. I'd never spoken to him before.

"No," he groaned, not looking up.

"I can call Safe Ride," I offered—Palo Alto's free taxi service for drunken teenagers.

"My bike," Guy grumbled.

"If I ride your bike for you, can you walk home?"

"No." He sounded like a very old man. "I'm so stupid."

"Listen, don't worry about it. I'll call Safe Ride. I'll deal with your bike. You just have to go home and sleep it off, you know?"

"He's right, he shouldn't leave that bike here," Jack whispered as we walked Guy outside.

The awkward way that Guy moved, like he hadn't yet grown into his six-foot-plus frame, was exaggerated in his drunken state.

"I'll have your bike for you," I promised as he ducked into the back seat of the white Toyota.

"*Oh my god*! I'm *so* sorry. That was *so* lame," Jack pushed back his dyed black hair.

"Don't worry about it." Jack didn't seem to understand what a score the bike was. "Thanks for calling me."

Jack wore eyeliner and tight black jeans, listened to Madonna obsessively. He went to Catholic school, so I didn't know where Veda had met him or where he'd heard I was interested in Guy. At a party on both counts, probably. Jack never missed a house party. He was usually the beer runner, particularly skilled in convincing Stanford students to buy alcohol for him at a minimal markup. "I am *so* not gay," Jack hissed, changing the subject. "Some jerk in there just *totally* called me a fag. That is *so gross.*"

"Who gives a fuck about that jerk?" I climbed on my bike. "Just tell him you're Madonna."

Jack laughed.

I rode off, steering my own bike with one hand and dragging Guy's brand-new ten-speed next to me.

"I'm Madonna!" Jack yelled after me.

In the platinum light of Sunday noon, Guy appeared sleepy-eyed on my doorstep. The house was empty except for Feral, who must have crept in after I'd fallen asleep and crashed out with a blanket on the floor. My parents were still at church, where my stepdad, John, gave Mass every Sunday to a motley mix of recovering Catholics. I blushed when I saw Guy standing there, head bent and hung-over. Surely he knew what a stalker maneuver I'd pulled, kidnapping his bike at midnight as Safe Ride whisked him away. But he was too grateful to be suspicious. "Thank you so much." He held up his large hands. "I'm so embarrassed."

I felt slightly nauseous. "How did you know where I lived?"

"I had to call that obnoxious kid, Jack."

I stepped outside, led Guy along the stone path that curved around the side of our narrow Spanish house, under the Australian tea tree, into the garage where I'd stashed the silver bike.

"Hey . . ." He grabbed the curved handlebars, eyes fixed on the cement floor. "I was just gonna go get some juice and chill someplace. You wanna come?"

One.

Two.

Three.

Inhale.

Do You Know Me?

N o one will ever understand you, Ariel," my mother said. "You are the last introvert in a world of extroverts." She was notably depressed that fall, had just been fired from her job teaching art on death row at San Quentin because she refused to wear a bulletproof vest and had gotten "too close" to the inmates. "They're so cute," she'd smile, then narrow her dark eyes, lower her voice to a raspy whisper: "They've been screwed by the system." She spent late hours in the candle-lit living room, rocking herself back and forth in her great pine chair, listening to Bette Midler sing "The Rose."

Every life-movie has its soundtrack.

John made dinners from his thick *Fannie Farmer Cookbook*, but left the house in the evenings on his ancient one-speed, carrying a satchel full of colored notebooks. He was working with an editor to harvest an autobiography from his meticulous journals—the story of a former Stanford chaplain, excommunicated from the Catholic Church after thirty years in the priesthood for marrying my mother when I was in kindergarten.

But I didn't pay much attention to my parents. I'd been fired from my own job at the Lick Me frozen yogurt stand for refusing to blow my boss and for insisting on calling him "Creepy Bob" instead of the simple "Bob" he preferred. I don't think my parents noticed when I stopped coming home for dinner.

I went to school in the mornings and met up with Guy in the afternoons. We smoked pot, wandered up and down University Avenue, went to anti-apartheid rallies on the Stanford campus, ate burritos, listened to Run-D.M.C. in his attic room.

When he walked me home late evenings along Byron Street or Hawthorne, police in passing patrol cars shined their spotlights on us. "I've never been checked out by so many pigs in my life," I laughed. But when I saw the look on Guy's face, I felt like an idiot. The *why* of the sudden scrutiny hadn't occurred to me.

"Sometimes it sucks to be black," he said softly.

In the dark of my room, Feral grilled me for titillating details. "You have *got* to be kidding," she sighed when I offered nothing. She sat at the edge of my bed, then, hands fluttering, and described her freshman affair with a pickpocket named Wolf. "It's why my mother threw me out," she half-sighed. "More like *dragged*. She had me by the hair. It's *so* cool that your mom doesn't make any of our business her own, you know?"

So cool. In my mother's eyes, all the other parents in Palo Alto were overprotective, their children woefully unprepared to spread their wings and fly away. If nothing else, my mother's children would learn self-reliance. I smiled.

Feral's eyes shone like she was on some mythical drug. She looked ageless, like a mermaid. I knew that one night I'd come home and she just wouldn't be there. She'd have swum away. "*Oh my god*, did I already tell you about Terrance? He's my new squeeze."

That night in dream, I walked a dry riverbed, hot sun on my bare shoulders. Around a bend, I spotted a toothless and wrinkled woman. Hunched over, digging in the red earth like an anthropologist.

"Whatcha lookin' for?" I wanted to know.

"Bones," she hummed.

With each beat, the heart pumps nearly three ounces of blood into the arteries—seventy-five to ninety gallons an hour when the body is at rest.

Guy turned sixteen in October, got his license. He came tapping at my bedroom window, 10 P.M.

"*Oh my god oh my god oh my god!*" Feral bounced up and down on the bed.

I grabbed the *Rain Dogs* tape I'd bought Guy for his birthday and forgotten to wrap.

"Do you need the room to yourself tonight?" Feral bit her lip. "Oh my god!"

"No." I climbed out the window, careful not to trip on the gardening bench that served as my stepladder. "See you later."

Guy shook his keys in the air like they were tickets to Disneyland.

I followed him out to the rust-colored '69 VW bug parked at the curb. "I've got it on indefinite loan from my parents. I guess it's mine until it blows up."

I concentrated on Guy as the car sputtered and spat along Embarcadero. I wanted to remember everything—the earnest way he held the steering wheel, the curl of his fingers, the squint of his dark eyes, the red and white Mexican blanket that covered the ripped upholstery on the passenger's side, the smell of mildew and weed, the way the night air hissed in through a gap in the closed driver's side window.

"This is so cool." I buckled the gray seat belt as we headed toward the Stanford campus.

Guy drove in circles around Angel Field, finally parked in

an empty lot. He turned off the ignition but left the headlights on, faced me like he was about to say something deep. He leaned in. His left eye wandered a little when he tried to focus.

I felt panicky. Maybe my logic was twisted, but here was my only clear thought: *What starts has to end.* "D'yawanna go to the beach?" I blurted out.

He pulled back, nervously ran his fingers through his loose Afro. "Um, OK—Pescadero?"

"Yeah." I gnawed on my lip.

We rumbled out of town, up over Skyline Boulevard, out along the winding highway through the redwoods, the VW's dim headlights illuminating just the two yards in front of us. We talked about immortality. Guy hunched over the wheel, watching intently for each twist in the road.

I rolled down my window. "Yes!" I yelled into the spin of dark scenery. The forest smelled sweet and cool, like life. The road turned. Sharp curves in the night.

When the salty air and smell of eucalyptus filled the car, I decided I'd been wrong when I told myself that everything had to end. *A wise traveler has no fixed plans and is not intent upon arriving,* Lao Tze said. How come I could only remember lines from unassigned readings? "Oh, hey—I got you this." I reached back to slip the Tom Waits tape into the boom box on the floor behind the emergency brake. Side two up, I pressed the rewind button. I wanted to hear "Blind Love" and "Downtown Train," the gravelly soundtrack I'd kidnapped Guy's bike to.

"Oh, cool, thanks. I don't have this."

Guy parked on the shoulder of Highway 1.

Outside, coastal winds raged. I grabbed the Mexican blanket from the passenger's seat.

"I think I have another one, too." Guy said, leaned into the back seat, produced a gray and blue poncho. He climbed down the steep trail to the beach, then turned back, held out his hand to help me down.

I hesitated, could feel my stomach tighten, exhaled, let him take my hand.

We sat close on the damp beach, blankets wrapped around us, looking out over the water toward the shadowy sea cliffs and a flickering lighthouse, trying to discern an invisible horizon in the indigo night.

"It was a good idea to come out here," Guy whispered, then leaned back onto the sand.

I curled up next to him as the waves crashed on the shore, one after another.

He closed his eyes.

I watched his face for a long time. His skin seemed to glow as if polished. His sweater smelled like dew. I reached over to touch his chin. He didn't move, so I leaned in, kissed him lightly on the cheek. I thought we were some otherworldly couple, shipwrecked survivors sleeping on the shore.

In Africa, I'd used a whole roll of film photographing a crimson sunset over the Kalahari. As that vast sky went dark, I'd told myself that Palo Alto would never be enough for me. My lovers would be the horizons. But now I wondered, hoped: Maybe Guy would hold me close, hold me down, hold me home.

"I guess we should go," he finally whispered. "It's a school night."

Back in my room, I found Feral thumbing through my thick yellow Wilhelm translation of the I Ching. She closed the book when I opened the window and climbed in. "I know, I know," she said. "Nothing happened?" She slipped the book under the bed.

I shrugged. "It's a school night."

❧

Since I'd started hanging out with Guy, I'd moved a half-circle in from my old post nearest the hole in the chainlink fence, lonely now that Sid and Veda were gone. And I went to class on time. Guy got straight A's in honors classes and believed that civilized people didn't smoke pot until *after* school, which for me was a revelation. I went to school on time—went at all—because of Guy, because I had nothing better to do, because Mr. Schellenberg's first-period creative writing class started at 8 A.M. sharp.

Schoolwork itself was easy. You know how some girls can talk to people and some can dance? I couldn't talk to people and I couldn't dance, but math seemed logical and I could churn out a five-page essay on a book I hadn't read in twenty minutes flat—two social studies papers during Spanish class if I had to. I was especially skilled at scoping out a teacher. I mean, was this someone who sincerely believed in memorization, or someone who secretly wanted her mind blown by a stoned teenage revelation? While reading thirty essays in a single sitting, was this the kind of teacher who wanted to be able to skim, pick out the pertinent elements he was testing for and move on, or did he want a cigarette break? Did he need an introduction, three body paragraphs and a conclusion, or did he long for a wild tale, free-associated from the original question? It's a good scam if you can pull it off, making A-minuses in high school without paying the slightest bit of attention. Notes on my progress reports: *Not working up to her potential. A good student when in attendance. Does not participate in class discussions.* Still, an A-minus is an A-minus is an A-minus.

The only wise guy to beat me at my own game: Mr. Schellenberg. He was short, wore faded jeans, talked through his gray beard even when none of us let on we were listening. On

17

the first day of class he said, "OK, everyone has an A in this class. No matter what you do, you have an A." And so, of course, I showed up every damn morning—on time and listening intently even as I feigned sleep. He kept his word, too, gave me an A. And his progress report note: *You are one of us.*

Guy usually sat with the Marxists at school, but he was the only kid I ever knew who could walk undaunted anywhere he pleased on that campus. I'd never met someone with righteous politics who seemed so undamaged. People tried to bug him, of course. Leroy, a rocker kid I'd gone out with for a few weeks freshman year, taunted him for being too "white." Cops and the occasional shopkeeper eyed him for being too black. But he wasn't like my other friends, he wasn't limping through it. Before I met Guy, I'd figured you had to be broken to be good—not ripped in half, but softly and cruelly broken. Like there was a little glass tube of compassion inside each of us. Halloween glow sticks. Dull and ignorant until some eager injustice grabbed us and snapped the tube and freed all that luminous liquid compassion to flow through our veins. Now I wondered if some people were just born alight.

Tuesdays and Thursdays, when Guy's friend Carl worked the cash register at the café in Town and Country Village shopping center across the street from school, we ate lunch there. Carl didn't make us pay for our French onion soup and lattes. He made up the difference in the till by overcharging the pinch-faced clueless bastard customers who wore buttons that said things like "Feed the Homeless to the Hungry." We were all mourning the slow death of our hometown. A whirlwind synthetic venom called silicon had spread through and contaminated the magnolia- and ginkgo-lined streets and alleys of our childhoods, transforming our hippie ghetto of broken-down boarding houses and old family fixer-uppers into a high-rent suburban wasteland of building permit lawsuits and computer debris. We were the new underclass in a town where falling-down buildings were demolished and replaced with new buildings painted to look like they were falling down. But who were we to complain about displacement? Settling other people's land is an American tradition. All of us suffering from a kind of economic and geographic attention deficit, not content to stay put and tend our own humble gardens.

"Why don't you just go back to Italy or someplace, then?" a central-quad girl hissed when I complained about the proposed installation of an historical plaque in front of an ivy-covered garage a block from my house. It would read: Birthplace of Silicon Valley.

"There goes the neighborhood," I'd muttered.

Carl charged the central-quad girl double for her nonfat decaf au lait and chocolate croissant.

Yeah, back to Italy, birthplace of my long-dead great-grandfather who'd left the homeland to join his cowboy cousins on the Tex-Mex border. I imagined I'd be damned welcome in Italy.

The quad girl flipped her stringy blond hair and walked out.

Carl wanted to talk about whether we should be anarchists instead of Marxists.

I suggested we toss a coin, but Carl and Guy just stared at me, not sure if I was kidding.

"Marxism doesn't have to be oppressive," Carl said, sitting down on the wooden stool behind the counter. He was white, a recent transplant from Toronto. "But it just so happens that all large-scale attempts at Marxism to date have gotten bogged down in their own authoritarianism."

Guy thought we could still be Marxists, or at least radical socialists. "How is the state going to take control of the means of production if there is no state?" He slurped the last of his French onion soup. "I'm not against having a state. I'm against having all these cops whose sole function is to perpetuate capitalism. They arrest two-bit drug dealers and sell their unpaid prison labor to corporate America. It's modern slavery."

Carl nodded. "And with anarchism, I guess the question we have to answer is, are most people basically good?"

"I think they are," Guy said.

Basically good. Walking back across the busy street toward campus, I tried to form an opinion on the matter. Basically good. I thought that people were basically assholes, but I wanted Guy to be right. Basically good.

Weekend nights we hung out at the New Varsity—an all-ages Mission Revival restaurant-bar-coffeehouse-concert-hall-movie-palace-last-holdout-of-old-Palo Alto where you could catch the Dead Kennedys or Tuck and Patti or *The Rocky Horror Picture Show*. The building swarmed with high school kids and punks and old hippies and rumpled Stanford students.

Guy and I sat upstairs, nursing milky coffees at a round wooden table as a balding folkie broke guitar strings onstage. Guy described a vivid dream where he climbed a stairway all night long—up, up, up to no place. I had a copy of *The Journey to the East* and read to him: *A similar thing has already happened to many other people. . . . Once in their youth the light shone for them; they saw the light and followed the star, but then came reason and the mockery of the world; then came faint-heartedness and apparent failure; then came weariness and disillusionment, and so they lost their way again, they became blind again. Some of them have spent the rest of their lives looking for us again, but could not find us.*

"That isn't going to happen to us, is it, Guy?"

He smiled, but didn't answer me.

A freshman high-school girl I'd seen smoking on the

northeastern rim of campus leaned on our table, giggling. "I'm
on acid." She smiled up at me. Her pupils were dime-sized,
green irises just an outline. "Do you know me?"

"No," I admitted. "Not unless you mean 'know you' in a
universal sort of way."

Bright flash from her eyes: "Know me in a universal sort
of way!"

People on acid were so easily delighted.

"In a past life I was an Amazon princess but Cortez slit my
throat," she laughed, throwing back her head to expose her
long, vulnerable neck. "My name is Harmony."

A skinny girl with translucent skin and dyed black hair
pulled Harmony away from the table. "Let's get out of here."
And they vanished like a hallucination.

Because Silence Frightens People

The rains came heavy that year and Guy's dad didn't want to give him the cash to rent a tuxedo for the winter formal. It wasn't so much a money thing. It was political. "That's such B.S.," Guy's dad said as he rinsed the dinner dishes. He was having a little bit of a midlife crisis because he'd ordered his FBI file under the Freedom of Information Act and discovered he was no longer worthy of surveillance. Guy described his usually aloof dad tearing through the house like a madman, cursing the last entry: *Married white woman, acquired professorship at Stanford, bought Subaru.*

"I mean, are *you* wearing a formal dress?" Guy's dad wanted to know. He was a slightly darker version of Guy, with a short, clipped beard.

"No," I admitted.

Guy glared at me.

"But, I mean, it's really fancy . . . what I'm wearing. It's—*like* formal."

"*Like* formal?"

"Stop it, Dad. It's formal," Guy pleaded. "She's just saying that because you're making her feel like a jerk. And the boys wear tuxedos, that's just what they do."

Guy's dad shrugged. "Sorry." He scratched his beard. "I don't know how you kids got to be so conservative."

Guy rolled his eyes, tugged at my elbow. As we headed upstairs to his attic room, he said, "Shit, do you think we're conservative?"

My grandmother sent me a hundred dollars as an early Christmas present, so in San Francisco I tried on black vintage dresses as my sister, Leslie, pulled me from shop to shop up and down Haight Street in the rain. Under an awning in front of the hologram shop, she bought a dime bag from a damp hippie kid who warned us that the CIA was trying to force all the pot dealers out of business with a drug called crack. "We're trying to organize a boycott." He squinted his stoner-red eyes. "I'm serious, man."

I finally settled on a white racer-back tank dress with black leather trim.

Leslie thought I should get a black beret to go with it, but I couldn't deal with a hat. "Oh well, it's really cute," she promised.

I spent the rest of the money on a shiny pair of combat boots from Buffalo Exchange.

Leslie sat down on a wooden bench to roll a joint. "You're fun to hang out with now, Ariel. You've kind of come out of your shell. You never used to talk. It was fully obnoxious."

What she said was true enough. The last introvert in a world of extroverts. Silence: my response to both emptiness and saturation. But silence frightens people. I had to learn how to talk. Out of politeness.

"Did you get hypnotherapy or something?" Leslie wanted to know. She was into all that—karmic cleansings and channeling dolphins and whatnot.

"No."

"Maybe you should try it. You might still have a blockage in your throat chakra."

I nodded. *Maybe.*

I took the Caltrain home, clutching my little plastic bag of *like* formalwear.

In my room, I slipped on the dress. I found my mother in

her studio out behind the house. I modeled for her, too excited.

She lowered her reading glasses onto her nose, looked me up and down. "Did you pay more than five dollars for that?"

"Yeah," I admitted. I'd paid sixty-eight.

"Well, that's a shame," she said, pushing her glasses into place and turning back to her charcoal drawing of a seated skeleton. "It looks like a man's undershirt."

I thought my mother could have been a silent-movie star with her Hollywood nose and her night-dark eyes. I wished I'd inherited even a fraction of her beauty or charisma, but what did she know about fashion? She wore all my old reject outfits, spiced them up with heavy silver and turquoise Mexican jewelry. I left her to her work.

I was supposed to meet Guy at a pre-formal party in south Palo Alto, so at 6 P.M. all made-up in my mother's Clinique (courtesy of Feral's experienced hand), I walked up the cement path to a green Eichler tract house.

Jack screamed from the couch as I stepped inside. "Oh my *god*, Ariel, you are so beautiful!" He rushed up to me, held both my hands out in front of me. Jack looked so cute in his pressed black tux and flamingo-pink cummerbund. "*Oh my god*, Jennie," he called over to his date, a bleach-blond punk girl I knew as a friend of Leslie. "Besides you, isn't Ariel the *most* beautiful woman in the world?" He pulled me over to the couch where Jennie sat in her faux-vintage black lace gown.

She nodded coolly in my direction. "What's up?"

"Where's Heartthrob? Where is he? Where *is* he?" Jack wanted to know. "Oh my *god*, Jennie, have you *seen* Ariel's boyfriend?"

"He's not my boyfriend," I blushed. "But he'll be here."

"Boyfriend," I'd rolled the word on my tongue nights when Feral was out. *My boyfriend.*

Half an hour late, decked out in his red and black rental, Guy carried a fogged-up clear plastic box containing a rose wrist corsage. He posed for a picture with his thumb and index finger holding his chin as if fingering a nonexistent goatee.

"You are so hot," I whispered. I could feel my face flush as soon as I'd said it.

Jack offered to smoke us out, so we all locked ourselves in a back bedroom. I didn't know whose house it was.

"Guy can't stand me," Jack whispered as he passed me the joint.

I looked over at Guy, who was zoning out on the unmade bed. It was true, but I shook my head no. I didn't know why Guy hated him so much, but I didn't ask. Jack could be seriously obnoxious, but if it was more than that I didn't want to know about it.

As soon as we walked in, I knew the dance had been a mistake. The whole central zone of campus had been transplanted into a pink hotel ballroom where some new wave band sang covers from the *Footloose* soundtrack under a glowing glass chandelier. It's not like I'd expected a punk band—I would have settled happily for Chaka Khan or Pat Benatar covers. We *do* belong to the night. But this was humiliating. Guy pretended he could detect a funk beat in the tunes, pulled me into the crowd to dance as though we fit in. And when I stood close to him, letting his body fill my field of vision, I almost forgot how much we didn't. He held me during a slow song. I tried to stand tiptoed in my combat boots to make up some of the height difference. But when the band started playing "Eyes Without a Face," I just couldn't take it anymore. I ducked into a gold and pink wallpapered bathroom. Two silicone girls were in there, wearing metallic China Doll wigs and snorting coke through dollar bills on the pale marble counter. "Oh my *god*," one of them sniffed. "Don't you know how to knock? You can't tell anybody—"

"You're in a fucking public bathroom. Ever occurred to you to go into one of the stalls?"

"*Oh. My. God.* And do lines on *what*? The *toilet* seat?" She was horrified.

Her twin looked up at me, wiping her nose. "Aren't you Leslie's sister? Leslie was really gross, too."

I didn't bother to pee. I found Guy at the punch bowl with his friend Carl, discussing strategies for introducing our fellow students to the merits of socialism through house music. I couldn't discern a trace of irony in their voices. They were so sincere. More than anything, I wanted to be like them. I wanted to believe that I could just reach out to the coke-sniffing bitches and get them excited about a revolution against themselves. But I couldn't even frame the thought without being cynical. *What was wrong with me?*

"Are you coming to the march in San Francisco next weekend?" Carl asked me.

"Definitely." That, I knew how to do.

"Right on. I think we're gonna block the federal building." Carl's date yanked him back onto the dance floor when the band started singing "Karma Chameleon," and mercifully, Guy was the one to suggest we leave.

Guy's friend Billy had invited us over for after-dance drinks. Billy's parents were out of town at an EST workshop, but he wasn't really having a party.

In the driveway next to Billy's stucco bungalow, Guy turned off the ignition, leaned right over the stick shift and grabbed my shoulders before I could panic. His jaw line was clean-shaven, his lips as soft as hope. His tongue tasted like citrus. His hair smelled like weed. I pushed my seat back. Guy readjusted his position to avoid the controls between us. I slipped my arms around his waist and felt him tremble, just a little. His hands fluttered nervously like the wings of a hummingbird on my upper arms, then my shoulders, settling for a moment at the nape of my neck. *Shh* . . . He leaned into me, seemed to melt. His hands steadied as he moved them down my back and ran his tongue over my chin.

I glanced out the car window. "Look," I whispered into Guy's hair as he buried his face in my dress.

Up at Billy's window, two pairs of eyes peered through an opening in the heavy curtains.

Guy looked so cute when he blushed. "We better go inside."

A tall girl with long black hair and short bangs swung the door open for us. "I thought you two would never come in! I'm Betsy!" She wore pink chiffon.

"Hey."

We sat at a low oak coffee table in the living room, playing quarters with short glasses of warm Guinness from Billy's dad's basement stash. Betsy laughed and slapped the table at my misfortunes—I could never bounce the quarter into the glass. "It's OK," she chirped. "Guinness is good for you!" and then she bounced her own quarter easily into the dark beer and pointed at me and slapped the table and led the three of them counting as I drank. I could never drink fast enough.

Billy slipped a Bowie record onto the turntable, kept the volume low. "You never come to band practice anymore, Guy." He shot me an exaggerated dirty look. "Just kidding," he laughed, trying to take it back. But I knew he was serious.

"Aw, man. I'm sorry," Guy said. "I'll come on Sunday, I swear."

"Ziggy Stardust" whispered out of the speakers.

"I'm spent," Guy said, and stretched out on the yellow upholstered couch.

I stayed on the floor, leaned back to rest my head on a couch cushion, heard Betsy cackle as she pulled Billy out of the living room and into the darkness of the hallway. I watched the slow rhythm of Guy's chest as it rose and fell with each breath. The light that seeped from him as he slept was like sunrise, so luminous I thought it could sweep back my shadows.

Betsy tapped me on the shoulder. "It's four in the morning," she whispered. "Do you need a ride home?"

"Yeah." I kissed Guy's forehead and tried to inhale some portion of his good light, then stood up too fast. "Are you OK to drive?"

"Me?" Betsy winked. "I only had one glass."

At home, I settled into my empty bed. I figured that Feral had gone out, maybe over to Terrance's to give me the privacy she hoped I'd need. She was sweet, Feral, but she always left little plates of eggs and half-eaten apples under the bed to rot.

I carefully stored my red rose corsage in an inner compartment of the black lacquered Chinese box my bio-dad had given me the last time I saw him. I fell asleep quickly, thinking of Guy's soft lips.

Just before 10 A.M., I crawled out of bed, walked barefoot down our long hall lined with many dictionaries and *The Collected Works of C.G. Jung*, found my mother sitting at the butcher-block table in the kitchen with her best friend, Roberta, who hadn't changed her hairstyle since the Nixon Administration. My mother looked up from the fruit and pastries between them and announced that Feral's mother had come to claim her in the night. "She's sending her to some boarding school in southern California."

"That sucks." I grabbed a little blue plate from the cupboard and helped myself to a soft croissant and quartered orange.

"It really does," my mother said, her elbows resting on the table. "That woman is a bitch."

I pulled up a stool. At least I hadn't heard "The Rose" in the last couple of days. My mother was cheering up.

"I hear you're seeing Professor Campbell's son," Roberta clucked, changing the subject. "You know, the professor is just wonderful."

"Yeah," I nodded.

Roberta had a weird look on her face. "I brought you a present," she said as she reached into her Guatemalan bag and produced a clam-sized, foil-wrapped something.

My mother started fidgeting with a can opener.

"Thanks," I said as I took the something from her and started to open it. The bready thing inside looked like a misshapen Christmas sand tart.

Roberta let out a low laugh, "It's a vulva biscuit!"

My mom put down the can opener, got up and opened the fridge, moved bottles and Tupperware containers around.

"Huh?" It did look like a vulva, now that she mentioned it.

"Are you on the Pill?" Roberta fixed her brown eyes on me. "No."

"Ariel, you need to get on the Pill."

"Um, yeah," I said. "OK."

She stared at me.

I took a bite of my buttery croissant. My head hurt.

"Oh my goodness—" Roberta gasped. "You're not sexually active?"

I stared down at my plate. It had little yellow fish painted around the rim.

"And he's still with you?" she sucked up a horrified laugh, like she'd never heard anything so ludicrous.

"Yeah. But, listen. I have to go. Thanks for the cookie."

My mom shut the fridge.

I picked up my plate and my vulva biscuit, leaving the foil on the wooden table, walked back down the hall to my bedroom. Roberta was worse than Feral. I mean, how embarrassing. And poor Feral, I thought of her sitting silently in the passenger's seat of her mom's old Ford, her wild curls in the wind, heading south down the 101 into the blue winter, stone-faced, careful not to give her mother the satisfaction of even a single tear.

Learning How to Navigate

The floods of February gave way to a crystalline March. The city blossomed like its heart was not breaking. Our gray cats yawned on the patio picnic table and my mother's irises bloomed in the cool spring air. Even the blue jays that pillaged seeds from our vegetable garden didn't annoy me. Guy became my singular fixation. He'd show up after band practice, dancing at my window. He'd pick me up at work—I had a job selling popcorn at a foreign and second-run movie house on Emerson Street, where we showed *Kiss of the Spider Woman* every night. I bought a book on walking meditation and counted my breaths from my bedroom window to Guy's doorstep.

I wore pants Leslie had made from a stolen American flag and a T-shirt scribbled with "Young American" on the free trains chartered by the Palo Alto Peace Center that took us to anti-Reagan, pro-Sandinista and anti-Pinochet rallies in San Francisco. I always recognized the old peaceniks Miriam Patchen and Laurent Franz on the train, said hello.

"Young American, huh?" Miriam muttered. "You *are* horrible."

No Business as Usual Day started out spirited but disintegrated into a mad rushing window-smashing looting spree down Market Street and through the financial district.

Guy tugged at the sleeves of angry white boys and tried to reason: "We're not here to vandalize small businesses."

They ignored him. Of course they ignored him.

We gave up, took a Muni bus to the lower Haight, inched up the hill. We stopped in front of a Caribbean restaurant to buy weed that glistened in its sandwich bag and turned out to be a clever mixture of oregano and tree sap. No matter. We planned a summer trip to Europe. *We'll get Eurail passes, go everywhere.* We handed a bearded homeless guy thirty bucks to buy two bottles of Jack Daniels—one for us, one for himself—then walked all the way back to the train station at 4th and Townsend, Guy air-drumming and singing "Earth Crisis."

On the platform, amid the *clip-clop chatter-blah* of commuters as we waited for the four o'clock train, Guy fished in his Levi's pocket and produced a tiny rose quartz heart. He pressed it into my palm. "I got you this."

On the commuter train, we drank and laughed. *Should we join Hands Across America? Would it be too lame?* When I threw up on the curb outside the Southern Pacific station in Palo Alto, Guy held my hair out of my face.

Naked, curled up next to me in my double bed, Guy didn't seem so tall. He slept with one hand on my belly. The owl in the oak tree outside my window sounded like a faraway train. I wanted to hide under Guy's glistening skin, in the rise and fall of his back. I tried to remember the words to an eighth-century Chinese poem cycle I'd once been able to recite in both languages, but I could only remember fragments: *A full goblet of wine at the right time / Is worth more than all the kingdoms of this earth! / Dark is life, is death. . . ./ On the little pool's still / Surface everything appears / Fantastically in a mirror-image / Everything is standing on its head. . . .*

I had recurring dreams of night trains, tangled streets. I wanted to live on Aphrodite Terra, the largest continent on Venus. My garden would be vast, stretching out for miles in every direction, lush, junglelike. Maybe I would keep an aviary there: rare tropical birds.

I believed in magic, in all the magics. The world would dangle a carrot: depression masquerading as realism. I wouldn't bite. I wanted to paint my room tangerine. I watched Guy in sleep, decided that sex had been falsely advertised. Not over- or underrated—just completely misrepresented on all those cologne billboards and cigarette bus-stop ads. Sex was supposed to be all fireworks and pinball. I thought it was sweet and primitive, like evening surf.

I saved my paychecks from the theater, read shoestring-budget guides to southwestern Europe, drew labyrinths on the unlined pages of my journals. Every week some faraway horror made Guy tear up—the bombing of Libya, the accident in Chernobyl and still no U.S. sanctions against South Africa.

Mornings before I headed out to school, John closed his notebook full of sermons-in-progress and sat with me in the kitchen. He ate granola with honey and no milk, told me stories from John Muir's memoirs and described high mountain trails. "I want to go backpacking with you sometime again," I told him. "Like when I was little." I was thinking of the glimmering black flecks in the granite boulders and cliffs of the high Sierras. I was thinking of the way John's pale blue eyes sparkled as we headed out of the city and up into the foothills. But somehow I knew we wouldn't go.

During fifty-minute classes at school, I stared out windows, listened to Tom Waits on headphones hidden in my curls. I met Guy for lunch on the lawn near the tracks. We ate take-out sushi. I swallowed tiny pink birth control pills with Diet Coke. "Isn't this the best weather?" I said, resting my head on his lap. "Sunny and cool."

My mother worked late nights in her studio, visited her old

students on death row at San Quentin during the day, took a new part-time job teaching painting at a halfway house. She found me smoking on the patio one afternoon, offered me five hundred dollars to quit.

I laughed.

"I'm serious," she said. "Name your price."

Guy's VW bug blew up on Highway 17 in early June. We hitched a ride the rest of the way to Santa Cruz in a white Cadillac with a double facelift woman who wore an Ollie North Is a National Hero button on her pink T-shirt. I hesitated when she opened the car door for us—surely this was what a serial killer looked like—but Guy shrugged and climbed in, so I followed him.

We poured quarters into the arcade pinball machines at the boardwalk. I started out strong, but Guy was the better player. I didn't realize how long we'd been there until the pockets of my rayon sundress were empty.

On the beach a half-mile down from the glow and clamor of the boardwalk rides, my ears rang. We sat close on the damp sand and watched the sun set purple-orange over the Pacific. "We still have to get your ticket to London," I reminded him. I'd bought mine for $330 the week before.

He reached over, gripped my bare thigh too tight, then let go. "Listen, I have to tell you something. I wanted to come out here to tell you something." He looked up at the sunset, then down again. "I've decided, well—I was thinking about it."

"Thinking?"

"Europe. I was thinking about Europe and I realized that I— well, I don't want to go. I mean, *Europe*. I realized—I think Europe is the root of all evil. I don't know why I told you I wanted to go."

My throat felt like I was trying to swallow tar. Three short inhalations through my mouth. A long, slow exhale through my nose. I turned to him, met his gaze. "Then I guess we don't have to get your ticket."

His whole upper body relaxed. He leaned into me. "You're not mad?" he whispered. "I can't believe you're not mad."

"Why would I be mad?" I clenched my jaw, quickly tried to relax. I wished the wind would stop blowing. "I don't want you to do anything you don't want to do."

"You're so great," he sighed, wrapping his arms around me as the last strokes of color faded from the sky. And all at once, I remembered what loneliness tasted like.

A pear-shaped and four-chambered hollow muscle, the heart's structure makes it an efficient, never-ceasing pump. From the moment of development through the moment of death, it pumps. The heart, therefore, has to be strong.

In Europe, I wore red lipstick and a dead woman's dress until both were stolen from under my dorm bed in Brussels. Then I wore a black minidress from a Swedish girl and a biker jacket from home. I slept in hostels and train stations, carried only what fit in my tiny black daypack.

In the gardens and cafés of Paris, I chain-smoked.

In Cannes, I swam topless in the warm Mediterranean waves, begged the old Gypsies to kidnap me. I showed them the contents of my money belt: seven hundred francs and one hundred dollars U.S. But they had no use for me. They were drenched in jewelry, carried no packs.

In Chartres, I walked the labyrinth of the Cretan Minotaur, counting my breaths.

At the grand arched prewar train station in Amsterdam, I ran into an old friend of my sister—a sandy blond boy who'd taken me to a 1920s theme dance freshman year. He'd been a senior then. Now his home was the road. We shared a piece of hash cake at a crowded coffee shop with yellow walls and tried to find our way back to the cheap Rajneesh youth hostel. "If we just keep going down this street, we're bound to get somewhere," I reasoned. As we walked, I lost all feeling in my feet, then my legs. I was floating, but it took focus to continue. We walked, but hour after hour under the three-quarter moon, we passed the same houseboats and bridges, the same tall building with the red neon announcement: Jesus Loves You. Amsterdam's circular canal streets.

One must know how to float as words do, Anaïs Nin said in unassigned reading, *without roots and without watering cans. One must know how to navigate without latitudes and longitudes and without motor.* By morning, I'd lost my black daypack, but not my money belt. I'd lost the boy, too. I stood in front of the train station. I had to figure out this navigation thing. Compasses were good and cheap, but compasses could be stolen. What was a compass, anyway? Just a magnet that could sense a pull towards the north. Why couldn't I learn to close my eyes, sense the pull, face north? The sun would rise in my right hand, set in my left. Maps were good and cheap, too—I studied them on trains and in stations—but a girl had to be able to place herself on a map, to figure out if she's even within its boundaries. I could examine all the maps in the world but, ultimately, I had to learn to find my way without latitudes or longitudes, without roots or watering cans, without Guy or anybody else.

I held my hands over my eyes like blinders to block my peripheral vision, stepped onto a platform, then onto a train. Maybe I passed out as it pulled away from the station, because just then a flash of a nightmare jutted into the day: a world of movie set facades, nothing behind them.

When I opened my eyes, a uniformed man leaned over me,

hassling me for a ticket or a passport in broken English. I shook my head, tried to wave him away. What was the end of that Anaïs Nin passage? *Without drugs and without burdens.* I had no luggage now.

When the train stopped, the uniformed man escorted me to the door and I stepped out onto a dusky platform. A few families milled around on the street below. I walked down cement stairs. The cloud-covered sky gave me no hint as to the time or my direction. An old man passed on his bicycle. France? Belgium? It might as easily have been southern Germany or northern Italy. Warm, almost humid. Maybe a light storm approaching. I closed my eyes, but felt no magnetic pull in any direction. A couple with a little yelping dog brushed past me, chattering unmistakably in French. I followed the narrow street in the direction that seemed lightest. West, I decided. I came to a tiny hotel with a blue painted door. The old woman let me pay in guilders instead of francs. And in the morning, she pointed me to a station.

I spent the last of my money on a bus to Calais, a ferry to Dover, a bullet train to London, arriving three days before my flight home with an empty wallet and a pack of Gauloises cigarettes. I slept soundly on the cold flagstone floor of Victoria Station, dreamed of a night train full of statues and an alarm clock ringing in a deserted station—no one to wake.

Whether it's a grand terminal or a humble platform, there's no better place to sleep in this world than a train station.

A chubby girl with bleach-blond hair snored next to me. She knew a place where we could get some food, she told me in the morning. Her name was Anastasia. If I waited at the foot of the clock tower, she'd come back for me. She promised. I waited through the morning in the cool summer rain, smoking, watching the crowd for the round girl with smeared kohl eyeliner.

As the clock sounded its noon bells, a short man in a tweed coat rushed up to me. "Anastasia told me to come for you." He spoke too quickly, his longish hair slicked back. "We must go now."

His broad smile scared me, but I was ravenous.

He led me down stairs and escalators onto the tube, which stopped and started with mechanical gasps, then back up to a street and through the Covent Gardens Market, down an alley and across a wider street, down another alley, up three stained flights of stairs and through a hollow aluminum door. He locked it behind us.

Anastasia was not inside the dirty apartment that smelled vaguely of turpentine. I didn't see any food. The man excused himself and disappeared into a back room. I stood in the cramped living room, the floor and coffee table strewn with Judge Dredd and Archie comic books.

The man reappeared wearing a red satin robe. He smiled his broad smile.

I felt nauseous. I turned, lunged for the door latch.

His small hand whipped past my ear, smashing my fingers against the metal lock. "Don't be afraid," he whispered. "I'm more comfortable in my robe." He slipped his other hand around my waist.

I elbowed him in the ribs as hard as I could, "Fuck you."

He made a groaning sound, loosened his grip on my hand and around my waist.

I elbowed him again. And again. "Fuck you!" In my mind's eye, I made him disappear. The little metal lock my sole focus.

"Little girl," he hissed. "I know you need the money."

I pried the latch open, yanked at the doorknob, rushed down the stairs. I imagined myself in a race, on an obstacle course, in a labyrinth heading toward the rose. My legs were strong—out into the August drizzle, back down the alley. I turned onto a cobblestone street, ran, no idea where I was. I concentrated on my stride, on the invisible magnetic pull. A glowing Underground sign appeared like an angel. I ducked into the Charing Cross station, jumped a turnstile, slid onto the tube.

In the crowd of pale evening commuters at Victoria Station, I tried to steady my breath. I begged two quid from a bearded busker who played "Hotel California" over and over again. I bought coffee and a sandwich roll, ate quickly as I scanned the crowd. In exchange for my last fifty pence I could take a shower, but as I approached the entrance to the washroom, blond Anastasia appeared at the edge of the crowd with the little man in his tweed coat. I pocketed the last of my sandwich, ducked onto the airport express train, took a seat, cried to the conductor that all my money had been stolen.

He didn't believe me. "Yanks can be a bit foolish," he muttered as he took down the home address from my passport. London Transport would send me a bill for their troubles.

I slept on a soft vinyl chair in the airport departure lounge. When I opened my eyes, I didn't know where I was.

A man with a shaved head and a red-orange robe stared down at me. "I am curious as to the state of you," he announced in his German accent. "My name is Hans."

I sat up slowly, nodded. "I'm OK."

Hans squatted next to me, surged into a run-on sentence about formlessness and the Universe and egolessness and the nature of consciousness and self-realization and oneness and inner peace and visions of an avatar.

"I'd like to hear more," I said. "Can you buy me breakfast?"

I ate eggs and biscuits drenched in butter, drank watery coffee and listened vaguely as Hans waved his orange scarf in the stale air and gushed about the glory of Lord Krishna. He trailed me all day through the fluorescent-lit airport, his robe falling open occasionally to reveal red-orange Levi's.

"So, do you just put all your clothes in the washing machine with a few packets of Rit Dye when you join?"

"Yes, yes." He nodded. On the way to my gate, he stopped to buy me a pack of gum. "For when your ears get plugged up," he said. "And Ariel—you'll always be safe with Krishna."

I folded a piece of mint gum into my mouth. I didn't know about Krishna, but I felt safe with Hans.

I slept unevenly in the blue hum of the plane as it soared over the Atlantic. Fourteen hours and I was back home in Palo Alto, where no matter how many computer companies moved in, the streets were still named after poets. My mother made Cornish game hens for dinner and when no one was looking, I licked my plate.

Later, I climbed out my bedroom window, wandered alone along Homer Avenue, up Bryant. I was tired, but I was restless, too.

I found Guy in front of Swensen's Ice Cream next to the New Varsity Theater. We shared his mint shake.

Our SAT scores had arrived in the mail while I was gone. "Whaddya get?" he wanted to know.

I'd already planned to lie up a hundred points in anticipation of his perfect score. "Twelve hundred," I said.

And I knew I was an asshole when Guy frowned down at his big shoes. "I only got eleven hundred."

I'd never lit a cigarette in front of him before.

"You're smoking a lot now?"

"Listen," I said, dragging hard on my Camel. "I think I'm going to drop out of school. If I get Mr. Schellenberg, I'll go to first period—but that's it."

Guy looked so sad. He put his arm around me and we walked through the warm night.

"You should quit with me. We could travel. Not Europe." I threw my cigarette on the sidewalk and crushed it with my boot.

Silence.

We walked toward my house.

"I am a black man," he finally said. "Maybe it's a prison to you, but fifty years ago I wouldn't have been allowed to go to that high school. You know I can't quit—can't waste my life."

I knew. "But I don't want to go without you," I whispered.

"No matter what happens," he said. "I'll love you forever."

In the glow from the streetlight outside my bedroom window, Guy's body was perfect—coffee-colored, long and muscular. I felt fat and pale. I turned over onto my stomach, let Guy scratch my back. "You have no waistline," he laughed.

"What?"

He cleared his throat. "When you lie down like that, it looks like you have no waistline."

As Guy slept, I plucked the hair out from the nape of my neck, one strand at a time. I dreamed I was falling, but when I opened my mouth to scream, I couldn't manage a sound.

I clipped the nail on my index finger short, threw up my food in our terra-cotta-tiled bathroom.

Maybe all I needed was a waistline.

The Forest Through the Trees

started working at the movie house again, running the
projector, gave Jack my job selling the popcorn. We were
screening a Varda film called *Vagabond* that made me cry
in the dark of the projection booth. I didn't understand why
the traveling girl had to die. I wanted Varda to come back and
give me a fifth act: *the resurrection of the vagabond.*

Dinner breaks, Jack came upstairs into the booth and I
smoked instead of eating.

"How come the more you love Guy, the more you hate
yourself?" he wanted to know.

I told him I didn't know what he was talking about. "That's
a mean thing to say, Jack."

He apologized, bit into his quarter-pound burger.

I didn't know what was happening to me, but I didn't think
Guy had much to do with it. It felt like a storm-tossed Pacific
wave had crashed over my head. I couldn't pinpoint when it
had started—maybe in Europe, maybe before—but I was
losing energy. Everything looked dull to me, but at the same
time I could feel a pressure building.

When Saskia, the girl who worked the box office, saw my
little pink birth control pills in my backpack pocket, she wrinkled her nose, frowned. "Those things'll make you crazy."

Maybe that's all it was. The little pink pills. Sometimes my
feet itched, or tingled as if asleep. I felt like crying, but I
sucked it up. *What did I have to cry about?* I wanted my gleeful

indifference back. My reflection in the glass window of the projection booth seemed so remote.

You all die at fifteen, Diderot said in unassigned reading. And maybe he was right, the asshole. Maybe I was every cliché.

I went to first period at 8 A.M. every morning, then to work. I earned eighty dollars a week plus tuna salad sandwiches and espresso in exchange for my midmornings at a coffee shop near the bookstore where John clerked, earned two hundred dollars a week plus Diet Coke and popcorn in exchange for my nights at the movie house. I didn't need the paychecks to live on. I helped myself to pocket money from the till at the theatre by selling both ends of the tickets to late showings of *Vagabond*. I worked all autumn, stashed my wages away like a hamster with its dry corn. I wasn't sure what I was saving up for. I was scared.

At home, John looked at me sideways as he wound the grandmother clock in the living room. "You seem a little out of sorts. Maybe you're working too much? Something at school?"

I shook my head. "I'm fine."

He said, "Someone called from the attendance office. You're being marked absent from everything but first period."

I said, "It's because I sit in the back of the classroom."

I don't think he believed me, but John chose his battles like a Taoist warrior. He wouldn't dream of allying himself with the attendance lady at school. And he only offered advice when asked.

On a Tuesday night after I got off work, Guy wanted to talk. I met him at the 7-Eleven on Lytton, stood at the nacho bar piling jalapeños on my chips while he mixed cola and cherry Slurpee in a big cup. "Should we try to find someone to buy us a six pack?" I tried.

Guy shook his head, leaned against the metal counter with his drink.

"What do you wanna do tonight, anyway? We could walk down to the creek?"

Under the streetlights, Guy's skin looked dull. He talked fast and nervous about college, music, his band, a book he had to return to the library. Then he went quiet.

I picked at my tortilla chips and fake cheese. "Is something up?" We kept walking.

"Yeah."

I dropped an orange goo-coated pepper down the front of my black T-shirt dress. "Shit."

"Listen," he said, moving out in front of me and holding up his large hands for me to stop. "Are you listening?"

"Yeah," I looked up at him standing in the middle of the sidewalk with his hands in the air.

"I think we should break up," he said.

"Uh huh?" I looked back down at the front of my dress, tried to wipe the cheese off with a stiff paper napkin.

"Are you listening, Ariel?"

I was listening, but I didn't know what to say. I was stunned. Resigned. Of course we should break up. Things start, end. "Uh huh?" I sat down on the curb, studied my combat boots.

Guy knelt down next to me, put his arm around me, then pulled away.

I stacked four peppers onto a chip and stuffed it in my mouth.

"Are you OK?"

"Yeah. I'm fine."

Guy stood up, awkwardly patted the top of my head. "Ariel, listen. I have to go. Can I walk you home?"

"No, that's cool." I didn't look up. "I think I'm supposed to meet somebody at the Varsity."

I walked down University Avenue, but no one I knew was inside the theater. I ordered a coffee, carried it out and around the side of the building, crouched against a graffitied cement wall, lit a cigarette. The warm wind hissed through the alley, carrying a ripped movie schedule. A kid I vaguely knew walked past me, then turned back. He wasn't a kid, really—maybe twenty-five—but he hung out with punks at Palo Alto High School. I'd seen him at the Varsity, his arms around the skinny girl with translucent skin and dyed black hair. "Hey," he called over to me. "What's your name?"

"Ariel."

"Oh, yeah, Ariel. Sorry I forgot. Hey, I'm Burke. Anyway. My roommate's having a party at our place—you should come over."

I followed Burke through the alley and out to his black Chevy in the parking lot. Maybe Jack would be there.

Dark apartment strewn with kids I didn't know. It smelled like puke. A blue-haired boy who claimed to recognize me from elementary school fixed me a drink in the dirty kitchen and I downed it in one gulp. "We're doing tequila shots in the back room." He tugged at my sleeve.

I sat on an unmade bed next to a girl with long braids. Another boy lay asleep or passed out in the corner. Burke crouched against the wall, unlaced his boots. He had on one black sock, one red. The girl in braids passed me the Jose Cuervo. I took a swig, stood up to hand the bottle to Burke. The blue-haired boy leaned his head back and held the bottle straight up, pouring tequila down his throat like water. "Stairway to Heaven" blared from the front room, the music pausing occasionally and screeching a little as someone tried to play the record backward.

"Would you ever do it for money?" the blue-haired boy asked the girl in braids.

"Sure," she said. "If the price was right."

I took another gulp from the bottle, leaned back onto the bed and looked up at the cottage-cheese ceiling. I felt queasy. When I opened my eyes, "Stairway to Heaven" was still playing, but the other kids were gone. Burke's red face seemed huge in my field of vision. It took me a moment to focus, to realize how close he was.

"Get off me, man." I tried to slide out from under him, but he grasped my arm hard.

"C'mon, honey." He pressed his shoulder into my chest.

I felt sick, couldn't breathe. I pushed feebly at his other shoulder.

He shifted his weight, pulled at my tights. He smelled like beer, sweat and tequila. "You know you want it. Or do you only like black dick?"

"Get the fuck off me, man." He was strong, but I was also too tired to fight. *What did it matter, really?* Maybe some people are overcome by outside forces, but I could feel my defeat bubbling up from within. "Can you just stop?"

He gripped my throat. "Shut up, bitch." His body dense above me.

I couldn't concentrate. I clenched my fists. It occurred to me to knee him in the balls, but I couldn't rearrange my position. Scream, but who would hear me over the music? I'd decided on the curb earlier that personal choice was a farce, anyway. Things just happened. Or they didn't. I closed my eyes. If I couldn't make Burke disappear, at least I could make me disappear.

It was two o'clock in the morning when I called Jack from the green phone in the living room. A shaven-headed kid was parked next to the record player, moving the needle back to the beginning of the song every time it ended. I didn't expect to find Jack home, but he answered on the first ring, wide awake. "Listen," I said. "I'm over here at the corner of Alma near your house. Sorry to bug you—can you pick me up?"

I'd hardly put the phone down and stepped outside onto the concrete steps when Jack pulled up on his shiny pink moped. "Oh my *god*, Ariel. You sounded *so* stressed on the phone. I *totally* didn't *even* fix my hair."

"Yeah," I climbed onto the back. "I guess I'm stressed." I could hear "Stairway to Heaven" starting up again as we pulled away.

"It must be something astrological. Everyone's *totally* stressed," Jack yelled over the buzz of the scooter. "D'yawanna do some coke, or are you still boycotting it?"

"Maybe another night. I don't feel so good." I wrapped my arms around Jack's waist as we sped through the night.

At home, I took a shower, washed with jasmine soap, climbed into my soft soft bed, watched the shadows outside my window. *What was happening to me?* I didn't have enough energy even to suffer. I thought I was in a surrealist movie, on a runaway train—the scenery spun past me in a swirl of strange colors. Or maybe the problem was with the projector, maybe my movie was playing too fast. I tried to hum the tune to "Footloose," but "Stairway to Heaven" played over and over in my head.

I was running out of metaphors. Almost winter now. And I couldn't figure out what had become of the spring.

The unnerving part was that the world and everyone in it just carried on. Something had happened. Or it hadn't. Everything was different now. And exactly the same. The moon rose and set. The magnolia leaves turned and fell. *Blue Velvet* opened at the theater. Well-scrubbed men and women in J.Crew sweaters ordered popcorn. *Small, medium or large?* It mattered to them. They wanted to know if we used real butter. They ordered Red Vines, Diet Coke. The punks huddled at the New Varsity Theatre in their black cotton rags and ghostly makeup. They fought, kissed. My mother slipped in and out between the house and her studio, floorboards creaking in the night. John woke up early, mixed juice, ate granola with honey and no milk. I did not give a shit. And the world and everyone in it carried on as if I did.

Numb. From the Old English "niman," meaning *taken* or *seized*, as by cold or grief. Loosely related to the words "nimble," "nemesis," and "nomad."

From Kenneth Patchen's play *Don't Look Now*, unassigned:

> AUNT CLEOBEL: *Because as more and more is offered without love, the area we can have real lives in grows smaller and smaller.*
> JOAN: *Until finally the only genuine feeling left to us is that we are not capable of feeling anything any more.*

A Hawaiian picture postcard of a pink hotel arrived in the mail from my bio-dad. I hadn't heard from him since my grandparents decided he was too crazy to have around anymore and shipped him off to Hawaii. All through my elementary-school years, he'd lived in their basement in Carmel. Leslie and I had visited him over summer and winter breaks. And then nothing. I tried to remember what he looked like, what he sounded like. Madman or sage? He'd drawn spirals in the margins and written:

Dear Ariel,

You can't see the forest through the trees. No one can. You just go around in your own little world and you don't know where you are.

Love, Dad

On Saturday, Jack called in sick to work.

I threaded the projector, clamored down the black stairs to sell popcorn, ran back up to start the movie, then down to sell more popcorn. A mad rush for fifteen minutes and then lights out in the theater. *Hush.* I crept back down the painted stairs.

I leaned against the wall behind the popcorn machine, started talking shit with Saskia, who sat smoking in the box office. She was moving to Seattle. "There aren't going to be any punks left in Palo Alto," I complained.

"Not a one," she smiled. "It's all about Seattle."

The skinny girl with translucent skin and dyed black hair pressed her face up to the box office window behind Saskia. The glass fogged up around her thin lips.

Saskia turned around. "Can I help you?" But the girl looked right through her, walked around the box office and pushed open the glass door from the sidewalk, marched up to the concessions stand. She leaned over the buttery counter. "You're Ariel?"

"Yeah."

"What happened between you and Burke?" She narrowed her gaze. She had the palest blue eyes I had ever seen.

"Nothing."

"Don't lie to me, bitch." She wore a dozen bangles on each wrist.

"Why do you want to know?"

"Because he's my fucking boyfriend, that's why. Because he just got arrested for raping my friend Harmony, that's why.

Because the detective wants to talk to you, that's why." She wiped her nose.

"Then the detective can talk to me."

"Shut up, bitch," she said as she turned.

Last show over. Lights up in the theater. The audience wandered away. I was rewinding the movie when Saskia appeared in the dark of the projection booth with bright scissors in her hand and a gleam in her eye like she'd been drinking whiskey in the box office. She wanted to cut my hair like the vagabond girl's. *Snip, snip.*

Cool midnight and we locked the theater, headed over to the University Creamery, where the junkie waitress yelled at us and the junkie cook yelled at her and we sat smoking Camel nonfilters. Saskia—little and elegant in her thrift store 1940s dress, safety pins in her ears, pixie haircut like Mia Farrow's circa 1968. She had the habit of wrinkling her nose and closing her eyes and covering up her beautiful face when she got embarrassed, which was often. We talked about the movie we'd make someday—an artistic response to Varda's *Vagabond*. *Sans Toit ni Loi* in French—*Without Roof or Rule*.

In Varda's film, the traveling girl is foul-mouthed, tough, lazy. She refuses to settle down, is found frozen in a ditch in the French countryside in wintertime. Freedom equals loneliness, equals death. *Fuck Varda*. In our movie, the vagabond girl wouldn't have to settle down. We weren't sure how, but she'd survive.

"What was up with that skinny girl at the theater?" Saskia wanted to know.

I lit a cigarette, shook my head. "Nothing."

If You Are Falling

Sunday morning early, the red telephone next to my bed rang like an alarm clock.

I put on too much eyeliner, took a SamTrans bus to the Menlo Park police station.

The detective met me in front of the cement building. She wore a miniskirt, smiled too wide. I followed her down a long, white hallway into a windowless room.

"Awesome of you to come down," she chirped as she opened a black binder on her desk. "First let's make sure we're talking about the same man."

"It wasn't really rape," I told her as I fingered the picture of Burke in the row of depressing mug shots. They looked like my mother's old students at San Quentin. "Screwed by the system," my mother seethed when she talked about them.

I sat dumbly on a wheeled gray chair next to an oversized file cabinet.

"You can just tell me what happened, then." The detective smiled as she closed her photo binder. I couldn't tell how old she was. Twenty-five? Forty? She looked like a picture of a beauty queen taken from far away. Pretty, but her features seemed vague and blurred, the color of old bone.

She stared at me, waiting. "I know this is harsh," she finally said. "But you can just start out with where you met him that night."

It bugged me that she used words like "awesome" and "harsh."

"Did you meet each other at the New Varsity?"

"Who told you that?"

"Nobody told me," she said, more seriously. "I know this man. I know how he operates."

I was silent. How did she know him? Had her cops been shining their spotlights on him as they passed in their patrol cars? They'd been watching Guy, not Burke.

"Listen." She screwed up her pale face. "Why did you come down here today?"

"Because you asked me to," I said. "I don't think it was really rape."

She looked up at the ceiling for what seemed like a long time, then suddenly slammed her palm down on the metal desk. "If you said 'no' and you had intercourse anyway, it was rape!"

I scooted back in my chair. It occurred to me that there must be something wrong with my head. I'd followed Burke to his car without a second thought, but if I met this woman in an alley, I wouldn't follow her anywhere. "I didn't use the word 'no,'" I told her. My hands and feet felt cold.

The detective leaned in, changing her expression again. "Understand me," she said. "You didn't even call the police that night. I have one witness who says you were drinking. Another witness says you left on a stolen motor scooter. You could be in some trouble for not cooperating, but I'm not like that. This man is going down with or without you."

Did you meet each other at the New Varsity? One witness? Another witness? How come strangers could follow the narrative of my life when all I could bring to mind was the warped screeching sound from the speakers when someone tried to play "Stairway to Heaven" backward? I stood up. "Then let him go down without me."

*In Chinese medicine, the disease known as "numbness of the heart"
is said to be contracted via external evil influences that cause anx-
iety, emptying the heart while the evil influences flow in.*

I walked the three blocks to Jack's house, found him sitting
on his bed, wild-eyed, fidgeting with a cassette tape box.
"What's going on with you, man? Are you really sick?" His
walls were covered with more Madonna posters than I knew
existed.

"I'm not sick," he sighed, wiping his nose. "What happened
the other night before I picked you up? You looked *totally*
bummed."

"I don't want to talk about it. I just think people are basically assholes, OK?"

Jack grabbed a baggie and a razor from his nightstand, cut
two thick lines on the plastic cassette box and set it on the bed.
From under the blanket he produced a cut drinking straw,
leaned over and snorted one of the lines. He said, "If Christ
came back—the *Messiah* in flesh and blood—who would offer
him the bigger ad contract, Disney or the Gap?"

He handed me the straw. I held one nostril closed and
sniffed the other line. "Disney. Absolutely."

He nodded.

"Have you just been sitting in here doing drugs?"

"Yeah," he laughed. "D'yawanna go out?"

We parked the moped in an alley behind a downtown apartment complex, climbed the fire escape to the roof. We sat
side by side, our feet dangling over the edge of the building.
The moon low on the horizon. "Is something going on with
you, Jack?"

He looked so anxious. He tried to smile, but his face fell. He
wiped his nose. "Do you think I'm *gay*?"

"I don't know, hon. I think you're you."

He looked down at his lap. "Do you have *any* idea how *gross* that would be? My mother would *die*. For real, die."

I shook my head. "She's your mom. I'm sure she wants you to be who you are." I wasn't sure, but there's always hoping.

"Do you think you get to choose?"

"No more than anything else," I shrugged. "Maybe not at all." I put my arm around him. My heartbeat felt electric. The silhouette of the rabbit on the moon stood out like a hologram.

"I just picture trying to tell her, like even if I'm grown up or *old* or whatever. I mean, like, we're *totally* Catholic. Oh my *god*, I'd rather lie down on the train tracks."

My neck hurt. "Wait to tell her until you know," I offered. "Until you're not stressing. I mean, it's not really about her. Not now."

He stared out over the town as blindness settled, tapped his fingers rhythmically on the edge of the roof and hummed the tune of "Live to Tell" too fast. "I'm gonna move to New York," he said.

"That'll be cool."

"I *swear*. As soon as I graduate." He lit another cigarette off his last. "Do you think you could die just by jumping off the building?"

"No. I think you could break your back and end up in a wheelchair."

Jack pulled his Ziplock out of his jean jacket pocket, dabbed his pinkie in the powder and sniffed it off his finger. He held out the bag. "You want more?"

I shook my head. Already wired, my mind raced. And all at once my life made perfect sense to me. "There are all these possibilities," I said. "You move into them like you move into the surf. You can ride a possibility all the way to the shore, or you can go under. The wave doesn't care whether you catch it or not, or how far you ride it. Nothing. It doesn't care. And when you glide to the shore, you just turn around and get back in the water, because that's the rule, you have to get back in the water. If you go under, then when you come up for air, there's always another possibility coming at you. And you catch that one. Or you don't. We're stumbling around in the foam getting knocked down by the tail end of every possibility there is, man. We have to get further out there, to the source of things." Perfect sense for the first time in my life. And no sense at all. Looking out over the suburb, it looked like a wave-tossed eternity—the streetlights just reflections of the moon over the ocean. "There's nothing worth dying over, Jack. Not on purpose, anyway. But whenever you feel like that, like your heart is going to explode, like maybe you should just lie down on the tracks and let the train take you where you're going or you feel like flying, like flying off the edge of a building, down into the city that tried to break your spirit—then that's it, the end of fear. But you don't have to die for it. You just get back in the water, come back up, because that's the rule, you have to come back up, but this time you aren't afraid of the big waves. You can ride a tsunami possibility all the way to the shore, only to turn around and get right back in there. Do you know what I'm talking about, Jack?"

He laughed, but this time his face didn't fall.

It made me happy to see him smile.

"I don't think I've ever heard you talk so much the whole time I've known you." He leaned his head on my shoulder and we watched the night.

As the sunrise broke over the eastern hills, I thought I'd seen god. "Why don't we have words for that?"

Jack shook his head. "Someday we'll have words for *everything.*"

"Listen, why don't you get a bus home? Pick your scooter up later?"

We scaled back down the side of the apartment building, walked to the University Creamery for coffee, smoking all the way. My jaw ached. I was still scared for Jack, but I left him at the bus stop and headed home to change my clothes for school.

The silver train was stopped between stations at the place where I cut across the tracks and through the hole in the chain-link fence to first-period creative writing. A blond cop stood by, scratching his head. Mystified commuters paced in the ballast gravel, craned their necks to see the mangled spectacle on the tracks.

On the other side of the fence, a crowd of punks were gathered around a tall girl who stood sobbing, inconsolable. I paused to watch the group until a Mohawk moved and I could see the crying girl's face—Harmony, the Amazon princess who'd busted Burke. Wailing, she sounded like a seagull. Some nights I'd wished I could cry like that.

Inside my classroom, I sat down at the little metal and wooden desk. Everyone around me whispered—the body on the tracks had been the skinny girl with translucent skin and the palest blue eyes. The last thing she'd said to me: *Shut up, bitch.*

Mr. Schellenberg stood in front of the podium, hands in his jeans pockets. He stood calm and silent, like he didn't know what all the whispering was about. He smiled under the fluorescent lights and described the day he'd moved to Palo Alto—the black squirrels that darted along the telephone wires, the sycamore trees and southern magnolias, leaves rustling in the wind. He held up a copy of a new paperback he liked, *Writing Down the Bones*. It had a black and blue cover, with stars. He read the introduction aloud to us, slowly. Writing meditation.

When the bell rang, I stole the slim volume off the podium, left without saying a word. Outside, I sat down on the wet lawn, slipped my shoes off and put them in my backpack. I lit a cigarette, pressed my toes into the mud. I felt like a Sierra river rock, bleached and worn down by the flow of everything. I was finished with high school.

Finally the silver train started up its engine and sounded its somber horn. I stood up, started to walk toward the tracks, pausing at the place where "Do it so it feels real" had been stenciled on the curb. I climbed back through the hole in the fence, stepped out onto a wooden crosstie between the rails and headed toward the station. The tracks stretched out in front of me like a highway. The gravel stuck to my bare feet and I knew I could just keep walking, forever. I could remember the times when I felt bigger than a lot of things, but now I felt sizeless, shadowy. Just before the Southern Pacific station, I stepped into the bushes to let a train pass, then kept walking until I came to the tallest tree. I set down my backpack, lay down on the tiny patch of dry yellow grass, gazed up the trunk of that giant twin redwood. A year earlier, this wild numbness would have been unfathomable. I could hear the train coming, and closer, *ch clack ch clack ch clack* over the San Francisquito Creek bridge. I didn't hold my breath. It sped past me.

I fell asleep.

When I opened my eyes, the stars shone like a candlelight vigil in the heavens. I wondered how many of those stars were already dead. The sepia moon hung there, silent. "I don't care," I whispered up into the darkness. "I don't care, do you hear me?" I yelled it this time, like the moon could make it true. But the moon—she'd heard it all before.

I walked home barefoot. Dull stupid town.

Wedged between my window and the sill, a piece of binder paper, college ruled and folded in three—a note from Guy: "Two paths, one goal?" he'd scribbled across the top. And further down: "I'll love you forever." It seemed like a missive from another world. *I'll love you forever.* What a fucking joke. I wanted to write a nasty letter, send it to Guy. Maybe cruelty could serve as a vacuum on his spirit and I'd get back everything that was mine.

In the quiet of my bedroom, I tossed three pennies according to the instructions at the front of my thick *I Ching.* I counted the lines to find my fortune: *Decay (maggots breeding in a bowl). Work on what has been spoiled. It furthers one to cross the great water. Before the starting point, three days. After the starting point, three days. We must not recoil from danger.*

I was thinking of the vagabond girl—strange how easily she laughed.

Before the starting point, three days. Maggots breeding in a bowl. It was true. After all that early-morning talk about possibilities, what was I doing here? Climbing a stairway up, up, up—to no place.

I inhaled. I had a choice: I could stay home and die young—keep on dying—or I could fly away to someplace completely foreign where I knew no one and where maybe I could figure out what was me and what was geography, what was me and what was circumstance. Maybe I could find a metaphor to make it all OK.

No firm plans—not even intent upon arriving. I fixed my mind on departure. I took the California High School Proficiency Examination, passed. I emptied my savings account, bought a one-way ticket, packed the contents of my room into the basement.

You know the rule, Joseph Campbell said in unassigned reading. *If you are falling, DIVE.*

Part II

Heartfelt

Located in the middle of the chest, behind the breastbone and
between the lungs, the heart rests in the pericardial cavity.
This moistened chamber is encaged by ribs.
The diaphragm, a thick layer of muscle, lies below.
The heart, therefore, is well protected.

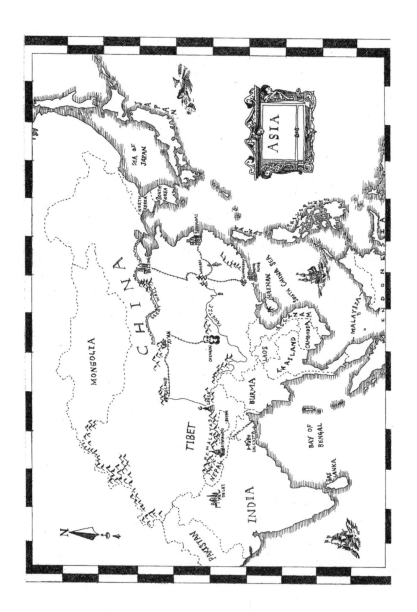

White Ghost Girl

From thirty-five thousand feet, just an ocean full of blues. Closer to the earth, I could make out a peninsula, an island. Closer still, laundry waved like flags off every balcony in the early evening light. The plane flew so low through the city, I thought we'd lose the tip of a wing against one of the concrete high-rises. Neon signs glowed in English and Chinese. Too many cars and double-decker buses and bright trams dotted the narrow streets.

I strolled through customs in a jet-lagged daze—nothing to declare.

"Business or pleasure?" a rumpled immigration officer wanted to know.

"Shopping," I lied.

He had a dark mole on his chin, rubber-stamped my passport with a red six-week visa.

At Thomas Cook I traded one hundred dollars U.S. for nearly one thousand in multicolored Monopoly money.

Outside the terminal, a silver air-conditioned bus with plush reclining seats took me into the city. "You stay Chungking Mansions?" A short Indian-looking guy wanted to know when I called out my stop. "Why you not stay nice place?"

The air outside felt like steam in my throat. Tourists carried shopping bags down Nathan Road toward the ferry dock. Young gangsters conspicuously patrolled the street corners. Backpackers wandered disoriented with their heavy loads.

Chungking Mansions—I'd dreamed this place before as a great waiting station in the sky. And now here it was in the dense world, an aging seventeen-story tenement complex of a thousand cheap guest houses, hostels, noodle shops, sari stores, salons, curry stands, apartments and sweatshop factories. My *Lonely Planet* guidebook had described it as a medieval town under permanent siege, a netherworld of sleaze and foul odors. "Take a look down the light wells off the D-block stairs for a vision of hell."

Behind a pink plywood door in C-block, I paid ten Monopoly dollars for a bottom bunk in a room that slept twelve. I didn't say anything as I walked in, crawled onto my bed, set my gray Swiss Army backpack at the foot. I'd brought only carry-on: black Levi's, blue Levi's, combat boots and sandals; two T-shirts and a gray sweatshirt; cotton duckie pajamas; a book on Buddhism and my *I Ching*, a hardcover journal and two black pens; three pairs of underwear and two bras; my broken heart; sunscreen foundation, purple lipstick, Great Lash mascara, Blistex, red Revlon nail polish and hair gel; Drum tobacco and rolling papers; groundless hope; a camera and film; my Sony Walkman; Prince, Tom Waits and Cat Stevens tapes; a half-pound bag of Peet's coffee; traveler's checks, my passport and maps; a toothbrush and a compass.

Back home I'd lied to my parents, said I'd been accepted to the Beijing Language Institute. It was like a study abroad program, I explained. My mother bought me the maps and said, "Remember: Anything that doesn't kill you just adds to the film quality."

Flying to mainland China would have cost me over one thousand dollars U.S., so I'd settled on a one-way ticket to Hong Kong for a third of that.

JOURNAL ENTRY #1
22°18′N 114°10′E
WINTER, 1987

> *self-portrait:*
> *moon faced, pale*
> *eyes like mood rings: gray or blue or green*
> *dark circles*
> *strong legs*
> *too fat for the pages of a magazine,*
> *too thin to survive a month in the desert*
> *fingernails chewed to the quick*
> *good toenails, painted red*
> *courage, cowardice*
> *dark hair*
> *freckles*

Bedraggled travelers on the other bunks rifled through their own packs, talked softly to each other about tickets, visas, changing money on the black market, Kuala Lumpur, a bar in Chiang Mai.

"How old are you?" an Australian in the bed next to me wanted to know. He had wide, dark eyes and a long beard like Walt Whitman.

"Sixteen."

"Canadian?"

"Californian."

"You're not loud enough to be an American."

I shrugged.

He offered me a Tsingtao beer. "Traveling can be dangerous," he warned me as I took it from him.

"California can be dangerous, too."

Beer bottles and traveler's tales circled in the windowless

room—everyone in transit here. I couldn't remember the last time I'd slept, but I wasn't tired. I downed my Tsingtao, left the hostel in search of food—back out into the mansions that smelled like fish sauce and sweat.

Gangs of Asian and African kids argued at elevator entrances, rodent-sized cockroaches scurried at their feet. Chinese, white and Indian men floated along a dark indoor alley of porn vendors. I made my way through the clamor and hum, through the corridors and stairwells, past the money changers and hustlers and whores and sleepy-eyed backpackers who warned of police raids and bragged that we stood at the epicenter of the gold-smuggling trade to Nepal and Korea. I found a red plastic chair in a ground-floor noodle shop, sat down and paid a few coins I didn't know the value of for a bowl of hot, salty ramen.

Outside the mansions, I walked along glowing streets, turning corners with the flow of the crowd. The traffic horns and shouting and music that streamed from nightclubs and record stores faded into a dreamy rumbling sound. I walked under scaffolding and dripping air conditioners, past a hundred Chinese and Indian food stalls. I followed a neon arrow into a dark building and up, up, up a narrow staircase to Jimmy Ho's tattoo shop. The old man sat crouched over a metal desk, sketching. A brown dog slept at his feet. I flipped through flash drawings, handed him one hundred Monopoly dollars, sat down on his wooden bench. I wanted a bird under my skin. If my body was not mine, at least some of the scars on it could be of my own choosing.

He leaned over me with his needle-tipped gun, leaving his mark on me in black and blue ink.

That night in the hostel, I dreamed myself soaring thirty-five thousand feet above the Pacific with black feathered wings. As I descended toward the water, my wings evaporated into soap bubbles. I landed on wet asphalt that glowed with the reflection of a city.

A hovercraft to Guangzhou three days later and I was finally in China.

At a busy noisy crowded gray train station, I changed money with a Chinese man who looked like a Gypsy and said he was from Ürümqi. Blank look on my face, so he clarified: *Far away.*

He gave me People's Money instead of the crisp Foreign Exchange Certificates non-Chinese were supposed to carry.

At the ticket counter, a stern attendant with a crooked nose wanted the bank-issued certificates, and wanted to sell me a first-class ticket. But I played dumb. "I do not understand," I said in English until she gave up and sold me a hard-seat ticket for the train to Beijing. The ticket itself didn't guarantee me any seat at all, but my white skin and curly hair attracted attention as soon as I climbed onto the People's Car. I tried to refuse the little brown fold-out seat next to the window, offered it to an old woman with leathery skin who hobbled on child-sized feet. But the crowd just laughed at me. "Sit down, White Ghost Girl," the old woman scolded in Chinese. I sat down and she leaned over another woman, grabbed my cheek between her thumb and index finger.

Thirty-six hours, then, the smoky train car overflowing with farmers, old people, chickens, a gray pig, children in Rambo T-shirts and imitation American baseball caps with team names like "Big Hit." Little cloth and plastic bags of jackfruit and flowers were stashed in every corner. Old men spat incessantly into the aisle. People leaned over each other, craning their necks to watch me. I felt like I should sing a song, provide some entertainment beyond White Girl with Mouth Hanging Open, but I was happy. The chaos made me feel strangely calm. *This is the way things should be*, I thought. *Overwhelming, real.* A middle-aged Indian man sat across from me, the only other foreigner in our car. "Canadian?" he asked.

"No, American. *Meiguoren.*"

"*Meiguoren!*" The news spread through The People's Car like a circus sideshow announcement, " *Meiguoren! Meiguoren!*"

Hours and days multiplied by miles, *Meiguo* seemed light years away—the distance making miniatures of everything. There hadn't been enough preparation time or truthtelling for anyone at home to tell me I "couldn't" go, but the "could," the "did," was just dawning on me. Images of the body on the tracks and the detective who wore a miniskirt and the Southern Pacific depot and the little bags of white powder and the late showing of *Vagabond* at the theater and all the popcorn I could eat and the hole in the chainlink fence at the edge of campus and Guy walking away and my parents waving goodbye all dwindled into *Meiguo*—a faraway place with a pretty name.

A little boy sitting behind me pulled at my hair. When I turned around to face him, he pressed a thumb into my cheek. "If she's American, why doesn't she have black skin?" he asked the crowd.

An old man with a deep scar across his throat offered me a piece of yellow cake as the scenes outside the train window dulled from green to gray, rice paddies and oxen to industrial flatlands and blue minitrucks.

By hour thirty-two, I was puking into a pink plastic bag. Three old women sharing a single seat across the aisle watched me like a movie, laughing and pointing and slapping their knees. "Look at White Ghost Girl," the one with a silver tooth cried. "She's far from home now!"

In My Country, We Might Think You Were Mad

The Beijing train station. Rivers of black and gray and blue. Stone-faced Chinese travelers all carrying many bags. I scanned the signs, recognized the character for "mouth," made my way out into the wintry noon. In every direction huge gray square cement buildings lined wide streets the same color as the smoggy sky. I wondered if I should have gotten off the train sooner, in the South, when the views from the windows were still chaotic, colorful. Across the street from the station, I ate white rice and broth in a restaurant that reminded me of a hospital cafeteria. Back outside, I felt slightly better, ready for the gray maze of bus lines and swarms of blue-gray and plain-gray-clad bicyclists, most of whom wore little white surgical masks over their noses and mouths. Gray. A girl can only use the word "gray" so many times, so after this I'll stop. If it was in Beijing, it was gray.

I studied my map as if it were a religious text. I knew where I was going, if not quite how to get there. I stepped onto an oversized bus and it lumbered away from the train station and past Tian'anmen Square, where huge color portraits of Lenin, Stalin and Marx had been erected alongside a painting of Mao. The bus squeaked to a halt and a horde of people crowded into the already full aisle. I couldn't see out the windows anymore. Elbows pressed into ribs, shoes overlapped. At every stop, more people crowded onboard. I felt like I was at a rock concert, could hardly breathe. When everyone finally poured out of the bus, I followed them. They scattered onto a dozen other identical-looking buses. A few people paused to stare at me, so I chanted my destination, *"Beijing Yuyan Xueyuan,"* in my best singsongy Chinese until a young man in a white button-down woman's shirt said, "Follow me," in English. I followed him onto another crowded bus.

I stepped through the cement pillars where my guide had pointed from our bus window, down a cement path and onto the misty green campus. My carry-on bag seemed heavy now. I sat down on a bench in front of what looked like a cafeteria. The grounds were so uncrowded, I almost felt like I was back in California. But it was cold.

A twenty-something Chinese man stopped his one-speed bicycle in front of me and leaned in cautiously. "Can I help you?"

I shook my head. "No." I had the feeling I was waiting for someone, and I hoped I'd know him when I saw him. I still wanted to learn how to navigate streets and foreign landscapes, but it seemed more important now to learn how to navigate among people, to be able to look at someone and know if he would lead me to a dead end, a dirty apartment with a lock on the door, or if he could—if he would—be a friend, help me.

A white woman slowed as she passed me. "Are you looking for somebody?"

I shook my head. "Thanks." I couldn't believe I hadn't thought about the weather, hadn't packed a coat.

A stocky African man stepped in front of me. High cheekbones, kindly face. "And you are waiting here as if it is a railway station for what purpose?" He spoke English with a French accent.

"For the purpose of becoming a student here." I stood up.

"Fair enough," he said. He was my height, with a square jaw and blue-black skin. "You will join me for lunch?"

We drank tea, ate fresh yogurt and fried noodles in the cafeteria. His name was Vincent. An acupuncturist, twenty-eight years old. He quizzed me: "You are Canadian?"

"No, American. From near San Francisco."

"You have been in contact with the school prior to your arrival?"

"No, I have not."

"How long do you wish to stay here?"

"I don't know."

"You speak some Chinese?"

"Yes, a little."

"You have money?"

"Yes, a little."

"Someplace to stay?"

"No, not yet."

Vincent nodded like a doctor making mental notes at an annual physical. As I finished my plate of greasy noodles, he announced the prognosis with a hesitant smile: "In my country, we might think you were mad. But I have never been to San Francisco, so that is not for me to judge. Wait for me in front of the cafeteria where we first met. I will return after my meeting in one hour. We will find you a room and, if we are lucky, we will make a student of you."

I sat on a green bench between the cafeteria and some tennis courts, checked my Swatch watch, fished around in my backpack, waited. Foreign students passed me in small groups speaking English or French or Arabic or Chinese. My tattoo itched under my sweatshirt. I'd been wearing the same thing since I left Hong Kong. Maybe I *was* mad. With no fixed plans, I'd arrived with only an address from inside my old green language textbook.

I'd started studying Chinese when I was seven years old because I wanted to talk to my bio-dad. When I visited him summers in Carmel, he hardly spoke to me. But during the school year, he sent me packages in the mail. He sent Chinese shoes and painted Chinese dolls and a gold and white spirit house I thought was Chinese, and books. *So many books!* All in Chinese. My mother explained that he didn't speak much because he was schizophrenic. But in my mind, he just didn't speak much *English*. I figured that if I could learn Chinese, then we'd have a special way to communicate—something in common, the way other kids shared a love of stamp collecting with their dads.

Over a dinner of bitter chicken mole on a September night in Palo Alto, I asked my mother if I could study Chinese. "Of course!" Nothing excited her more than an eccentric interest. Within a week, she'd found me a Chinese school right in Palo Alto. I went every Friday night from 6 to 9 P.M., tried to read and draw characters alongside the second-generation immigrant kids who spoke Chinese at home but had to learn the written language. I studied my strokes and worked hard on my pronunciation all autumn. Winter break arrived and my grandparents picked my sister and me up in their shiny new Lincoln Town Car, and amid small talk we drove down the 101 toward the Monterey Peninsula.

I found my bio-dad sitting on the sand in front of my grandparents' yellow house on the Carmel beach. He wore a paint-splattered windbreaker and long crazy wig, held a clarinet. I ran right up to him, *"Ni hao ma?"* I stood there, hands clasped behind my back, proud—excited.

But he just looked to the side of me and smiled. *"Ni hao ma?"* he answered flatly. And then he went silent. He brought the clarinet to his lips and started playing a jazz standard. Because as it turned out, *"Ni hao ma?"* was the only Chinese sentence my bio-dad knew.

I looked out over his shoulder at the ocean and all at once I understood: Past the blue there was more blue.

After that, I kept going to Chinese school on Friday nights because I'd made a friend named Eileen Chang, and because we got almond cookies at recess. I hadn't studied much in the past few years. But now here I was, waiting for an African doctor in the mist. I lit a cigarette.

"What are you grieving?" Vincent wanted to know when he sat down next to me on the bench.

"Grieving?"

Vincent nodded. "In Chinese medicine we understand that if you are grieving but cannot shed sufficient tears, you will crave heat on your lungs. That is why so many Chinese smoke. They are grieving, but they cannot cry. Follow me." He stood up, led me down tree-lined cement paths, past dozens of little lawns surrounded by foot-high metal fences, into a square building. "His name is Teacher Wang," Vincent whispered as we stepped through the door. "But let me talk."

In a dark room that smelled of incense, Teacher Wang played pool by himself.

Vincent picked up a cue stick.

Teacher Wang made the break shot. He wore a crisp white T-shirt and blue slacks.

Vincent spoke fast in Chinese. I only understood bits of what he said: *This girl . . . Old Gold Mountain . . . study . . . sleep . . . little money . . . I think she is quite young . . .*

Teacher Wang had the ball in hand, spoke quickly.

Vincent translated the situation for me: Tuition and a dorm room in a cement building would set me back nearly nine hundred dollars U.S. for the semester, a little less if I agreed to tutor a Chinese student. Classes would begin in February, after the New Year's celebration.

I said a silent prayer and counted out nearly half my traveler's checks as Teacher Wang pocketed the eight ball.

We walked back along the cement paths, past hundreds of parked one-speed bicycles, into a square cement foreign-students building, up a narrow staircase and down a stark hallway. Vincent jiggled the key and opened the door to room 212.

As it turned out, this was the white foreign-students building. The Muslim students were housed in a slightly older cement building nearby, the Africans in an older building still. The worst accommodations were reserved for Chinese students, where half a dozen kids shared each room. Foreign students all slept in singles or doubles.

Room 212, crammed full of furniture: two single beds, two dressers, two wooden chairs, two desks with two big red thermoses on them. Hardly space to walk between the beds. "I'll come for you at dinnertime?" Vincent said, handing me the key as he turned to leave.

"OK. Hey—thanks a lot, man."

A huge white suitcase was stashed under one of the beds, piles of paper and Chinese trinkets on the desk next to it. I slid my pack under the other bed, stretched out on top of the flowered wool blanket and closed my eyes. Vincent would come for me at dinnertime. It seemed kind of pathetic to me that no matter where I went, everything still revolved around eating and sleeping. I imagined myself in a puffy white space suit. I could be on the moon and have no more pressing thought than my own hunger. I fell asleep.

When I opened my eyes, a girl with icy blue eyes stared down at me. "Are you my roommate?" An orange barrette held her hair out of her face on one side.

"Yeah. Hi. I'm Ariel." I started to sit up.

"Fuck." She jerked her body away from me, spun around,

kicked one of the desks. "Fuck! Fuck! Fuck!" The whole room seemed to vibrate when she screamed.

It occurred to me that I might be dreaming. "I'm sorry?"

"Fuck," she said, kicking the desk again. She reminded me of a horse. "I wasn't supposed to get a fucking roommate. This is *my* room."

"Oh—hey, I'm really sorry. I can ask them to move me. They just gave me this key—"

She threw her arms up. "And I'll bet you've already been through all my stuff?" Her accent was American, but I couldn't place it. Northeastern, maybe.

"No. I just came in here and went to sleep. I was tired. For real, I didn't touch anything." I lay back down, closed my eyes. I couldn't deal with this shit.

"Fuck," she spun around again. "Well, fucking fine then." She threw books and clothes and tapes and Chinese porcelain figurines into her suitcase. "I'm fucking leaving."

Vincent appeared, wide-eyed, in the doorway. "Excuse me— is there a problem?"

Her laughter sounded mechanical. "Don't pretend you don't know," she hissed, leaning in too close to him. "They've sent in another spy." She turned back to me. "And you! Don't look so smug. Even if you're watching me, don't think they're not watching you."

Vincent stepped out of the horse's way as she dragged her huge suitcase out of the room and down the hall. "Fuck!" I heard her yell as she clamored down the stairs.

"What happened?" Vincent sat down on the girl's unmade bed.

"I have no idea. She just started freaking out on me when I woke up. Do you know her?"

"I've seen her around," he said. "Sometimes the American students go a little mad here. It is true that they are watching you. They read your mail. You just have to accept it, do not talk about politics, ignore it." He unfolded a small poster. "I brought you this to decorate your room." A drawing of a bald man, some kind of an acupuncture guide. Next to each point were the Chinese characters for its corresponding ailment or body part. It reminded me of a toy voodoo doll my great-grandmother had given me on my tenth birthday.

According to Chinese medicine, we actually have five hearts: one in the chest, one in the palm of each hand, one in the sole of each foot.

In the foreign-students cafeteria, we sat at a round table with a half-dozen African men. Vincent introduced them quickly by name and country: Ben from Ghana, Leopold and Mr. J from Burundi, Tekatel from Botswana, Jon from Sierra Leone, Sam from Swaziland. Most were lighter-skinned than Vincent, and younger.

We drank tea, ate fried rice with meat.

"What kind of meat is it?" I asked no one in particular.

Ben from Ghana laughed. "It is just meat."

That's what it tasted like—plain, tough. Just meat.

"When they say 'just meat,' they mean it is *dog*," Leopold from Burundi laughed, and they all laughed with him. I wasn't sure if they were joking.

I hadn't expected to find Africans in Beijing, but it made as much sense as anything else. The men were all studying Mandarin in preparation for graduate school in China. Mr. J from Burundi would study agriculture. Tekatel from Botswana and Leopold from Burundi would both become engineers. Vincent had already studied acupuncture in Zaire, but was going for a specialization in heart troubles. "At university in Shanghai," he explained. "I will study the broken heart to learn how the normal heart functions."

I smiled.

"Funny?"

"No. That makes sense."

Another group of Africans spoke French at a table in the corner and a small group of white women were gathered near the entrance, but most of the tables in the cafeteria were empty.

"Are there any African women studying here?" I asked.

Vincent shook his head. "In my country, we understand it is a privilege to send even one son to university."

"This is the black and white cafeteria," Tekatel from Botswana explained. "Chinese eat in another cafeteria, and Muslims in another. You've arrived during break. More American students will come after Spring Festival, but not very many of them will eat here. They will stay at the Beijing Hotel and eat at Maxim's."

I shrugged. I'd had enough of Americans.

The Year of the Rabbit

T ime confused me, I slept odd hours, wandered restless along the streets near campus where there were no
stores, just a few open-market stalls selling nothing I
needed. I met the Africans in the black and white cafeteria for
lunch and dinner. New Year's eve snuck up on me. Vincent,
Leopold, Tekatel and Mr. J came banging at my door. "Today
we make *jiaozi*," Leopold announced when I opened it. The
tallest in the group, he stood with his shoulders hunched over.

"I thought we'd go to Tian'anmen."

Vincent shook his head. "The Chinese students may march
against the foreign students today. Teacher Wang has invited us
to his home."

I laced up my boots.

"We brought you a present," Mr. J piped up.

From his little plastic bag, Vincent produced a thick green
Chinese army coat.

"Oh, god—thank you so much." I still had to figure out
how to shop.

Outside the school gates, we piled into a blue taxi and sped
through the freezing drizzle past hundreds of featureless high
rises. Red paper lanterns hung from some of the streetlights
and awnings, but even the decorations for Spring Festival were
sparse. Beijing seemed like a place where it would be hard to
feel things. Sprawling, remote. The streets on the outskirts of
the city were practically carless—just a few taxis, buses and

blue minitrucks. The sidewalks swarmed with pedestrians and bicyclists, their baskets full.

"Why would the Chinese students march against us?" I wanted to know.

"Because—" Mr. J started to answer, but Vincent held up his hand from the front seat of the taxi.

"I don't like politics. I like life," he said without turning around.

We found Teacher Wang on the top floor of a cement apartment building drinking tea from an enamel cup. "Happy New Year!" He smiled when we walked in. His hair was cut too short around his eyes. He held out a red bowl filled with little white candies. "For the Year of the Rabbit . . ."

Vincent presented Teacher Wang with a bottle of *bai jiu*, strong Chinese rice wine. "From all of us," he said. "May the Year of the Rabbit bring you much good fortune."

The Year of the Rabbit—I'd read all about it on a little red and gold poster my crazy roommate left in our room: *After the tumultuous and seemingly never-ending Year of the Tiger, the peaceful Year of the Rabbit gives welcome relief to all. Less energy is required; persuasion is preferred over force. Problems are smaller, though we tend to overindulge. Rest now and avoid unpleasantries because the Year of the Dragon begins an electric time of extreme ups and downs.*

But I still needed New Year's resolutions! I'd floated through the holidays at home on stoned autopilot. The Western calendar's 1987 began without fanfare. I didn't even stay up to watch the ball drop on TV. My first new moon in China was my last chance.

We crowded around the kitchen table and folded pork and cabbage stuffing into little rounds of dough. Teacher Wang poured us tea and instructed us on arranging the folded dumplings in concentric circles on a huge platter. "You like Beijing?" he asked.

"Yeah, so far it's great." I did like it. But I'd expected it to be prettier. I wanted cherry blossoms and pagodas, picture postcards. Maybe I wanted the Avenue of Eternal Peace to be paved with jade, but even little bourgeois trappings would have pleased me.

"What is your name again?" Teacher Wang wanted to know.

"Ariel."

"I-lee-o?"

Vincent laughed. "They called her White Ghost Girl on the train. She liked that."

Teacher Wang covered his mouth, but even his dark eyes laughed. "Well, then, White Ghost Girl, it is fairly cold, but this is the Spring Festival. I hope you will study hard in the coming months. You would not want to let the spring down."

Teacher Wang's apartment was sparsely furnished and tiny—just a kitchen and a bedroom with closet-sized bathroom and balcony. Cement floors and walls bare except for a Phoebe Cates calendar that hung in the kitchen.

Tekatel stepped out onto the balcony to smoke a Chinese cigarette while Vincent, Leopold and Mr. J exchanged sad stories about trying to get their monthly stipends from their embassies. I ducked outside to smoke with Tekatel.

"Vincent tells me you've been to Botswana," Tekatel said as he lit my cigarette.

"Yeah, summer before last. I stayed mostly in Gaborone." *Botswana*. It seemed like a lifetime ago.

Tekatel had a wistful look in his eyes. "Do you know the ambassador's daughter, Carmen?"

"No. I stayed with my friend Rosa. I met her boyfriend, Dirk. And the Rojas girls."

"Ah, the fast-car crowd. And so you danced at Club X?"

How weird that he knew the place—strange little American-pop-culture-themed discotheque where we danced to Prince and Sheila E. I thought it would be cool to spend my life like this, traveling around, meeting random people who become family in a matter of days. Maybe it wasn't so weird that he knew the place. Maybe when you made your way into a world of traveling kids, there weren't six degrees of separation anymore—maybe there were only two or three.

"Did you know that Club X was raided last summer?" Tekatel asked.

I shook my head.

"They arrested some arms dealers on their way through to South Africa. Killed some kids. And Rosa's boyfriend Dirk finally crashed that car. He's dead."

I didn't know.

In the kitchen, we dropped the dumplings into a huge pot of boiling water on the stove and fished them out with a strainer. Teacher Wang mixed soy sauce, vinegar, sugar, red chilies, garlic and ginger in a pan. From a high metal cupboard he produced six tall bottles of Chinese beer. "Doesn't anybody care about you?" he asked as he opened a bottle and handed it to me.

"Sure," I said. "My parents care about me. Maybe a couple of other people."

"And yet they have allowed you to travel halfway around the world unaccompanied?"

I didn't know what to say. Even I was surprised that my mother and John hadn't made a move to stop me. One minute I'd had a hair-brained idea. The next, I was on a plane. I said, "In America, it's different."

Teacher Wang sipped his beer, stirred his sauce. "Yes. Different."

"Marco Polo was only seventeen when he set out for China. And they didn't even have planes and trains back then," I tried, then remembered he'd been with his father.

Teacher Wang sighed, skeptical. "Well. I suppose that's what we fools all want. More freedom than years. More freedom than wisdom. No matter. Traveling will help you deal with your sadness."

Maybe it was because I was famished, but the *jiaozi* tasted like heaven—like a hearty meal cooked on a Sierra campfire after a long day's hike. Or maybe my taste buds were just thankful for something other than dog meat. *What the hell was I doing here?*

After dinner, I followed Teacher Wang and the Africans out to the balcony and up a wobbly metal fire escape onto the roof. I had a strange thought when Vincent offered me his hand to help me up: *What if trust were something I could build with my own hands?* On the roof I shivered a little, even with the army coat on.

"I thought surely I would die when I came here from Zaire last winter," Vincent said. "It doesn't even get this cold in France."

We sat in a row, our feet dangling off the edge of the building. Only the hotels in the city were lit up. "There's the Lido," Vincent said, pointing to one bright building. "The new Sheraton. And there's the Beijing Hotel. And Maxim's."

I thought about the lion dancers and all the red dragon puppets that would be making their way up Market Street in San Francisco for Chinese New Year, the baton twirlers and the light shows and the sparklers and the crowds of partiers drinking beer and eating sweet-and-sour pork from white cardboard takeout boxes. I might be rushing laughing onto a BART train with the punks and dropouts from Palo Alto High School now. The illegal fireworks would go on and on into the night.

My resolutions: *To learn how to navigate among people. To do things I am afraid to do. To trust life, trust in the bigger pattern even when I'm too close to the earth to see it.*

"I think there will be fireworks soon," Teacher Wang said as he passed the bottle of *bai jiu* down the line. I followed the men's lead and didn't so much sip the drink as pour a little down my throat. It tasted the way lighter fluid smells. We could hear a few firecrackers going off on the streets below us, but no grand displays lit the sky.

Do Not Talk About Politics

The Beijing winter wasn't kidding. The cold just would not let up. The metal furnace in my box of a room sputtered and buzzed, worked or didn't work at random intervals. I started praying to the Holy Trinity, to Buddha, to the Goddess of the Eastern Sky—it seemed to have as much effect on the heater as anything else.

Sublime: standing under the stream of hot water in the white women's communal showers, which were usually empty. But I regretted my indulgence as I shivered under my wool blanket, trying to get warm and dry. I almost wished I'd packed the green travel-sized hair dryer my mother had tried to force on me before I left home. It helped to drink *bai jiu*, and it helped to hop back and forth in the narrow space between the beds in my room until my downstairs neighbor banged on her ceiling and screamed curses in Chinese and English out her window.

That's what I was doing—hopping back and forth between the beds in my room—when a wispy Chinese girl pushed my door open—"Knock knock." She wore a white button-down shirt and baggy cotton pants. I'd almost forgotten that I agreed to tutor a Chinese student.

"My name is Kuan," she announced. "You must be I-lee-o."

"Yeah, I'm Ariel—come on in." I set up the two wooden chairs at my desk. Pretty girl, she had high cheekbones and an uneven bowl haircut. "What do you need help with?"

She scanned the contents of my cramped room, stared at me like she was trying to navigate something. "We are reading *The Adventures of Tom Sawyer* now," she said. "But truly, I must work on my conversation in English."

I was glad I didn't have to admit that I'd never read Mark Twain. "Your English sounds really good," I told her.

She blushed. "It is terrible."

Kuan wanted to know where I came from, so we talked about California, the way it has no seasons. And Chinatown in San Francisco. Kuan had grown up in Beijing. She would learn English, then go on to Beijing University to study literature or whatever field she was assigned to.

"Mondays, Wednesdays and Fridays," she said. "Those are the days I shall come, unless you dislike them."

"Nope," I assured her. "I like those days fine."

"What does mel-an-choly mean?" she wanted to know.

"It means sad. A soft, steady sad."

We lounged around my room. I didn't know what else we should talk about.

"Why are the Chinese students marching against us?" I asked.

"I do not know," she said flatly. "Maybe they do not like you." She pushed her bangs out of her face.

I didn't press the issue. "Do not talk about politics," Vincent had warned me, squinting his round eyes.

On Wednesday afternoon, the fog held heavy outside my uncurtained second-story window, but Kuan wanted to go for a walk. We wandered down narrow cement paths, blowing our breath like smoke in the wintry air. We stepped over shrubs and a low metal fence onto one of the bigger lawns. Kuan looked down at her black flats. "Those students are not marching against you," she finally said. "They are marching against the government. They want social reform. The general secretary of the party, who supported reforms, has been fired."

"Do you want social reform?"

Kuan was quiet. We walked through the fog. "You ask a lot of questions," she said, then looked away. She touched her finger to her red nose. "I want to live. I want to study hard and help the motherland move forward. I want to get married and have a son."

We sat down on one of the green benches. My ears felt like they were frozen solid. "In America we march for more socialism," I told her.

Kuan covered her mouth when she laughed. "More socialism!" But then she squinted her eyes, looked more serious. "What do you do when you march for social reform in America?"

I shrugged. "We have sit-ins, where we won't move out of the way. Sometimes we block a certain building. My boyfriend used to tell the other marchers to stay focused because sometimes people just come to riot. We make signs, chant stupid slogans. We want the press to take notice, so there is always some street theater, costumes. It's no revolution, but it does have an impact. Little by little."

"And you aren't afraid?"

"No," I said. "Not really. What's the worst that can happen? Even if it's just for our own peace of mind, we have to march, complain, tell our own truth."

"Your own truth?" Kuan tilted her head to one side. "I do not understand. You make it sound like there is more than one truth."

"I guess that's what I believe, that there are always different truths. There isn't just one, or even two or three. But maybe I'm wrong."

"You have a boyfriend?" Kuan blurted out, like she'd just realized I mentioned one.

"I used to."

Kuan stuck out her lower lip. "What happened?"

"I don't know. We were different."

"Sad," she said, hunching her whole body into her frown. Kuan was seventeen, but her mannerisms made her seem younger.

"Yeah, maybe sad. But that's how it goes. Listen," I wanted to change the subject. "We're going dancing at the Lido next Friday. Do you wanna come?"

Kuan laughed, shook her head. "They don't let Chinese into the Lido."

"But they let Hong Kong Chinese in. We'll dress you up. You could look like a Hong Kong Chinese girl. Easy."

"No," she laughed. "Certainly no." And then she grabbed my hand and squeezed it hard. "You are my American friend."

A few more white foreign students started trickling into my building, but I wasn't assigned a new roommate. An English girl who lived in Taiwan took the room next door, and Alice, a psychology student from Harvard, moved in across the hall.

A girl with puffy eyes who'd lived in Guangzhou, the daughter of Christian missionaries, invited me to an American party downtown. "They're airlifting McDonald's in from Hong Kong," she chirped when I met her outside the black and white cafeteria. The thought of eating a Big Mac flown in from Hong Kong made me feel queasy. As if my own white privilege in Beijing didn't already taste foul enough. "No thanks," I told her. And she never spoke to me again.

Classes started on a cloudy Monday. I sat under the fluorescent lights in a small white room with a dozen other white students as Teacher Wang led us in reciting the *pinyin* alphabet and taught us to say in Chinese "The plum trees will soon begin to blossom" and "Deng Xiaoping, the illustrious leader of the motherland, is a fine man."

There were rumors of student protests, but everyone who would talk about them had a different story. Chinese students had circulated a letter calling the African students "black devils." The African students had better housing, got stipends from the Chinese government. Some African men were dating Chinese students, buying them gifts that Chinese men could never afford. Chinese students marched against their status as third-class citizens on campus. African students marched against racism. And Chinese students marched for democracy, against Deng Xiaoping. Nobody would explain why the Chinese students weren't marching against the white students—we were treated even better than the Africans. And every time I heard rumors that protest was about to be staged, Vincent had other plans. We were going to the Summer Palace. Or we were going to the Beijing Hotel to eat in the dining room that didn't allow unescorted Chinese. Or we were going to Shanghai for the weekend. Or we were going to see someone at an embassy. "If you want to make trouble," Vincent told me, "you stay with the whites. My boys and I, we cannot afford any trouble." We rode the crowded blue buses, went to stores and scoured the near-empty shelves, bought *bai jiu* and pretty communist propaganda posters of happy workers, young space travelers and civic-minded police officers. In the Beijing Hotel gift shop, I bought silk long underwear from a Chinese sales lady who wouldn't be allowed in if she didn't work there. I should have been boycotting the place, but I wasn't sure if anybody cared whether or not I shopped there. Surely it was owned by the same government that owned the People's shops. If I was going to boycott the Beijing Hotel, I'd have to boycott the whole country. At a metal table outside Maxim's, Pierre Cardin's swank restaurant, Vincent and I shared a sandwich and drank real coffee with cream. An American with food between his teeth leaned over our table and stared at Vincent. "Where ya from?"

"Zaire." Vincent smiled politely.

"Zaire, eh?" the American scratched his three-day beard. "I hear your President Mobutu went through all the churches and replaced the pictures of Jesus with portraits of himself."

Vincent scooted back in his chair. "I don't know anything about that," he said sternly. "I don't like politics."

"Ah." The man leaned in closer. "An apathetic African?"

Vincent muttered something in French, dropped some People's money onto the table, stood up. "Let's go."

I gulped down my coffee, grabbed the rest of our overpriced sandwich, followed Vincent as he cursed in Chinese, French, English and a language I didn't recognize. "*Merde* . . . call me a pathetic African . . . *ni*! . . . I call you pathetic motherfucker . . . stupid shit man . . . I guess it is easy to be righteous when you are carrying an American passport . . . *ni*! . . . *merde*! . . . stupid shit man . . . *Oh, hello! I am American, so I know everything.* . . ."

Vincent was strange, but I liked him.

We toured the Forbidden City, talked about the Chinese healing points in the Inner Court. "They are the same as the killing points," Vincent explained. He was wearing a felt hat, black suit pants and a plain white T-shirt. "It's all in your intention." Peering into the imperial concubines' little rooms, we wished our dorm rooms were as fancy.

In the stark hallway at the Zairean embassy, we waited for Vincent's stipend money that never materialized. We browsed in an English-language bookstore where seemingly random passages were blacked out of the books, drank tea in clean restaurants that served little else. I hadn't seen any homeless people in Beijing, or any beggars. But I didn't understand why the city had to be so anesthetized. Why weren't there little altars to Buddha and the Moon Goddess tucked in every corner, like in Chinatown and Hong Kong? I thought people could handle sputtering heaters that never worked, but no gods? Here was where the communist line always lost me. *Religion is the sigh of the oppressed people*, Marx said, but also, *the heart of a heartless world*. Was this really what he meant? That utopia could be ugly, could do without a heart? Giving up beauty and faith seemed like too harsh a trade, even if you were bargaining for food and shelter.

Alice, the psychology student from Harvard with henna-red hair, was as curious as I was about all the protests. So one afternoon we followed a fresh rumor, skipped lunch and rode a crowded bus along the dull streets to the university out near the Summer Palace. "The scale of this city is all wrong," Alice said. She wore three hooded sweat jackets over her I (heart) Beijing T-shirt. "The boulevards are too wide for the few buses, the sidewalks too narrow for all the people on foot. The bicyclists don't know where to go. It makes me feel like I'm always in a dream."

Quiet campus. Even more square cement buildings and geometrically trimmed shrubs than at the language institute, but traditional buildings too—pagodas and red columns. We wandered aimlessly among the buildings, wondering whether the rumor had been a false lead. Then we heard the voices, turned a corner. A small group of Chinese students marched down a cement path, shouting almost politely. It seemed more like a pep rally than a protest. And the Chinese students complained in puns. Were they saying "I love Deng Xiaoping" or "Smash Xiaoping into a thousand pieces"?

"We like dialogue," one student called toward us in English when he saw us, but none stopped to talk. I snapped a few pictures.

Back on the Beijing Language Institute campus late that afternoon, Teacher Wang and a man with big round glasses approached Alice and me as we sat on the bench near the tennis courts. They smiled broadly with anger flashing in their eyes. Teacher Wang introduced the round-glasses man as Teacher Fu. Teacher Wang asked us how everything was going: Did we like our rooms? Were we studying hard? Then he mentioned, almost in passing, that Teacher Fu was headed downtown to get some film developed. Did either of us need any prints? I dumbly handed over my roll of film. And I never saw my prints. Of course I never saw my prints.

Later, Alice wanted me to ask after the film, demand my pictures from Teacher Wang. "He tricked us," she insisted, screwing up her freckled face. "You have to confront him."

But I thought better of it. Every setting has its own structure, after all, its own rules. And if you want to find your place, you'd better understand those rules. *Do not talk about politics.* Simple enough. But here, everything was politics. So my place was on the outskirts. Again. Always.

On Friday, Kuan brought me a pack of Peacock cigarettes. I'd been trying to avoid Chinese cigarettes, but I thanked her, lit one, pretended the tangy smell alone didn't make me feel like puking. "What do you want to talk about today?"

"I do not know," she said as she sat down at my desk, picked up my cork-covered journal.

She read a few pages slowly, then put it down. She pushed my three tarnished pennies off my *I Ching* book and flipped through the warped pages. Somehow the book had gotten damp in my bag. "Why do you have this?"

"For when I need to make an important decision. I ask it

what I should do next. Or I just throw the coins to see what it will say."

Kuan shook her head.

"For real," I said. "Here's one I got the other day." I paged through the thick book to find the Wanderer. I pointed out the text I liked: *Strange lands and separation are the wanderer's lot. . . . When grass on a mountain takes fire, there is bright light. However, the fire does not linger in one place, but travels on to new fuel. It is a phenomenon of short duration.*

Kuan raised her thin eyebrows. "You are just like an old Chinese woman, I-lee-o, but you use your American pennies instead of the yarrow sticks. I should take you home to my grandmother. You two can drink black tea and she can tell you ghost stories and you can sit outside on barrels and smoke like men and make funny of all the children who do not believe. Teacher Wang call you White Ghost Girl, but I will call you *laolao*. Come on, Grandma, use your head to make your choices." She laughed this deep belly laugh that seemed somehow out of character, like it came from someplace inside her that was tougher than she looked, more mischievous.

"This is for real, Kuan." I read to her from my hexagram: *A wanderer has no fixed abode; his home is the road. Therefore he must take care to remain upright and steadfast, so that he sojourns only in the proper places, associating only with good people. . . . Fire on the mountain / The image of THE WANDERER / Thus the superior man / Is clear minded and cautious. . . .*

Kuan covered her mouth when she laughed. "And who is the superior man, *laolao*?"

She was kind of pissing me off. "No one," I said. "They just say that when they mean to suggest how you should act when you get the hexagram. They tell you how the superior man would do it and then you know you should do the same."

Kuan smiled. "Maybe if you studied your characters, you

would not have to lug around that big translation." She pointed to the character for the Wanderer, scribbled it on a blank page in my journal, then wrote out a few older versions of the same character and pointed. "Look. Two people seeking shelter under a tree. Travel. Make friends. That is all your oracle is telling you. Now," she closed my journal, "when do we go to the Lido?"

Beijing Tricky

Teacher Fu stood outside the white foreign-students building, smoking. I nodded hello as I passed him. I wondered what classes he taught.

Vincent seemed less than excited when I sat down next to him in the cafeteria with my plate of greens and generic meat and announced that Kuan was coming to the Lido with us. "She's just showering now—I'm gonna help her dress up." I was so psyched. I could make her look like a Hong Kong Chinese girl, no problem!

"Now," Vincent said, tightening his jaw a little, "please do not get into trouble under my name."

Tekatel and Mr. J just sat there, silent.

"You think we'll get into trouble for taking her?" It hadn't occurred to me to ask Vincent and his friends whether I could invite her. And I hadn't thought of myself as doing anything under Vincent's name. He'd gotten me a room, what more responsibility did he have? Navigating subtleties.

Vincent looked at Tekatel, then at Mr. J.

"It's OK by me, man," Mr. J offered. With his gold chains, oversized Afro and lapel, Mr. J looked like a '70s *Soul Train* throwback.

"Maybe you can take her in a different taxi?" Tekatel suggested.

"OK." I nodded.

Vincent took a few more bites of his greasy greens. "All right," he finally said. "Bring her to Lido tonight, we can meet you both there. But tonight, that's all. We will not start taking her all around town where Chinese don't go. And tonight, Ghost Girl, you do not leave her side." Mr. J and Tekatel nodded as Vincent pointed to them. "We three would not take a Chinese girl out. And we do not need anybody saying otherwise."

"OK—listen, I'm really sorry." I was. "I didn't realize it would be a big deal."

Vincent waved his hand in the air, tried to laugh it off. "No, it's not a big deal. . . ."

When I got back to my room, Kuan was wrapped up in a white towel, grinning. "You have hot water!"

"You don't have hot water?"

"Yes, but not on Fridays. On Tuesdays."

I rifled through my drawers and handed Kuan my black Levi's and black T-shirt. "You wear my combat boots. I'll wear your shoes." She had black farmer flats no Hong Kong Chinese girl would be caught dead in. My clothes were baggy on her, but not as baggy as her own. She sat on my bed as I lined her eyes with black kohl liner I'd bought in the open market outside school, applied layer after layer of Great Lash. Her skin was smooth, perfect. I hated to cover it with my pasty foundation. I slicked her short hair back with gel, applied a heavy coat of purple lipstick. "Let me see your fingernails."

She offered me her unwrinkled hands. Her little fingernails curved downward just like Lee Press-Ons. I painted them red, and she fluttered her hands like butterfly wings until the polish dried.

Kuan closed her eyes as I led her by her shoulders to the square mirror above my dresser.

"Open your eyes."

"*Ay-ah!*" She covered her face with both hands.

"You look positively New Wave." I smiled at her in the mirror. "For real, Kuan."

She hunched her shoulders. "I do not know, *laolao*."

"Well, you do have to stick your chest out a little more. You have to walk taller."

"Walk taller?"

I lay down on top of my wool blanket and tried to coach her as she walked back and forth between the metal beds. "Head up, shoulders back, you have to lift your feet off the floor when you walk. And wiggle just a little bit. C'mon, you're a rock star. You're the queen of Hong Kong."

"*Ay-ah.*" Kuan slouched down next to me on my bed. "It will never work."

"No. Come on. You look perfect."

The wind was strong, but the night was going to be just right. In the little blue taxi, Kuan tapped her foot nervously on the floor. "So far you like Beijing?"

I watched the night fog from the car window. "Sometimes it seems harsh to me," I admitted. "All the cement block buildings, and the streets laid out like a perfect chess board. It's strange—when I left home I was afraid because I was feeling things less and less. And here I've come to a place that matches my insides—a place where it's hard to feel anything."

But Kuan shook her head. "Do not be fooled by what you can see," she said. "There is a great underground city here, blue tunnels cut by hand from the living rock. When I was a little girl, there was a secret entrance in the alley where my family lived. I climbed down, down, down. It could be very wet down in the tunnels, but it was my own world. The greatest bomb shelter ever built—it could house all of Beijing—schools, hospitals, statues, supplies for many months. The central tunnel is a subterranean highway leading out of the city to the western mountains. My mama caught me climbing down the stone steps one time, and I was forbidden to go. But I already knew. Plain face forward is just Beijing tricky."

The Lido was supposed to be an exact replica of the Holiday Inn in Palo Alto where my grandmother used to stay when she visited, but the Lido seemed so much fancier. Kuan squeezed my hand as I paid the cover and we slipped easily past the Chinese doorman and into the club that smelled of sweat and perfume. Strobe lights flashed in the dark room, and a disco ball spun from the ceiling, casting colored lights on the walls. Black, white and Asian kids danced to a remix of "I Melt with You," shouting over the pulsing music, letting out shooting stars of laughter. I pulled Kuan toward the bar, offered to buy her a drink.

"Let us share," she whispered. But I ordered two. She sat on the stool next to me, still holding my hand. Looking out at all the kids dancing, she beamed, swayed to the music, tried to sing along here and there.

If we'd been at a Palo Alto High School dance, I would have been dying. But the excitement on Kuan's face peeled all that away. She wiggled on her stool. "Thank you," she whispered. We slurped the sweet tropical cocktails through fat white straws, and Kuan stared blankly, pretending not to understand when the bartender said something to her in Mandarin.

Vincent, Leopold, Tekatel and Mr. J appeared at our side in a cloud of aftershave, and I bought them a round. "Congratulations," Vincent said, smiling, impressed at Kuan's transformation.

When Tina Turner started singing "Better Be Good to Me" through the speakers, Kuan wanted to dance. She plucked the red toothpick umbrellas from our empty glasses, gave me mine and pocketed her own as she climbed off the stool. "We have to save these!"

It's hard to say which one of us was the clumsier dancer, but we didn't care. We circled each other on the smooth floor, she spun me around and I couldn't help laughing when she tried to do a little moonwalk. She flailed her thin arms in the flashing lights. She put one hand on her hip, wagged her index finger, pursed her purple lips and tried to look extra tough as she shouted along with Tina Turner. She raised her fists over her head, marched in a circle. We were doing some awful cross between disco square dancing and break dancing. She laughed without covering her mouth. Her eyes shone like a little girl in a wondrous amusement park. In the strobing light, she looked like an old-fashioned movie star. I'd never seen anyone so beautiful. The song faded into Madonna singing "White Heat," and Kuan shook her fist in the air, shouted, "My love is dangerous!" She placed a thin, manicured hand on my arm, rested her head on my shoulder, fell into me, already drunk. Blur of softness. We slow danced under the disco ball, the music pulsing too fast.

"Door," Vincent whispered as he leaned in between us, then slid away.

I looked up. A uniformed officer and a man in brown stood next to the doorman, talking, looking right at us. A fourth man stood with them. I recognized him. Was it Teacher Fu? I squinted to see. His glasses flashed under the strobe lights, but I couldn't be sure who it was. I pulled Kuan into the crowd. "What would happen if you got caught here?"

"What?" she shouted over the music.

The man in brown made his way through the dancers and lights, shot me the coldest look, grasped Kuan's shoulder.

Her face fell as she turned to face him.

I didn't know if he was a cop, someone from the hotel, someone from school or what. We were still holding hands. I wasn't going to let go of her. I scanned the crowd for Vincent, but he was nowhere. If anyone on the dance floor noticed what was happening, they didn't let on.

The man in brown spoke to Kuan in Chinese.

Her cheeks reddened.

I couldn't hear what he was saying.

This time Kuan didn't pretend not to speak Chinese. She pulled her hand from my grip. "I must go," she said soberly.

I followed them as the man in brown pulled her off the dance floor. "No," I blurted out. "Wait—"

Kuan shook her head, shooed me away with her hand.

I wanted to know who the man in brown was, where he was taking her. "Wait!" I yelled it this time. "Where are you going?" When the man in brown glanced back at me over his shoulder, I saw Burke's face.

I thought I could see Kuan's eyes fill with tears as they neared the door. I was screaming now, the doorman held me back with one arm. "Where the fuck are you taking her?" Seismic panic. I jumped forward a half-inch when I felt a hand press into the small of my back.

"You will hold your center," Vincent said softly.

I don't know what song was streaming from the speakers. I heard "Stairway to Heaven."

"You will hold your center," Vincent said again.

"Center?" Who'd held his center at Maxim's? What the fuck was going on? "I have to go with her. Come on, Vincent— where are they taking her? We have to go—who is that man?" I was supposed to stay at Kuan's side. Now I was stuck between Vincent and the doorman.

Vincent didn't answer me. "You will hold your center," he

said again. And then, after assuring the doorman that he didn't need to call another cop to deal with me, "I think she will be all right."

"But where did they take her?" My tears tasted like the ocean.

"I do not know," he said. Then, smiling a little, "You forgot to teach her not to dance like a Chinese."

Great Wall, Subterranean Highway

I t was nearly midnight when I got back to my room and slipped into bed with my clothes on. The furnace wasn't working. I rubbed my hands together and breathed into them, remembered the bottle of *bai jiu* in my dresser. I was getting used to the taste of the stuff. It warmed my throat instantly and the heat spread slowly across my chest. Kuan had been ablaze at the Lido. Where had they taken her? I'd wanted to show her an American-pop-culture-themed discotheque. Now I might never see her again. Panic congealed into dread. I knew Chinese weren't allowed at the Lido, but I had no clue what the consequences might be.

I woke up with a headache. Hammer on my skull, a knocking at the door. It took me a full minute to focus. I climbed out of bed.

Pretty Alice stood in the hall. "I picked this up for you." She held out a brown paper-wrapped box from home.

March 22, 1987

Tiniest Ariel,

In your letters, you praise the Chinese government. Surely you understand the human rights abuses, the political prisoners, the lack of basic freedoms! Educate yourself, Tiniest!

Now. I was talking to a friend at church who spent some years in China. He mentioned that the dental care there is simply abhorrent. I mentioned this to John and he, in turn, mentioned that he didn't think you'd had braces on your teeth for about a year before you left. Neither of us could remember you getting them off, so this morning I called your orthodontist. Our conversation was very enlightening. Your orthodontist told me that NOT ONLY did he never take the braces off of your teeth, but you hadn't been to see him in over a year. I repeat: Over a year! WHAT HAPPENED TO THE BRACES, TINIEST?

I ran into Guy and your friend Carl at a protest at the Concord Naval Weapons Station on Saturday. We stopped the trains carrying weapons to Central America! Guy is off to Howard University in September. Isn't that exciting? They both asked about you.

Last night John and I went to see a wonderful film called Beverly Hills Cop. (Actually, John didn't enjoy it at all. He says I only liked it because I'm from Beverly Hills, but I thought you would have liked it, too! If it comes to Beijing, you ought to go and see it.) Your friend Jack said to tell you that you are sorely missed at the theater. He sold us our popcorn. (Is he on drugs?)

In the bad news department, Leslie won't be going back to college next fall. John and I can't afford the tuition, and your grandfather has completely screwed us over. It's simply a tragedy, and one I will never forgive him for.

In the good news department, John's book, Alive Into the Wilderness, *has just been published by Coast Light Press here in Palo Alto. Even though the book makes it sound like I forced him to marry me (which I did not!), I think it's very exciting.*

I am still spending time visiting my guys at San Quentin, and helping one friend there with his appeal and considering how we might make a movie about his case. Also working to promote an exhibition on the refugee experience—it's rewarding, but terribly time-consuming. The most difficult thing is that I don't get to spend much time in my studio working on my own projects these days.

Here is your care package for now. Enclosed you should find:

1 razor, which you asked for even though, as you know, shaving your legs only makes the hair grow in thicker

2 boxes of Stop-It, a homeopathic remedy that will help you quit smoking

3 Tiger's Milk Bars

2 boxes of dental floss

1 toothbrush (I went to the Stanford pharmacy and insisted on THE BEST toothbrush. It was not cheap.)

1 book called The Life of Poetry *by Muriel Rukeyser— John thought you would enjoy it*

3 crystals (one on a chain) for your protection

1 travel-sized hair dryer, which you forgot to pack

Well—that's all my news. Take care. And, Tiniest, don't go out with a wet head.

Love, Mom

My braces. I'd forgotten all about those metal tracks I'd pried off one by one with pliers from John's toolbox in the garage. I'd been surprised how easy it was. Just a little pressure on the bracket—and *pop*. Then the next. *Pop*. The glue itself proved more resistant. I could still feel little clumps of it on some of my teeth.

I took a shower, didn't even consider taking the hair dryer out of its box. My mother had never understood about my whitey Afro: Blow-drying made me look like Angela Davis circa 1970.

I found Vincent out by the tennis courts, but he didn't want to talk about the Lido, didn't want to go check on Kuan. "I am sure she is fine," he said. "We do not go into the Chinese-students' building."

I wasn't sure if Vincent's weird rules were designed to protect me, Kuan or himself. *What was he afraid of?* "I don't understand," I admitted. But the conversation was already over. He took my hand, led me onto a green minibus headed for the Great Wall at Badaling.

The wall was wider than I'd imagined, and packed with Chinese and foreign tourists. An old woman in a Mao suit leaned against the railing, cool as a punk rocker, eating an apple. Giddy Europeans posed for pictures. Little kids in red sweaters waddled and tripped on the giant stone steps. Young Chinese couples strolled along in their carefully pressed Western clothes, hopelessly out of fashion. We walked, climbed, walked more, past the first tower, and the second, and the third. The crowd thinned. We kept walking. The elaborate brick and granite road that zigzagged east and west along the rocky green mountains. I'd heard that in China, there were even bigger ancient pyramids than in Egypt. But they were closed off, secret military bases. I wanted to hike the thousands of miles the wall stretched, but at the fifth tower, we were exhausted. We sat down, peeled wax paper off the pork buns Vincent had packed.

It seemed a little bit sad to me as I chewed on my lunch— this thick wall to keep the foreigners and nomads out, the great underground city where the people of Beijing could hide from blacks and whites, strangers and invaders of every kind. They'd thought of everything except the attacker they knew, the one who spoke their language, the one they'd follow without a second thought.

"What are you thinking about?" Vincent wanted to know.

gotten her in trouble once—looking for her now would only make things worse. When the knock came at the door I figured it was Alice, or Vincent. I almost didn't answer. I wanted to be alone. But I opened the door.

"Knock knock." Kuan wore a little white headband and her favorite baggy cotton clothes. She had my Levi's, T-shirt and combat boots in a pink plastic bag. "I'm so sorry I had to leave early on Friday," she said calmly, holding the bag up for me.

I couldn't believe she was apologizing to me. "Holy shit, Kuan—I'm sorry. What happened? I've been totally worried about you."

She sat down on the edge of my bed. "It was time for me to come home," she said. "That's all." She looked sad, but her calm made me feel even more panicky.

I just stood there in front of her. Surely I was losing my mind. I thought of my crazy old horse of a roommate. Now her antics didn't seem so strange. I wanted to kick the desk, scream "Fuck!"

Surfing waves of Beijing tricky.

I sat down at the head of my metal bed, leaned back onto a red silk pillow I'd bought at the open market. "Well," I finally said. "No more dances for us, huh?"

"No," she whispered, and then curled up next to me, rested her head at my waist. "No more dances for us, laolao."

I watched her sad breath, the way it made her back rise and fall. She seemed so little. I reached for the Sony Walkman on the table, pushed play and turned the volume all the way up. We could hear "Purple Rain" playing out of the headphones. I rested my hand on her soft hair just above her headphones. I whispered, "It'll be OK."

The ancient Taoists said: The heart is like the bud of a lotus flower. It governs the blood and houses the mind. It opens to the tongue, "the

"Nothing much. Just what enemies look like," I lit a cigarette. "Vincent? How come you don't like to talk about Zaire, about politics?"

He stood up, brushed off his pants, folded the brown paper bag he'd brought the pork buns in, gazed out along the snaking wall. "Because I like life," he said slowly. "In my country, I have seen the dead bodies of my brothers, the ones who liked politics. So I made a promise to my mother. I keep my head in my books so she will not see my head on a stick in the square."

On the way back to campus, I stared out the window of the minibus. I know I promised I wouldn't use the word "gray" again, but I have to. Because here, making our way back through town, my whole memory of Beijing dissolves into gray. Pigeon-gray, pencil-gray, ash-gray, beach-gray. As if the whole city was carved from a single gray stone. People tell me it isn't like that anymore. People tell me I wouldn't recognize the city with its prostitutes, beggars, backpackers, fresh millennial splashes of color. But that's how it was half my life ago. Gray. Even the language institute that is so Eden green in my memory—I look at the color snapshots now, the ones that weren't confiscated, and they picture unrelenting gray. All that gray, it makes you nervous, and pretty soon the nervousness dissolves into a mild but steady gray paranoia. Maybe it was the surveillance, the martial law, the real danger we wouldn't fully understand for another couple of years (blood-stained gray). It was all of that, for sure, all that we didn't know and didn't understand and couldn't talk about. But more than anything else, it was the gray.

That night I dreamed I found a door at the back of my closet. I opened it, heard the rush of streaming water. I climbed damp concrete stairs down, down, down. I wandered through the blue tunnels under Beijing, turned left, then right, then left again, running now, through milky puddles toward the sound of a river. I was looking for a friend from home. I was looking for Kuan. I had to get to a class. Someone was following me. I could hear the splash of footsteps, but I couldn't see anyone. Cold tunnels. The chill reminded me that I was alone. The footsteps went silent. I had to find the subterranean highway.

In class on Monday, Teacher Wang led us in reciting the *pinyin* alphabet and taught us to say in Chinese, "It was nearly midnight last Friday when the dance was over," and "The teacher is very concerned about his students."

I wanted to learn how to say, "Where the fuck are you taking her?" But I didn't ask any questions. I had to learn not to get into trouble. I tapped my foot lightly on the dull white tile floor.

"Bye-bye," Teacher Wang said to each of the students as they filed out of the fluorescent classroom.

"Bye-bye," I started to say, but Teacher Wang held up his hand to stop me.

"White Ghost Girl, I-lee-o," he said softly. He looked down at his shoes, then looked up. Smiled, then frowned. He put his hands in his pockets, cleared his throat. "As you know, it was by special arrangement that you were invited to join our school. In the future, when you have a question about the way we do things here, you may come to me. We can work together to find your answer."

I nodded. "Thank you, Teacher Wang."

That afternoon, Kuan didn't come to my room. I lay on my wool blanket, waiting for her, smoking my tangy Chinese cigarettes.

～～～

JOURNAL ENTRY #17
39°55′N 116°25′E
SPRING, 1987

strange place, no art—and waiting now—what is
dance worth?—sometimes the americans—they g
mad—don't let the spring down—fuck!—i was su
take care—to remain upright and steadfast—cle
and cautious—you will hold your center—you wi
center—you will hold your center

I wrote letters home on the backs of my pr
propaganda posters and I scrawled "I love C
and Chinese on the blue and white airma
it's not like I didn't love China. The Am
plained endlessly ticked me off. But the
Nothing added up. I didn't understand
segregated. I didn't understand why n
about the polite student protests.
marchers were making China look ba
want the foreign students to get inv
some merit in shielding the Chin
Western influences. But doing a
Turner just didn't seem that pro
there a dance club in Beijing at al
gerous? I would have been such
Maoism, but they didn't even
understand any of it. Mostly
couldn't dance with Kuan.

By Wednesday afternoon, I'
again. She'd been disappea
like the constant chill, like

sprout of the heart," and is reflected in the eyes, "mirror of the heart's spirit."

I guess you could say I let the spring down. But it felt more like the spring let me down. She was a no-show. The plum trees never blossomed. Or they blossomed and the blossoms fell from their branches in a single morning breath. I missed the whole thing. The Goddess of the Western Sky delivered the thick heat of summer on the wings of an April dust storm that cloaked the city in a surreal layer of desert earth.

Kuan brought me a little surgical mask to wear in the haze. Sitting on my unmade bed, we talked about the weather, about the English language. We talked around things instead of through them. What did the word "freedom" connote in English? And why did we have so many words for it: "liberty," "independence," "sovereignty," "autonomy"? And "free"—why did it also mean something you didn't have to pay for?

Free. From the Old English "frēon," *to love.*

Evenings, Vincent tried to teach me to play tennis with borrowed rackets. Love meant zero in that game, too. Love meant losing. I always lost.

Vincent had exams coming up, so in his cluttered room that smelled of panax ginseng and chrysanthemum tinctures, I quizzed him with flash cards. He had to know the characters for the ventricles, the mitral valve, the atrium, the aorta, contraction and dilation.

According to Huang Di, the Yellow Emperor of China, the heart was the sovereign of all organs, representing the consciousness of the being. "The heart disdains being scattered," Vincent announced, quoting from his *Classic of Medicine.* "One should consume bitter herbs to keep the heart flow contained."

In the black and white cafeteria, we ate pickled cabbage.

Almost everywhere I went on campus, I ran into Teacher Fu. I nodded hello. He nodded back. We never spoke. Beijing was an exercise in not mentioning the big gray elephant in the living room. I wanted to poke at it, find out what kind of beast it was. Asian and African elephants were different—as were America's extinct mammoths. I wanted to measure its body, pet its wrinkled underbelly, feed it peanuts and apples, taunt it, find out what it would do to me. But I was learning restraint. *Trust in the bigger pattern*, I'd whisper to myself when I opened my eyes in the dusty morning.

I read my book on Buddhism, started trying to meditate in my room, but my mind wandered home and away. I was swimming in the ocean at Santa Cruz, I was riding a smoky Chinese train to the end of the western line. I wanted to take the Buddhist refuge vow. *Becoming a refugee is acknowledging that there is really no need for home, or ground*, a Tibetan master said in unassigned reading. *Taking refuge is an expression of freedom, because as refugees we are no longer bounded by the need for security*. I was suspended in no man's land, and maybe that's the way it was supposed to be. I forced myself to sit, hands resting just below my bellybutton, thumbs touching and not touching, staring at a low spot on the wall, listening to the chorus of cicadas outside. It seemed to me there must be a difference between proper meditation and this agitated spacing out, but I didn't know what that difference might be. To take the refuge vow, I'd have to change my attitude to pure nonaggression— nothing to prove; I'd have to change my "mark," which I didn't quite understand, except that it might follow naturally my change in attitude, and that it had something to do with gentleness, with a kind of politeness that wasn't just bullshit or self- protection; I'd have to change my name, too, but that had already been taken care of—I was White Ghost Girl. I was White Ghost Girl, and I had no need for home.

The Cold War Café

On a scorching Saturday while Vincent and Tekatel sweated on the tennis courts, I wandered off alone to catch a bus downtown for some real coffee. I missed a connection, ended up in an unfamiliar part of the city where outdoor vendors shouted, selling ice cream, Popsicles, tangerines, broccoli, mushrooms, snow peas, live animals. I bought a bag of produce, wandered up the road in the direction that felt like east, like downtown. People stared. A middle-aged woman with short, uneven bangs reached up as she passed me, patted me on the side of the head, chuckled. A man pointed at me, covered his laughing mouth. I felt like some endearingly ugly little dog everyone had to stop and pet.

"What time do you usually eat dinner?" someone in a blue Mao suit wanted to know.

I'd heard the question fifty times before—it came straight from the English lessons broadcast on the Voice of America. "About six o'clock."

He laughed a surprised laugh, like he hadn't expected to be understood or answered.

An old woman patted me on the stomach when I paused at another produce stall. "So fat!" she said in Chinese. I weighed all of 110 pounds.

Around a corner, down a narrow stone alley where a street

cat had killed a mouse and a raven glanced right and left, nervous as a shoplifter, before flying off with it, I spotted a black and white stenciled sign in English: The Cold War Café.

I followed an arrow that pointed down cement steps to a red metal door halfway underground.

Dark, windowless space. An electric blue lava lamp glowed in the center of the room. A Chinese singer who sounded like Laurie Anderson rumbled out of the speakers. Blue and pink light bulbs flickered overhead. Wall-to-wall black carpeting covered the floor, vinyl booths lined the gold and red dragon-papered walls. A black platform stage opposite the bar, empty. A dozen bleach-blond and Mohawked Chinese kids leaned over tables, whispering to each other or playing mahjong with dominoes and dice. A few paused to check me out as I walked to the bar, sat on a high black stool, ordered a Dragon beer. "I didn't know there were punks in Beijing," I said to the bartender in my pidgin Chinese. I didn't know the word for "punk."

He had a floppy black Mohawk and safety pins in his ears. "No," he laughed, dragging on his Marlboro cigarette. "No fuckin' punk in Beijing." He spoke English with a heavy accent, but I could understand him. He gestured toward the kids in the booths. "This ones only fuckin' punk in Beijing. You go Wuhan. Chinese punk all live Wuhan. Maybe Wuhan fuckin' punk come play music Cold War Café sometime. You fuckin' punk?" He picked up an empty beer bottle, wiped down the wooden counter.

"No," I admitted.

"You hate fuckin' everything?"

"Not really."

"I hate fuckin' everything." He smiled like it was a lie. He pointed to a red and black painted sign on the floor behind the bar. "I make that," he said. The sign was stenciled, in English: Be Yourself or Die. "I make one outside also."

I liked this place. *Be yourself or die.* Who was I now? White Ghost Girl refugee. Neither centered nor cautious. But I wanted to hang out down here in the bomb shelter where people knew how to decorate a room on the cheap.

"How much you want for your fuckin' Levi's?" the bartender wanted to know.

I looked down at my faded blue jeans that glowed purple under the colored lights. "They're not for sale."

"Fuckin' everything U.S.A. for sale. How much?" He leaned against the wall. I surveyed his outfit: a red T-shirt stenciled with "Wuhan Punk" and cool old four-pocket Chinese army pants. The black and white camouflage design looked like clouds against a pea-green sky.

"I'll trade you outfits," I offered. I thought he looked about my size.

His face lit up. "You joke me, right?" He had a deep scar under his left eye.

"I would never joke you," I promised.

We hid behind a worn red curtain next to the stage, traded pants, then T-shirts. I was wearing a plain white one with a V-neck. But it was made in America. "I stencil this one, too," he said. "I stencil 'Chaos'."

A few bleach-blond Chinese kids had gathered at the bar. They wanted to know if I had anything else for sale. I shook my head. "Sorry."

"You ever fuckin' go back U.S.A.?" a slight blond guy with half-inch black roots showing wanted to know. "We give you Foreign Exchange Certificate. You buy us thing."

The bartender opened another Dragon beer for me. "What do you want?" I was thinking I might be able to get some things sent over for them. And also that I probably shouldn't get into it. I felt weirdly protective of them. Communism might suck. But did they know that America sucked, too? Would they be happy at the New Varsity Theater in Palo Alto?

They consulted each other, three guys and a girl, spoke too fast in Chinese. I couldn't understand what they were saying. Finally the guy with his roots showing piped up: "We like Levi's, Nina Hagen, Bukowski."

"I like Throwing Muses," the girl added as she sat down on the stool next to me.

Levi's. Nina Hagen. Bukowski. Throwing Muses. Fair enough. I could get behind worldwide dissemination of good jeans, good music, good poetry.

"I can try," I said. "You won't get into trouble?"

The stencil-happy bartender laughed. "We fuckin' like trouble! How much you want for all that?"

I thought about it for a minute. What could I charge them? "Mahjong lessons," I said.

In my room, Kuan read the letter from my mother, shook her head, put the pages down on my desk. "Perhaps I do not understand her language," she frowned.

"Oh, you probably understand it fine." How could I explain my mother to Kuan? That she was controlling by nature, but loved A. S. Neil? Radical child-rearing meant complete freedom. How else would a kid learn self-reliance? Once, my mother ran into Guy outside a gallery on the Stanford campus. He was fretting because he had a college application due and he couldn't find his father to read it over for him. She laughed in his face. "You're so helpless, Guy! My children survive with complete neglect."

Free, from the old English "frēon," *to love*.

"Do you want anything from America?" I asked Kuan.

"No," she said as she fixed my Walkman headphones over her ears and pushed play. "Certainly no."

Vincent had a hot plate, so we skipped dinner in the cafeteria and I made vegetable curry with spices borrowed from the Muslim dorm. Vincent's roommate had been sent home to Uganda—something about a Chinese girl—so he was sharing his double with Leopold now. We sat on their beds, ate from enamel bowls, shared a giant bottle of beer, talked about Kerouac. Leopold was reading a worn copy of *Satori in Paris* that an American student had left behind. His English was perfect, but he wasn't sure he understood. "Maybe it is because I am neither a Catholic nor a Buddhist," he offered.

"Maybe."

He pointed at Vincent. "He is a Catholic—a Jesuit."

Vincent smiled, shook his head. "You keep your head in your Chinese books, Leo."

But Leopold just let out a throaty chuckle.

What can you tell about people by the clutter they keep in their tiny cement dorm room ten thousand miles from home? Vincent and Leopold had a hundred books in English, French and Chinese; a hundred bottles of Chinese remedies for everything from sinus infections to PMS; one warped Michael Jackson record; year-old tabloid newspapers in every language. No pictures from home.

"Vincent is here to study medicine," Leopold said, looking serious now. "And I am here to become an engineer. You are just here to study Chinese. But really we are all here to escape our destinies. Isn't that true?" He crossed his long legs.

"Or fulfill them," I offered.

"Yes," Leopold took a swig of beer. "We are each the same in that way. We each rejected destiny's first offer."

April 25, 1987

Dear Mom and John,

Thanks so much for all the goodies! There are a few more things I could use if you're wondering what to send me for my birthday:

All my Levi's, plus an extra pair or two if you're at the mall

Nina Hagen albums—as many as they have at Tower

A Throwing Muses album

Bukowski books

Dep hair gel

The latest Michael Jackson album

A Sony Walkman and a Modern English tape

Say hi to everyone for me. I love China!

—Ariel

"I want to take you someplace you'll like," Vincent announced over a rare lunch of fresh steamed vegetables in the black and white cafeteria. *Someplace I'd like.* I couldn't think of any tourist spots we'd missed. A model communist factory? Or maybe an old temple.

"Close your eyes," he said as we climbed onto the bus.

As if I'd know where we were going even with my eyes open. I was wearing my Chinese army pants and Wuhan Punk T-shirt.

Vincent had a bottle of *bai jiu* in his pants pocket. I felt more eyes than usual staring at us, but maybe I was imagining things. We switched buses at the terminal, rode to the end of the line.

"Keep your eyes closed," Vincent said as we stepped off into the dust. He led me a block or two down eerily quiet streets and onto gravelly ground. "You can sit," he finally said. "Open your eyes."

How did Vincent know what I'd like? The cool thing about the rail yard was that save for a few characters painted on the reddish-brown freight cars, it wasn't Chinese. It wasn't American, either. Or European. Or African. When you sit in a rail yard, you enter a world between worlds. The ballast gravel, the rusted iron tracks, the wooden or concrete rail ties. And no matter what time of day it is, when you sit in a rail yard, it becomes dusk.

We leaned back against a cement wall. "I do like it here," I whispered.

"I think," Vincent said, unscrewing the rice wine bottle cap, "I have fallen in love with you. If you were not so young, I would ask you to marry me."

His announcement took me by surprise. *Love.* I looked at Vincent's face. His smile accentuated high cheekbones. He didn't seem to be waiting for an answer. He just looked out across the hazy tracks. It occurred to me that Vincent was happy, not just here-now happy at the rail yard, but basically contented, and with no real reason to be so. I wondered if he was born that way, or if he had to work at it. "How'd you get to be like that?"

"In love?"

"No. Happy."

Vincent shrugged, stood up, took a few steps out from the wall, turned to face me. He was just my height. "Why not be happy?" He stretched his arms out, wrists bent upward, palms flat, and held them that way like a tai chi pose. He was a silhouette with a golden aura against the setting sun. "We are alive, you and me, and so many others!" He smiled, flexed his hands into the shape of talons—fingers bent at the joints, thumbs tucked in. He took a deep breath, raised his arms over his head and held them there, exhaled as he brought them back down to his sides. "I curse when I am angry, cry when I am grieving, and then I breathe and I am happy again."

He made it sound so simple.

Two bleach-blonds and the bartender with the floppy black Mohawk were appointed to teach me to play mahjong at the Cold War Café. We sat at a round table in a red vinyl booth. The bartender cast the dice, then directed us all to reseat ourselves. The blond with his roots showing chain-smoked and explained: "Four guy. One sit east, one sit north, one sit west, one sit south. You sit west. What you name, anyway?"

"White Ghost Girl."

He didn't laugh. He sucked on his cigarette, pointed to his nose, then motioned toward the other two players. "All three of us guy named Joe. Anyway. Play mahjong." Great clattering of tiles and counting of bones. We built walls with the Chinese dominoes as Joe kept talking. "East throw dice, count around wall. Land on wall to break. Like seven mean break north wall. Then north throw dice to see which spot in wall break. Now he pick up these two tile, he put them on top of wall just right side opening, these two tile now call loose tile."

He gestured at walls and tiles, his pale face pink under the lights. I was completely confused, but he kept on explaining.

"Wall break, deal tile, start east, each guy draw two stack tile from left side opening until every guy have twelve tile, then each one draw one tile, make thirteen tile. East draw fourteen tile. East discard one tile he no like. Then every guy draw tile from wall or take tile other guy no like until one guy make complete set. Then he fuckin' yell, mahjong!"

"Um," I sipped my beer. Basically, it started out like Battleship and ended up like poker. "OK. Maybe we should just play?"

Shouting, more clattering of tiles. We rolled dice, broke walls.

"You like your President Reagan?" the bartender Joe wanted to know.

"No—hate him." I studied my tiles. I didn't know which I should discard, what I needed.

"You know Chinese fuckin' discover America a thousand years before Columbus?" the quietest Joe asked. He had olive skin and round, almost Western eyes.

I didn't know.

"Sure," he said. "The Buddhist missionary go. They no need big ship. They fuckin' take good boat, get eastern wind. From China they sail up past Japan, past Korea, come along south part Alaska, go down coast U.S.A., meet painted people. Then they fuckin' go down Mexico, come back China on western wind. No problem."

It occurred to me that the quietest Joe might be planning a trip.

"Mahjong!" the bartender yelled.

The game required more concentration than I seemed to be able to muster.

We rebuilt our walls, started over.

JOURNAL ENTRY #43
35°55′N 116°25′E
SUMMER, 1987

WALL:

> *polite society   sun   day   outer beauty*
> *desert   buddhism/catholicism   activism*
> *dull   hope   happiness (stupidity)   warmth*
> *railyards————————————————love*

crazy   secret   intelligence   isolation
ocean   dream (solo travel to invisible world)   war
underground   moon   night   depth

I'll Be Back Soon

When the school year ended, Teacher Wang said there wasn't any room for me in the summer session. I thought he was lying, but I packed my bag. Vincent wanted to go see him, play a round of pool, argue my case. But I told him not to bother. "You could move into my room," he suggested. "Stay for the summer. I'll take care of you. Then in September we move to Shanghai for medical school." The offer was tempting. As weird as the language institute was, I felt safe there. The combination of being constantly watched and holding an American passport meant that as long as I didn't get kicked out of the country, nothing bad could happen to me. Teacher Fu was always around a corner.

"I'll think about it," I agreed. I just had to go to Hong Kong to get another visa.

When the care package arrived, I took a taxi straight to the Cold War Café, unloaded four pair of blue Levi's and three pair of black; the Throwing Muses album; *Nunsexmonkrock, Fearless* and *Nina Hagen in Ekstasy; Post Office* and *Ham on Rye* uncensored by Charles Bukowski; a four-ounce tub of lavender-tinted Dep hair gel.

The bleach-blond girl and two of the Joes were there. They huddled around me in the smoky dark. "This a lot of shit for few mahjong lessons," the bartender said as he slipped *Nunsexmonkrock* onto the turntable, played "Antiworld."

I shrugged. "I'm leaving Beijing," I told him. "But I'll be back soon."

He dug his fingers into the slimy Dep gel. "You go U.S.A.?"

"Naw. Hong Kong."

He smiled. "Wuhan number one! You stop Wuhan, say hi Wuhan fuckin' punk from Beijing fuckin' punk. You tell come play music sometime Cold War Café."

Vincent had spent another day at his embassy waiting for the check that never arrived. I wondered why he bothered to go at all. The money wasn't coming, simple. Anyone outside the situation could see it. But Vincent didn't seem to know anything about giving up hope. He had the eyes of a little boy: glistening with trust, always expecting some magnificent turn of events. My money wouldn't last forever, either. But how could I earn a living in Beijing? I drew a blank. Whites only worked as teachers, and teachers only seemed to earn their keep. I could have made the punks pay for their Levi's, but how much could I have charged them? Twenty bucks a pair? They charged me less than fifty cents for my Dragon beer. And it was one thing to write to my parents for Nina Hagen, even Bukowski. But how could I ask for money without explaining the braces? Without explaining why I'd only lasted a semester at the Beijing Language Institute?

I slept naked with Vincent in his single bed, read Leopold's Kerouac books by the pink glow of the Chinese lamp. Vincent read his textbooks on anatomy and the human heart. Lights out at midnight and he'd climb on top of me, whisper in my ear. I lapped up his warmth. He smelled of Bay Rum. But I just couldn't get into it. I couldn't focus. Or unfocus. He was sweet, whispering, "Do you want this? Are you OK?" And I'd smile under his sturdy weight and say, "Yeah. It feels good." And it did. It felt fine. But passion was like an early-morning dream I couldn't quite remember. I closed my eyes, tried to imagine it—*passion*—what did it taste like? What did it smell like? What was its texture? Thick and sweet, like molasses maybe. Or airy, like smoke.

Passion. From the medieval Latin, "passio," *to suffer.* Loosely related to the words "passive" and "pathos."

Maybe I was thinking too much. If I counted my breaths, would that put me back in my body or carry me further out? When Vincent came, smiling dumbly and soaking me with sweat, I was thinking about night trains—about where I'd go next.

According to Huang Di, the Yellow Emperor of China, the heart rules all of the mental and creative functions. It is associated with fire, and high noon. Heart troubles are best treated after the summer solstice. "If it doesn't get better in summertime," he was fond of saying, "it will get worse in wintertime."

July fourth. There would be fireworks at home. I kissed Vincent goodbye, whispered, "I'll be back soon."

He cocked his head to the side. "I do not suppose that is a promise."

"No."

He rubbed his hands together quickly, lifted my T-shirt and placed his hot palms on my stomach, closed his eyes. "I want to remember your skin," he said. He circled my waist with his hands, held them at the small of my back. "And you remember to hold your center—OK, Ghost Girl?"

Thirty-six hours on the train from Beijing to Guangzhou, I took a hard sleeper this time. Top bunk. Like a youth hostel on iron wheels. The weak overhead fan no match for the suffocating heat. But I slept soundly, the low thundering heartbeat of the train like a lullaby. Then a hovercraft across the water.

Three days in Hong Kong, where the sky never darkened, in transit there, waiting for my new visa. I bought a Polaroid camera from a street vendor off Nathan Road, lavender body lotion in a tiny drugstore, a pea-sized piece of hash from an African kid at the docks. On a giant screen in the Hong Kong Space Museum, the space shuttle *Challenger* launched and blew up, launched and blew up, launched and blew up. Failed America as all-day entertainment. I drank iced coffee with sweetened condensed milk. On a rooftop at Chungking Mansions, I rolled the sticky hash with tobacco and smoked, staring up into that red red sky.

In the pale light of morning, I took a ferry to Lamma Island, where there were no roads. I walked a quiet cement path through the hills. Yellow signs with green painted eyes next to garbage cans warned: "Hong Kong is watching." On the far side of the island, the path turned to dirt, led up to an abandoned scout camp on a low hill. I wandered through the empty rooms, sat down in a corner and rolled another joint.

Outside, I climbed down a rocky path, tried to imagine how beautiful the little beach would be without the tall cement power station. Across the blue: ancient junks and sparkling cruise ships and fishing boats and ocean liners. I left my clothes on the charcoal sand. As I walked into the water, tender waves lapped at my belly. I closed my eyes, imagined it all unpolluted. This calm sea held the same water that crashed furious on California shores. *I could live in Hong Kong for a while*, I thought. Maybe I'd set up a squat at the scout camp.

Back in my room on C-block, an English girl with henna-red

dreadlocks was stretched out on the bunk next to mine. "You smuggling?" she asked.

I rolled the last of my hash into a cigarette, took a drag, passed it to her. "No, just waiting for a visa. You?"

She turned over onto her stomach, puffed on the joint, studied my face. "I'm smuggling. But this is my last run. I'm gonna get a bartending job when I get back here."

"How much do you get paid for smuggling?"

"Five hundred dollars U.S. each time." She passed my joint back to me.

"What do you smuggle?"

"Clothes."

"Clothes?"

"Well, if there's something else hidden in the lining of the suitcase, I don't know about it." Freckle-faced, she looked about twenty-five.

I nodded. *Five hundred dollars U.S.*

"If you need money, you should call Mr. Wong. Tell him Djuna sent you." She jotted a phone number on a ripped piece of red paper.

I slipped it into my money belt.

"Beats fucking for a living," she said.

I counted out my traveler's checks. I had $480 left. I didn't have to worry for another season.

On the train back to Beijing, I was wearing my red Wuhan Punk T-shirt. A woman and her little boy sat on the brown fold-out chairs near the window, stared at me. I watched them, too. "How old are you?" the woman asked me in Chinese. Her long black hair tied in two loose buns behind her ears. Her rough hands made me think of farm work.

"Seventeen," I told her. That sounded so much older than sixteen to me. Like I'd been this naïve someone ever since I stopped being a kid, but now I had calluses on my feet. My skin was thicker, cracked at the edges.

She thought about that. *Seventeen.* "Your mother is crazy," she said.

Better my mother than me, I thought.

"Where are you going?" Her son watched me while we talked. We spoke Chinese, but occasionally the mother had to repeat words for the boy. My accent wasn't quite right, but she understood me.

Where was I going? Back to Beijing. I liked Vincent. I wanted to beat the three Joes at mahjong. I wanted to say goodbye to Kuan. But the truth was that I was going back to Beijing because it felt safe. Simple. I knew where to eat, where to drink; I was learning what not to say. I thought of my New Year's resolution: *To do things I am afraid to do.* I looked down at my shirt. *Where was I going?* "Wuhan," I said.

Halfway between Hong Kong and Beijing, then, I climbed off the train into a Chinese picture postcard: Yellow Crane Tower, East Lake, the Guiyuan Temple. Big city, yes, but no dust swirled in Wuhan. The sun was setting, painting things orange. I sat in the back seat of a bicycle rickshaw, bumping along a serpentine route to the grand Xuangong Hotel.

"You have time for a circus?" My rickshaw driver wanted to know. "*Hao bu hao?*" He pulled the bicycle cart over into an alley and turned back to look at me, smiled a sly smile.

I nodded. "*Hung hoa.*" There's always time for a circus.

Through a maze of alleys, then, down into a basement theater, air thick with smoke. My rickshaw driver led me through the dark to a fold-out chair near the stage. Under an emerald green light, a kid in a monkey costume juggled fire sticks and shouted in staccato dialect. A trio of old men in Mao suits played marching songs on a flute, a drum and a little stringed instrument I'd never seen before. My rickshaw driver sat next to me, smoking his Peacock cigarette, grinning. A kid in white tights and white pancake makeup appeared behind the monkey boy, raised her hands over her head like she was about to dive, and up she flew—up over the little wooden table at the back of the stage. She landed with a somersault on a red mat, bounced to her feet, turned around, raised her arms again, dove back over the table. The monkey boy bowed, pranced offstage, and the green light shone directly on the little acrobat. She used the table like a gymnast's vault, flipped back and forth to the gasps of the grandpas in their fold-out chairs. Handstand on the table, she yelled something in dialect, and the audience yelled back. A final dive off the table, a perfect somersault landing. All the smokers stopped smoking long enough to cheer. She rushed off-stage. The monkey boy lifted the table onto his back, hurried after her. The marching music. Now the acrobat girl again—on wheeled sneakers. She pulled another girl from behind the curtain and they waltzed and spun and lifted each other up in the air like figure skaters. I held my breath through the revolutions of their single, double, triple axles. Drum roll and the skating girls parted, stood stage right and left, gestured grandly toward the empty center. Another drum roll and, from the dark above, an albino midget descended center stage. The monkey boy rushed back and forth with planks of wood painted black, rigging a box around her. Lights off, lights on, lights off, lights on. The albino midget stood perfectly still. Darkness. Single spotlight. A guillotine blade glimmered terrifying green. A gasp from the audience and a final grand drum roll. Lights off, lights on. The blade sliced through the midget's neck, and her head fell to the floor with a thud. Lights out. Silence except for a child crying in the back of the room. I could hear my own heartbeat as it quickened. Green spotlight on suddenly, and the music. The unbeheaded midget threw her arms up in the air, beamed to the whistles and cheers.

I stood with the crowd, applauding as the kids took their bows.

When the lights came up in the theater space, I could see that I was the only white girl in the room.

The albino midget spotted me immediately, rushed toward me from the stage, shrieking and pushing people out of her way. She jumped up and down in front of me, shouting something. I knelt down to make eye contact. She patted me on the head, giggled, rubbed my cheeks, pulled at my hair. Taking my hand, she ran my fingers across her dry dry skin. She wore no makeup. She squeezed my hand, laughed. I looked up, realized that the full crowd had gathered. The albino midget jumped, pointed at me as she yelled something to them, and they all laughed together.

My rickshaw driver stood by, arms crossed, grinning proud. He'd brought the biggest freak of all to the circus.

From my pack, I produced my new camera.

"*Eeeyyyaaakk!*" the midget leapt at it.

My driver snapped the shot.

The crowd watched wide-eyed as our image emerged from the Polaroid blur. Two ghost girls in a smoky basement theater.

The midget's hand quivered when I gave her the picture.

Away through the alleys, dark now, my driver laughed and muttered to himself as he pedaled and sweated. Back out onto the busy streets, all the way to the grand Xuangong Hotel— former revolutionary headquarters for the People's Liberation Army. At fifteen dollars a night, the Xuangong was my greatest extravagance to date.

1950s-style coffee shop off the lobby. I sat at the almost empty bar, ordered a beer. The emerald green circus show swirled in my head. I didn't know where to start looking for my Wuhan punks. A twenty-something Chinese man sat down next to me. He wasn't a punk. He looked like a student, but he wore a fake gold chain. "What time do you usually eat dinner?" he wanted to know.

"About six o'clock."

From his pocket, he produced a small pile of crisp Foreign Exchange Certificates, placed them carefully on the counter. "For sex," he said. He looked in my general direction, but didn't meet my gaze.

For sex. I thought about that. His smooth, almost translucent skin. Small body. I imagined his chest, slightly concave. His hands. Would he tremble? I wondered how much money he'd piled there, but I didn't count it. Sex. Smuggling. It was good to know I had two things of value: my body, my passport. "No thank you," I said.

He blushed, bowed his head. "My apologies." He took the money off the counter, replaced it with a yellow pack of 555 cigarettes. "I misunderstood your business here. My name is Xiao."

I took one of his cigarettes. "White Ghost Girl."

He snickered behind a feminine hand. "Canadian?"

I shook my head. "I came from the sea. I took a train here."

He lit my cigarette, then his own. He puffed on it, but didn't inhale. "And you are here in Wuhan because you want to take the boat up the Yangtze River to Chongqing?" he guessed.

I studied the Formica counter, gulped the last of my beer, thought about the river I'd seen in a hundred brush paintings. A boat headed upstream. "Yeah," I said. "That's my plan."

Part III

To Have a
Change of Heart

The eastern hemisphere of the heart is responsible for accepting
oxygen-depleted blood and pumping it into the lungs, where
it receives oxygen. The blood then flows through
the mitral valve and into the western hemisphere.
From there, the nutrient-rich blood is pumped
into the aorta, which carries it away from the heart.

MY UNDERGROUND CITY

Now Subtract a Little Oxygen

In Sichuan Province, I dreamed of azaleas and woke up to the song of the *dujuan* cuckoo bird. They say the *dujuan* cries until she spits blood. They say the first to hear her song will surely lose a lover. *Is this how it would always be?* Traveling. Saying goodbye—*goodbye* and *I'll be back soon*—and meaning it, for real, meaning it like the best kind of lie. Because right then I knew "I'll be back soon" would always be a lie.

I took a train to the end of the western line, changed money in a dusty alley where I thought the sun would never set. The only guest in the cement hostel, I had a whole dorm room to myself. I slept naked.

In the morning, I slipped on my Chinese army pants and a black T-shirt, ate a tasteless steamed bun from a sidewalk vendor. An old man with matted hair who looked more Turkish than Chinese pointed me to an unmarked stop, and I waited for the beat-up blue bus that would spit and rumble out of town, out along the half-paved Tibetan highway. Thirty-seven hours, then, in the bright heat and dust. I watched the world out the window like a movie, the brown-green desert in the shadow of clouds lying low. I couldn't decide if the soundtrack should be Buddhist chanting or Italian arias. I was thirsty. A monk in a red-orange robe sat next to me: huge brown eyes, coffee-peach complexion. He smiled all the way, smiled wide-eyed like he alone knew the punch line to god's supreme joke on the world. The bus stopped in the middle of wild nowhere and another monk climbed onboard. Under his robe-cape, a baby-blue T-shirt with "Super Monk" in white iron-on letters. I nodded off and woke up. Dry throat. My whole body ached. Thirty-seven hours. I glimpsed the fat-headed panorama of snowy mountains on the horizon at dusk. As we passed nomad tents made of yak hair, candle-lit from within like sputtering lanterns, I jotted a note to myself in my journal: *Never do this again.* I nodded off and woke up. And at last—bright blue-sky morning—the bus rolled into Lhasa.

All the colors had changed again. And all the smells. Vivid yellow awnings. Inky blue alleys. A grand white and gold palace. A red temple. Jasmine and mint. Smoke and incense wafting through the dry air. Pilgrims and locals and nomads and tourists in their brights and blacks. Not a shade of gray on the palette.

At the cheap hotel's registration desk was a big hand-painted sign: Don't Shit in the Shower. A leathery-skinned Tibetan woman sat at a wooden table sipping yak butter tea. Two dollars a night in Foreign Exchange Certificates for a dorm bed. How strange to be in a place so not-Chinese. And how strange that they still used Chinese money.

Unclassified traveler's ads cluttered a bulletin board on the wall: *Sleeping Bag for Sale; Jeep Car-Pool to Everest Base Camp; 2 Bus Tickets to Kathmandu; I Need a* Lonely Planet *guide for Thailand; Lost Watch; Vagabond's Kid, Age 7, Looking for In-Town Playmate;* and *Has anyone seen Sheila from Brixton?*

The hotel woman led me through the courtyard, opened the orange door to my room. Dirt floor. Four single beds against four brown walls. A window that opened to an alley. In the middle of the room, like a centerpiece chandelier, a white woman with two long braids hung upside down from a rope swing rigged to a ceiling beam. Eyes closed, pale face flushed, hands in prayer, she chanted. The hotel woman looked her up and down, turned back to me and shrugged, pointed me to the vacant bed.

I lay on my stomach and watched the hanging woman for a long time. She wore acid-washed black Levi's and a striped T-shirt. Finally she curled her thin body upward, grabbed the swing ropes, awkwardly flipped herself over, landed on the floor, bowed in my direction. She looked like a grown-up Pippi Longstocking. "I thank you for your quiet and respect." She spoke English with a soft French accent. "I am Martine."

I nodded hello.

"You do not speak English?"

"Oh—yeah. I speak." I sat up.

"You appear tired—you have just arrived?" She had a strange café au lait birthmark like a small hand across her neck.

Sleepy nod. "This morning's bus."

She pulled at one of her braids. "I have something," she finally said. "A welcome to our room. A thank you for your quiet. You can keep a secret?"

I nodded. "Uh huh."

"Lock the door," she whispered.

Unquestioning, I went to the door, grabbed the little metal latch, locked us in.

From under her bed, Martine produced a small camping stove and a pan she filled with bottled water. She reached into her green military backpack. "You are ready?" And with a wave of her arm like she was pulling a rabbit from a hat, she produced a black one-pound bag of coffee. "Word gets out I have this and it will be gone in one hour. You cannot tell a soul."

Coffee. Had it only been a couple of weeks since my last real cup? Surely it had been longer. "Not a soul," I promised.

"You only just arrive, but there are travelers here who have no coffee in six months. I bring this from Paris nearly eight weeks ago. Still, for me it is fresh." Martine winked at me as she dumped some of the grounds into the boiling water. "I like you," she said. "Tens of travelers come and go through this room. You are the first to see my coffee."

"I appreciate it."

She handed me a steaming Sierra cup. "You are a Buddhist?"

I sipped the bitter coffee. "Not really," I admitted.

When Martine frowned, I wanted to take it back. Maybe she hadn't meant to share her sacred coffee with a heathen. But she just shrugged. "No matter. Walk with an open heart and sooner or later the Buddha will touch you. I give my own life to the Buddha after I crash my Fiat in Paris and he reveal himself to me. I wake up in Pitié-Salpêtrière Hospital, my head split open. I should die, but the Mother of All bless me and save my life. In return I give my life back to her and to the everlasting Buddha."

Martine's visa would last another month, but she had no plans to leave. "I never return to France," she said. "There I am TV producer."

In Lhasa, I had to give up smoking. At fourteen thousand feet, the thin air made me lightheaded. I had dreams in broad daylight as I walked barefoot through the streets. Maybe they weren't dreams, exactly. Maybe they were more like foreign images superimposed onto the main film. A woman in white walked in front of me and I knew she had always and never been there, that I wasn't wandering aimlessly—I was following her. I walked through daydreams of weeping willows, leaves that shimmered in the sun the way things shimmer when you drink vodka in the morning. Bright lotus flowers appeared spontaneously in the cracked earth. A white leopard lumbered along next to me. I'd never thought of it before: The path to enlightenment might just be a matter of subtracting a little oxygen.

A bearded man with a blue bandana tied around his head sat on the tattered couch in the courtyard at the Don't Shit in the Shower Hotel, breathed through a mask and complained that Tibet was ugly. "I understood I was coming to Shangri-la," he moaned. "There's nothing here."

Turn off your damn air, I thought. *Beauty is in the eye of the gasping beholder*. If the woman in white became visible on the streets of Lhasa, surely god would reveal herself on the trail up Annapurna or Everest.

In the smoky-dark Jokhang Temple, I waited hours in line with the pilgrims to touch the golden statue of Buddha. Outside in the square, a giant furnace of incense fumed. I bought a beaded locket from a woman with turquoise ribbons in her hair. She had a blue painting of a Buddhist goddess who looked to me like the Virgin Mary. A group of monks played pool on an outside table.

A young Chinese man sat on a low wall bemoaning his fate: Tibet was the Siberia of China. *What had he done to deserve being sent out here into the nothingness?* He said it like he knew what he'd done, but he didn't offer up the explanation. "Someday I will go home to my province!"

I traded my Swatch watch for six silver bracelets.

All of Tibet ran on Beijing time, so everyone was a slacker. Even the sun didn't rise until it was good and ready—8 A.M. and dawn just breaking.

An hour later, and all the travelers finally awake, Martine hung upside down from her rope swing. A Swede named Mats, who had little claws for hands and claimed to be 100 percent enlightened, skulked around our room. He'd been in Lhasa for a year now, had probably outstayed his Chinese visa. "One time," he admitted, "I shat in the shower."

One hundred percent enlightened.

He smelled of sardine oil.

He said: "I got conned into taking the Bodhisattva Vow, so no nirvana for me. I have to stick around here with you lot in samsara until every last one of you is enlightened. Bloody bad deal, if you ask me."

The fourth bed in our room belonged to a wild-eyed Dutch man with long black hair who came and left at odd hours. He played Talking Heads on his little black boom box, didn't care if Martine was chanting. David Byrne and Martine made an unsettling duo: the Buddhist heart sutra and "Road to Nowhere."

Rumor had it that outside the police station and in the square, Tibetan monks and nuns and lay people were protesting the Chinese occupation. But I was always late to the demonstrations.

I ate momo dumplings in a tiny café near the hotel. The yak butter tea tasted like beef bouillon. The barley beer was potent—between the altitude and the alcohol content, a single bottle made me laugh and laugh and laugh.

Evenings in the courtyard, I sat with Martine, listened to the travelers' tales as they circled. Dirty kids told of epic journeys from Golmud, from Ürümqi, from Chengdu, back from the Pakistani or Afghani border, from far-flung Buddhist monas-teries and cold cold caves. An older woman whose prominent brow reminded me of a crow had taken a forbidden road with no alien travel permit, dodged the Chinese police. A lanky hippie kid from Toronto had seen the great pyramid outside Xi'an. I opened a bottle of barley beer, offered Martine a sip but she held up her hand to refuse.

"I can't believe all the yak products these people consume," one kid was saying. "And they call themselves Buddhists. . . ."

"Yeah," someone else piped up. "It's like they've never heard of soy protein."

Everyone knew of a cheap bungalow in paradise. Here was the address. And everyone had giardia or malaria or cholera to go along with their elevation sickness. I was young by the travelers' standards, but not shockingly young. They were twenty-two, twenty-five, thirty-six, fifty-one. They carried their own toilet paper, Western cigarettes, tattered books. They carried stashes of weed, of hash, of liquid acid. Did I want some? *No, thanks.* The wispy air was drug enough and the last place I wanted to end up was in a Chinese jail on the Tibetan Plateau.

At night when the sun wouldn't set, I curled up in my bed with a worn copy of a book about Henry Miller that a Chinese punk had traded me for my Swiss army knife at a bar in Chengdu: *We are all guilty of crime the great crime of not living life to the full. But we are all potentially free. We can stop thinking of what we have failed to do and do whatever lies within our power. What those powers that are in us may be no one has truly dared to imagine. That they are infinite we will realize the day we admit to ourselves that imagination is everything. Imagination is the voice of daring.*

Martine sat facing the wall in meditation. I watched her, listened until she exhaled heavily and turned to face me.

"Martine?"

She clasped her hands behind her head, leaned against the wall. "Yes, Ghost Girl?"

"What happens when you meditate?"

"I try to quiet my mind." She looked blissed out and I wished I could meditate like she could, turn ecstasy on like a light.

"Do you succeed?"

"In meditation, no success or failure. I watch my thoughts. Sometimes, eventually, they quiet. You try?"

"I've tried, but my thoughts don't really quiet or stop or anything."

She nodded. "This is OK. You just sit. Do not worry what happens. Just sit."

"Martine?"

"Yes, Ghost Girl?"

"Do you think you're living your life to the full? I mean, is that what you're trying to do here?"

She readjusted herself on her bed, looked up at the ceiling beams. "Hmm. I never think about that before. Maybe not. No."

"So you don't think so much about your potential?"

"No. No potential. Maybe—" she pulled at her braid. "You speak of a kind of ambition. Any kind of ambition cause you suffering."

I lit a blue candle on my nightstand. "But you have an ambition to be a good Buddhist, no?"

She looked at me for a long time, then shook her head. "I sit. I do not think about this thing. You should try."

I nodded. "I don't know. I like my thoughts. And Buddha wants you to stop your thoughts."

Martine laughed. She had a gold tooth near the back of her mouth. "The Buddha want nothing from me! Only my heart in nonaggression!"

I thought about that. Aggression wasn't really my problem, or was it? It seemed to me that if the Buddha wanted my heart in nonaggression, he already had it.

"Ghost Girl," Martine said. "Life is suffering, yes? But the cause of suffering is only your endless wants and desires. If you sit, soon your thoughts quiet. Soon your interior become so very light. Soon your endless wants begin to float away. Then someday soon you have no more desires. No ambition for this full life. No more suffering."

The Dutch man had crept in while Martine was talking, curled up under his brown wool blanket.

"I sleep now," Martine said. "We talk more in the morning."

I went back to my book, read a few pages before Enlightenment Mats stumbled into our dark room, drunk on barley beer. "Fucking samsara," he mumbled. I set my book down, watched him as he made his way to my bedside. He stood over me. Was it just the reflection from the candle flame, or hadn't I noticed it before? The whites of Mats's eyes were yellow.

He surprised me when he leaned over, grabbed my tit and squeezed it hard. "I bet you're a tiger in bed," he growled.

"And I bet you're a date-rapist," I said, loud enough.

The Dutch man turned over in his bed.

Martine sat up. "What is going on?"

Mats fell back a step, then crawled onto his own bed. He crossed his arms in front of him, frowned. Pouty little creep.

After that, the Dutch man wouldn't speak to Mats anymore, wouldn't meet his yellow gaze. And Martine wouldn't leave my side. "You humiliate him," she said. "There is no telling what a humiliated man will do."

No telling, but I wasn't afraid of Enlightenment Mats.

On a late-September morning, Martine woke me before sunrise. "Up, up, up," she whispered. "You come with me."

Disoriented: "Huh?"

"Do not ask," she said. "The place we go is of importance."

I felt around at the foot of my bed for my Levi's, pulled them on. Sweatshirt. Then boots. I followed Martine out through the still-dark courtyard, out through the city, out into the starry night. She wore a green cashmere sweater over her striped T-shirt. Near the outskirts of town, she finally spoke: "The everlasting Buddha touch your heart yet?"

"I don't think so," I admitted.

"You see the Mother of All, receive from the milky ocean of her blessing?"

"Maybe I've seen her," I was thinking of the woman in white. "But I don't know that I received her blessing."

Martine nodded. "It is all right."

A mile? Five? We passed the nomad tents, darkened now, followed a narrow trail across the tiny trickle of a stream, hiked into the icy dawn. We walked for an hour, maybe two. I wondered what Martine's doctors back in Paris thought about her. She called it "awake." They probably called it "severe brain damage." I felt bad. Martine so wanted to convert me. And it wasn't that I didn't want to be converted. I was jealous of the Buddhists. They had texts and traditions to mark their paths. And they did make a more compelling case than the Marxists or the Maoists. Still. It was one thing to love the delicacy of the eightfold path, stand in line with the pilgrims at the temple, admire sweet idols. But when it came time to fling myself onto the dusty ground—prostrations to the everlasting one—I just couldn't get into it. I looked up at all those stars, made a wish and forgot it. We walked on.

At first the far-off chanting didn't seem real. I thought I was hearing things. Louder, then. And bells. Maybe Buddha in his boundless compassion was finally reaching out to me. Then silhouettes on a dark hill up ahead. Monks or pilgrims. A fire.

We made our way across a rocky field, but when I looked down in the pale red predawn light, they weren't rocks under my boots—they were bones. Prickly awestruck trepidation. I followed Martine.

At the fire, we sat behind a half-dozen Berkeley-style Europeans dressed like nomads and a Japanese kid in jeans and glasses. At the edge of the flat rock, flames illuminated a pile of bandaged bodies. A man—big for a Tibetan—wore a white apron, held a huge ax. The sight of him with his blade kicked up my adrenaline, but I sat still. As the stars faded into the bluing sky, a dark bird circled. I breathed in the cold air, watched as two other Tibetan men picked up one of the bodies, swung it onto the fire. The flames sputtered. Most of the onlookers held incense, but the perfumed smoke was no match for the smell of burning bandages, burning hair, burning flesh.

They chanted. Louder. And then ax man! Three corpses at the edge of a smooth rock. All at once he went at them, hacking the bodies to pieces as blood turned his white apron the color of the sunrise. The other men silently carried strips of flesh away from his fury, laid them out on another flat stone.

Martine leaned over, whispered in my ear, "The bodies will go back to nature in the mouths of the vultures."

I'd only seen one other dead body in all my life—and it had only been a few weeks earlier. Bloated. Floating in the Yangtze. Dusk. My boat pushed slowly upstream toward the famous gorges. The old *ma* who had adopted me as her own, offering me chocolate orange slices our first night onboard, tugged me onto the deck to show me all the beauty that was China. But I looked down into the river instead of up ahead. And there, a few yards below in the water, the body, blue and unrecognizable. It could have been anyone. Male or female. White or Chinese. Just a body floating down the Yangtze at dusk. And now this dry dawn. Surreal red haze. The raw morning. More bodies. The vultures circled.

I closed my eyes and it occurred to me that no one in the world knew where I was. And then, almost simultaneously, it occurred to me that maybe no one was wondering. I could die here. My body could be bandaged, burned. Or hacked to pieces, splattered across a white apron. No trace of me. I'd return to nature in the mouths of the vultures.

Geography and Circumstance

JOURNAL ENTRY #73
29°40′N 91°09′E
FALL, 1987

*china: no revelries, no beauty for beauty's sake, no gods. tibet:
no bank, no milk, no train. i'd sooner give up efficiency than
faith but i'm spoiled—i want it all. maybe the other travelers
and i just see the world as a shopping mall of philosophies,
cultures, religions. even the guidebooks call the tourists in
tibet vultures. we circle the temples and the celestial burial
sites, taking. martine is more optimistic. she says it's all in
our intention. if we approach the sacred rock with quiet
respect, we have as much right to be there as the stars and
the rising sun, as much right as the tibetans. we're all citizens of this earth, after all. i want her to be right, but even
she thinks i should be a buddhist. she waits, patiently.*

In October, Enlightenment Mats packed up his belongings,
said he was moving into a private room. He clutched his red
duffel bag close at his shoulder: "Some other bodhisattva will
have to save you lot. You've been nothing but a pain in my ass.
There's more than precipice and storm between you and your
Everest." He tried to slam the door behind him, but it swung
back open.

I rolled my eyes. "What a jerkbutt."

Martine smiled, "Though I like the bit he say about Everest. . . ."

The Dutch guy, who'd finally introduced himself as Christoffel, shook his head. "That was just a quote from the poet Cecil Day Lewis: *Those Himalayas of the mind are not so easily possessed. . . .* That guy is full of shit."

Martine shrugged. "Oh well." Then whispered: "Lock the door."

I jumped up to lock it as Christoffel shifted his gaze from me to Martine and back again, nervous. His dark locks looked like tangled weeds now. I thought he could use some conditioner.

Martine set a pot of water on her camping stove to boil.

"What are you doing?" Christoffel wanted to know.

"You'll see."

He'd finally earned in on the secret coffee.

The grounds were stale by now, but the coffee still tasted like heaven. I sipped from my cup, eyed my backpack. I had laundry to do. I wanted to take a shower.

But Martine had other plans: "You will come with me?" She wanted to go see a certain nun who lived in a certain cave just outside of town. I was wary of another Martine excursion, but I couldn't refuse her. Her coffee and her hope for me. Martine: the closest thing I had to a friend.

We rode in the back of a flatbed truck out into the flat, flat desert. "I think you are bodhisattva," Martine shouted over the roar of the truck's engine.

"How do you figure?"

"There are many bodhisattvas who do not know they are Buddhists in this lifetime."

"Really?" I was sitting on a tire. My butt hurt like hell.

"Maybe you take vow last lifetime. Maybe you take vow a hundred lifetimes ago. Maybe you take vow over and over and over."

I looked out over the desert. "Maybe so." The truck turned

abruptly, headed up a hill and past a crumbling monastery. I was getting used to the thin air. I wanted a cigarette. I wondered if lower altitudes would shock my system when I finally climbed down.

The truck driver left us on the bank of a dry salt lake. Martine paid him in Chinese money, asked him to come back for us in two days. She led the way across the red earth to the sacred cave's entrance marked by fading prayer flags.

Inside, the nun couldn't have been cuter. Sitting there surrounded by blankets, cooking gear, a pale green thermos. Wide-eyed in her brick-red robe, prayer beads wrapped around her forearm.

Martine spoke in French. The nun spoke in Tibetan. I couldn't tell whether or not they understood each other. I grasped none of their words, only their gestures. The nun showed us some unfinished pages of Sanskrit text. She was working on a secret autobiography. The cave felt like a walk-in fridge. All that heat outside, and the high air just couldn't hold it. I put my sweatshirt on, rubbed my palms together. The nun poured us tea and Martine wanted to chant, so we chanted. Or they did. I closed my eyes, tried to follow along. It sounded like a cross between a Chinese opera solo and a dying cat. Two days. *What was Martine thinking?* I wondered if the nun had a cigarette, gave up on the hope before it had even fully formed in my mind. I closed my eyes tighter, tried to let the weird wind sound sweep me along, but I hoped it would end soon. *If I'd stayed home, I'd be a high-school senior by now. I'd be applying to colleges, maybe. Still working at the movie theater.* I wondered what was playing. I wondered what my parents were doing. And Leslie. And Jack. I inhaled, tried to concentrate on the operatic dying cat. I opened my eyes. The single shaft of light penetrating the darkness through the cave's opening had shifted a little. I closed my eyes again, tried to accept the fact that the chanting might never end. *Everything is a great lying projection.* Which unassigned reading was that from?

As they chanted, I tried to imagine it: spending lifetimes here in this cave, breathing the wispy air, shooting the shit in the moonlight with the Mother of All. I could stay here like the nun. I could meet the pilgrims as they passed through. I could lie about my history. I could grow old, look back. I'd shave my curls. My skin would tan, wrinkle. Only my Italian nose and mood-ring eyes would give me away—a foreigner. I'd wear red-orange robes, drink salty butter tea, chant. Maybe Martine would stay with me. But even as I projected our futures here, I had to face it: My mind just would not empty. What kind of Buddhist could I ever be? Daydreamer. Worrier. As they chanted, my thoughts wandered to California, to Beijing, to the scary place in my imagination where I ran when I didn't want to feel things anymore. My underground city. That place had felt like detachment to me, but now I could see that that place was not empty, either. It was full and rich and grotesque and hungry and somehow cut off from the rest of my body. There were damp tunnels down there, labyrinths of blame, a room where some sadistic projectionist waited for me, ready to play back on film every stupid thing I had ever said, ever done. Not empty. More like the place in my dreams where I opened my mouth to scream but couldn't manage a sound. More like the silent moment when someone lifted the needle off the record, the moment in between "Stairway to Heaven" playing forward and "Stairway to Heaven" playing backward. More like hope as it fell away—the inhalation with which I'd realize that my lover's good light would never be enough to sweep back my shadows. More like this. More like sitting in a cave on the roof of the world reeling through similes in my not-empty mind, seeking refuge in a religion that would never be my own.

In Buddhism, the demons seemed to be ego and indulgence and desire. In my religion, the demons would be self-hatred and numbness and soul-sale. What had my desires ever done to me, anyway? My endless wants didn't cause me suffering. Assholes caused me suffering. Bullshit caused me suffering. Maybe I didn't want inner peace after all. Maybe I just wanted to live a real life—ego and indulgence and desire and all.

The women were still chanting when I climbed from the cave into the warmth outside. The paper-white peak of Mount Kailash rested regal on the horizon. The slow drifting of a single cloud across the blue blue sky reminded me that I'd be leaving soon. I walked toward the dry lake. In my bag, *The Life of Poetry*. I hadn't opened it since it arrived in the package from home. I had no particular interest or disinterest in it—a non-fiction book by a dead American woman I'd never heard of. But it was the only book I had now. I opened it, started reading. And here was the dead American, Muriel Rukeyser, leaving Spain at the start of the Spanish Civil War, bound for the first port at peace. Earlier, in a leafy square, she'd gathered with other travelers. The beginning of a war. And they wanted to know: *What is the foreigner's responsibility?* The answer came in a voice, deep and prophetic: *Go home: tell your peoples what you have seen.*

Back in the cave, Martine and her nun sat facing the wall, silent.

I fell asleep under thick woolen blankets, thinking of the sea—cold and low and blue.

First icy morning light through the cave's opening. The shadows of prayer flags, still in the windless dawn. My nose cold and dry. The women already chanting. I could smell the yak butter tea hot in my cup. I'd slept soundly, clutching *The Life of Poetry*.

I crept out of the cave, sat down at the edge of the dry salt lake.

The desert sun still low in the sky, I turned back to the beginning of the book and started to read it again: *The only security that matters is the security of the imagination.*

I'd never thought of myself as a poet before. "Poet." I rolled the word around on my tongue. "Poet" had always sounded like a profession to me, or a talent. But the dead American made it sound more like a faith, more like an exercise. Like meditation or chanting.

In California, people called me introverted—shy and strange. On the road they mistook me for Canadian—*too quiet to be an American.* But maybe words were never meant to be scattered like wildflower seeds on asphalt, wasted. Maybe words were precious, dangerous, delicate. Maybe I could make patterns out of the scraps and sentence fragments of my life. The Buddhists were all about living in the here and now. Martine only spoke in the present tense. But maybe there was something to living in the past, too—to knowing and remembering my own power. And in the future—a light at the end of every underground tunnel. Precious, dangerous, delicate. Maybe I didn't have all the words yet. Maybe all the words didn't exist yet. *All the poems of my life not yet made.* I closed the book. And it occurred to me as though I'd known it all along: There is geography. And there is circumstance. And then there's me. Changing. And roughly the same.

I stood up, *The Life of Poetry* in hand, and all at once the strangest sensation: I could feel my feet on the ground, feel the sun on my head. And I could feel something else, too. A magnetic pull. Not a pull in any particular direction, but a pull just the same. Like a rod of energy flowing from the fiery fierce sun to the crown of my head, right through the middle of me.

And from the bottoms of my callused feet to the fiery fierce core of the earth. The strangest sensation—I longed to hang on to it, but even as I let it fill me, I knew it wouldn't last.

Moments don't last.

But memories do.

Words do.

JOURNAL ENTRY #79
A CAVE NEAR 29°40'N 91°09'E
FALL, 1987

> sometimes i want to go home, but then i wonder/realize:
> maybe it's not home i miss, maybe it's my childhood
> not ritzy stupid shallow alto silicon valley
> but spring fairs at the peninsula school, hippie shows at
> the stanford amphitheater
> darting under picnic tables, blowing dandelions
> the smell of california weed, the palo alto of harold and
> maude
> the sierras, the tumbled granite and lodgepole pines, cold
> blue lakes
> the santa cruz beach boardwalk
> the tallest tree
> catching tadpoles in the san francisquito creek
> taking them home in mason jars, air holes hammered
> through the lids
> waiting every day as they grow fat, grow legs
> taking the jar back down the steep and brambled trail to
> the water's edge
> and letting them go again, but now they have legs
> and they have names
> because i've named them

they leap away, i wonder if they miss being tadpoles
i doubt they miss their mason jar
do they know that i've named them?

In the back of the flatbed truck, Martine and I sat on our tire, watched the landscape in silence. "We all sin so much," Martine finally said without looking at me. "But we cannot take back sin. All we can do is add good, just as you add more potatoes after too much salt in the soup. You just hope in the end the good will outweigh the sin. Even if the Buddha never touch your heart, Ghost Girl, do good, OK? If you sin, it is OK. You just add more potatoes. And whatever happens, do not waste your energy insisting you are right. OK?"

We passed the last nomad camps on the outskirts of Lhasa. I must have been spacing out, because we'd driven a good quarter-mile into town before something struck me as odd: All the shops were closed. No pilgrims or locals or tourists out on the street. A Chinese soldier wandered alone toward a temple. I wondered if a holiday had cleared the city. Our truck stopped abruptly at an intersection. A green-brown tank rolled past. I looked at Martine for a clue, but she just stared back at me. Our truck growled on, past the empty square where incense still billowed from the furnace. Another abrupt stop. Engine off. A soldier approached the cab, exchanged quick words with the driver. Martine pulled at one of her braids. The truck's engine started up again. I tried to remember what day it was, what date. The truck stopped finally at the entrance to the Don't Shit in the Shower Hotel, now guarded by a baby-faced Chinese soldier. Martine paid the driver in Chinese money and followed me past the guard. I glanced into the reception room where the old hotel woman sat stone-faced at her wooden table, drinking her yak butter tea.

In the courtyard, the travelers huddled, whispered. The crow-woman looked up as we approached. "We're all getting kicked out of Tibet," she announced. "The protests have gotten violent."

"Is anyone . . . hurt?" Martine stammered.

And all the travelers went quiet.

I could hear David Byrne singing "Heaven" from our room. I sat down on an arm of the tattered green couch.

Yellow-eyed Enlightenment Mats, with a scowl on his sun-burned face: "Not hurt, you fucking fool, *dead*. A hundred dead."

A tear rolled down Martine's pale cheek, streaking it clean, and I wished someone would shoot Enlightenment Mats. What difference would it make? A hundred and one dead.

The crow-woman whispered more news. It had started with monks protesting the Chinese occupation. Arrests were made. More protests. Rumors of torture. And then this morning, hundreds had gathered in front of the police station to demand the release of the political prisoners. They threw rocks. The cops responded with machine-gun fire.

Martine's thin shoulders shook as she cried.

"It is our moral duty to stay and fight for the Tibetans," someone said. "We will not be expelled."

"There will be more demonstrations," came another voice. I looked up. It was the hippie kid from Toronto. "Tibet will finally be liberated!"

Martine listened as they all said their bits. Finally, slow and shaky: "We stand in front. If Chinese want to shoot Tibetans, they will have to shoot us first."

Nods from Enlightenment Mats and two other men.

But the bearded guy with his oxygen tank, who sat just outside the circle, shook his head. "I'm leaving here. The Chinese are assholes. They'll kill you all. They don't care."

The hippie kid stepped out of the circle.

Martine wrapped her fingers around my arm, moved closer

to me, whispered in my ear, "I cannot believe we not here today. You stay and defend Tibet, Ghost Girl, yes?"

Maybe I was a coward, but my relief tasted like sweet coffee. *We missed the massacre.*

Enlightenment Mats: "Are you with us?"

Nods from Martine and the two other men, but I shook my head. "Did any Tibetans ask us to stay?"

Mats flicked his hand toward me as if shooing a fly away. "What should we expect from an American?"

"You must stay," Martine whispered. "It is of importance."

I wanted to feel torn. Stay and fight. Or go. But I'd already seen enough bodies. This wasn't my war. All I wanted to do: Collect the sentence fragment. Go home. Tell what I'd seen. And what had I seen? A soldier wandering across an empty street. Chants and prayers in an unhidden cave. Strips of flesh on a sacred rock. Travelers and pilgrims searching, faithful. A circus act in an alley theater. Banned music underground in the Cold War Café. Talk of the future in a gray city. Strobing lights, pulsing music. A single, forbidden dance. The secure imagination finding its shelter.

A few stayed to fight. They escaped the baby-faced guard by climbing out the back windows and into the alley behind the Don't Shit in the Shower Hotel.

In our room, I gave Martine a quick hug. She'd washed her face clean. She wasn't crying anymore. "Ghost Girl," she knelt down by her bed, gathered up her camping stove, pot and coffee. "Take these with you."

"I can't take your coffee." It was bad enough I was leaving her with Enlightenment Mats.

"I have to travel light now," she whispered. "It give me pleasure if you take."

"All right, then," I agreed. I packed my bag to David Byrne singing "Once in a Lifetime."

Like heading off into the blue again.

I settled my bill at the Don't Shit in the Shower Hotel, said goodbye to the old woman at the desk who smiled at me, baring rotting teeth.

I could imagine streams flowing underground.

And I climbed into the first gray thing I'd seen in months— a beat-up bus headed south toward the border.

Like this was the way it had always been.

A gray bus headed south toward the border.

Would always be.

Nomads

We passed dusty villages and modest camps. Families of three and four rambled across the desert without packs.

Nomad. From the Greek "nomas," *wandering in search of pasture*. Akin to the Anglo Saxon "niman," *to take*; the Old English "numin," *seized*, as by cold or grief. Loosely related to the words "nimble," "nemesis," "numb."

A white woman my mother's age sat next to me on the bus, shoved her maroon LeSportsac bag under the seat in front of her, smoothed her clean Guatemalan shirt over her jeans. She had jet-black hair with inch-long gray roots. "The situation here is just horrific," she was saying. "Just horrific."

I nodded.

"I've been all over the world," she said. "Never have I seen such overt oppression. The human rights abuses are beyond belief. *Beyond belief*." She looked me up and down like she'd just noticed she was talking to someone and that someone was me. "What are you?" she wanted to know.

"What am I?"

"Yes, *what*? A tourist? A Buddhist? A student?"

I hesitated. What was I?

So she dropped it. Back to her. "I belong to the Unitarian Church in Portland, Oregon. As soon as I get home I swear I am going to *get involved* once and for all. There are letters to be written, my dear. My congressman is going to get a letter from me about this. I can guarantee. Were you *there*?"

"There at the demonstration?"

"Yes, *there* at the demonstration, what did you think I would be asking about? Of course you were *there* in Lhasa. So was I. So were we all. I intended of course to take part in the demonstrations, but my Tibetan guide had the habit of giving me the wrong times. So of course I didn't see the worst of it. But still. I shudder to think. The Tibetan people are just so sweet, so open. They dig their own graves really, being so trusting." She yawned, adjusted her silver hoop earrings. "I said to my Tibetan guide, 'You watch your back, Sonny.' But he of course couldn't comprehend the idea at all, he was just so warm. These people, they aren't fighters. And I can respect that. I'm certainly not a fighter. What did you say you were?"

"Huh?"

"Right. So you understand. I'm not a fighter of course either, but when someone tries to oppress me, well, I just quote Joan Crawford. I say, and pardon my language, but I say, 'Don't fuck with me fellas, this ain't my first time at the rodeo.' And I told my guide as much. And, well, as you can imagine he just laughed at me. And I said, 'I'm serious, Sonny. Sometimes you have to be tough.' Of course his name wasn't Sonny. I never could pronounce his name. Not that he could pronounce *my* name, either, which is Dominique. . . ."

Oh, man. Americans really did talk more than anyone else. Like they just could not shut up. One or two pertinent things to say and they couldn't just leave it at that. The trip took the better part of two days. Two days of Dominique.

Nostalgia for the operatic dying cat.

She yammered on and on, imparted more and more of

nothing much. I closed my eyes, woke up to the sound of sweet rain against the window.

"I came to Tibet because I had to see for myself," Dominique was saying, "a place where spirituality isn't just some small part of the culture, it *is* the culture. And I saw for myself, all right. My congressman is going to hear about *all* of this. I said to my Tibetan guide, 'You and your people better wake up before you're wiped out, Sonny.' But he just laughed at me. Can you imagine? The food was just abominable, don't you think? No variety. I wonder if that's the Chinese's doing or if Tibetans have always subsisted on that greasy soup they call tea. Where did you say you were from, dear? Canada?"

Relief: The bus stopped abruptly.

"*Meiyou,*" was all the driver said. *No more.*

The road fell off into a gorge just short of the invisible line separating China from Nepal. I filed off the bus behind Dominique and the others, hiked down a steep trail. And we eased over the border clutching our North American and European passports as the Tibetan refugees all waited in the rain. Crazy belated monsoon.

Borders are such bullshit. Every last border in the world, bullshit. And passports—bullshit, too. Why could we cross the line when they couldn't?

Along the slippery path that descended into the valley, grapevine news about what had happened in Lhasa got worse. More protests. More machine-gun fire. Five hundred, six hundred, seven hundred dead. Holy men and bandits, lay women and their children. A French tourist shot in the back. Countless wounded. All the foreigners and journalists expelled. A ragtag group of unarmed white freedom fighters holed up in a cave somewhere. The border closed indefinitely behind us. The Himalayan air was thick and misty with all those ghosts rushing out and into the mountains. *But the green!* And I wasn't hallucinating. More green than my eyes could take in, comprehend. Men in near-rags carried refrigerators on their backs. Women with scarves dyed in rich tangerines and pinks. Fuchsia saris.

Mercifully, Dominique had found a new ear at which to aim her monologue: "The airline had better just *fly* me out of Kathmandu," she was saying. "No questions. Just *take* me home. Sorry I'm in the wrong city, but I am *not* buying another ticket over all of this. If they want more money, well, they can just send a bill to the Chinese government. I belong to the Unitarian Church, you know. In Portland, Oregon . . ."

I knelt down in the thick mud at the side of the trail, Annapurna vast and clouded in front of me. I wanted to breathe it all in. The green. And the birds: a blood pheasant with her rusty throat, a shimmering emerald dove, a three-banded rosefinch. I felt miserable—elated. Everything so gorgeous, I wanted to run away.

The other travelers from the bus trudged along. They needed to get some miles between their feet and the border, between their feet and all the death. They thought they could make it to Kathmandu in a day, maybe two.

But I just waited at the side of the trail until they'd passed, made my way alone to the first village, bought a pack of Yak cigarettes. I wasn't in any hurry to get where I was going. *Where was I going?*

In a café where portrait-plates of the Nepali king and queen graced a flowery altar like images of the gods, I sat down on a wooden stool, ordered chai tea and dahl bhat from an ageless Nepali waiter in a plaid shirt. I was thinking about reincarnation, about the way baby booms might follow massacres, when a mischief-eyed little boy with round, prominent ears appeared in the doorway, made a beeline for my table. He dropped a huge backpack at my feet, jumped up and down in front of me like a wind-up toy: "Whitey! You take me Kathmandu!" He wore a button-down khaki shirt and matching shorts that didn't cover his skinned knees. "You take me Kathmandu, Whitey!"

I shook my head, smiled at him. "I'm sorry." I was having enough trouble taking myself from unknown place to unknown place.

But the boy's face fell. He sat down on the stool next to me, slumped over, exaggerating his defeat. "Where you go, Whitey?"

"I don't know." My jeans were caked with mud. Dull cramps, and I knew my period couldn't be far off. *Where was I going to get a tampon?*

The little boy cocked his head to one side. "You no go Kathmandu?"

I lit a cigarette. The smoke tasted faintly of cardamom. "Well. Maybe I go Kathmandu."

Broad smile. "Yes!"

When I finished my chai, the boy rushed to get me another steaming cup. He was missing one of his front teeth. And I was a sucker. "You want some food?"

He ordered orange Fanta and dahl, soaked up every drop of the spicy stew with naan bread. And when he finished, he offered to shine my shoes.

"No," I said. "No, thanks."

The boy couldn't have been older than ten, but he claimed to be thirteen.

"Where are your parents?"

"Mother in village! I go Kathmandu sell shoes!"

I thought his mother was crazy, letting him run off to Kathmandu by himself. But what did I know? "Your name?"

"Krishna!"

I downed my second chai, studied Krishna's sweet face,

considered the reality: I had three hundred dollars U.S., and Krishna knew the way to the city. We were a team. "We'll go in the morning, then?"

Toothy smile: "Only 110 kilometers Kathmandu!"

"Do we have to walk the whole way?"

Krishna shrugged. "Maybe. Maybe not."

I changed money at the café, took a room behind the kitchen.

Blood circulates through the heart and blue tunnels of the body three times per minute, traveling a total of twelve thousand miles every day.

Twenty-five kilometers on foot in the rain. Two hours in a taxi that sped around slippery curves like the driver had a death wish for all of us. Fifteen more kilometers on foot. I tripped and slid through the mud to keep up with Krishna. Night on a straw mat in a candle-lit shed that passed for a hotel. An hour and a half on the back of a dirt bike. Twenty kilometers on foot as the sun battled the monsoon with mystic shards of light. Two hours in a crowded bus that smelled of curry and sweat. We arrived on Freak Street at dusk.

Incense and tapestries.

"Hey, sister!" came a voice. "I love you, sister!"

Children with their fluttering prayer wheels.

Tiny health food stores and head shops.

"Coke, hashish, brown sugar, change money?"

Rose and patchouli.

Stoned Western hippies in mirrored dresses.

Nepali salesmen in Adidas T-shirts.

Statues of elephant- and lion-headed gods.

Colorful posters of Kali, Shiva, Bob Dylan, Cat Stevens, Duran Duran.

"Hey, sister!"

"I love you, sister!"

My feet ached in my boots. I just stood there holding my pack, mouth open. I thought I was on Haight Street shopping for a formal. I thought I was at a Dead show on the Stanford campus—waiting in line to buy a purple balloon full of nitrous. Freak Street, Kathmandu: a perfect, ridiculous replica of home.

"Coke, hashish, brown sugar, change money?"

We ducked into a tiny hotel with a red painted sign: Namaste Lodge. One hundred fifty rupees got us a huge cement-floor room with two twin beds. Another hundred for a lasagna dinner in the low-ceilinged café.

"How'd you get to be so rich?" Krishna wanted to know.

"In America I made almost six dollars an hour—three thousand rupees a day."

His eyes widened. "What did you do?"

"I worked at a cinema."

He took a bite of his lasagna, grimaced. "I never see cinema. Tomorrow I sell shoes."

In our second-floor room, Krishna spread out his goods: black patten leathers and worn-out sneakers, muddy hiking boots and platform party shoes, woolen moccasins and brown sandals, a pair of Birkenstocks and child-sized Chinese farmer flats.

"Where'd you get all those?" I asked him.

"I collect. You have extra shoe?"

"No." Even my combat boots looked like shit now.

In the morning, I followed Krishna up Freak Street and across Basantapur Square, into an open market where women and men sold clothes, pipes, shampoo, disposable diapers, makeup, statues of Buddhist and Hindu gods, bootleg tapes, paperbacks in a dozen languages, tampons (thank the gods), incense and silver jewelry. I thought we would spread out a blanket like the rest of them, sit there all day with the shoes, but Krishna had a better idea. He'd sell to the vendors. He argued bitterly with an old man whose teeth were stained red. Some of the shoes were American, I pointed out. The red-toothed man was not impressed. The shoes were old—what could he sell them for? A woman with a bindi between her eyes winked at Krishna, offered him twice the rupees for his collection. The red-toothed man was back at it, yelling in Nepali and waving the woman away. Finally, a deal was struck: less than thirty dollars U.S. for the whole pile. But Krishna skipped all the way home down Freak Street to the Namaste Lodge, counted his money and laughed.

After breakfast, he led me around the city through huddles of stupas and shrines. He posed for a Polaroid portrait next to a vermilion-smeared statue of Tara, the sexy goddess of compassion. We approached a fancy hotel, but the doorman shooed us away. In dirt-floor shacks down mazes of alleys, we visited the boy's distant relatives or family friends. From a cement rooftop on the far side of town, we admired the royal palace. "King good man, Queen good woman," Krishna said, "but Prince brown sugar lord."

With a crowd of pilgrims and tourists, we waited in a court-yard at Kumari Bahal for the living virgin goddess to open her balcony window and look down on us. Beautiful girl, maybe ten years old, she wore a golden headdress and dark kohl makeup around her almond eyes. Expressionless, she stared out over the crowd. And for a split second, she met my gaze. Took my breath away. An incarnation of Durga, she wasn't allowed to laugh or smile.

Sacred is sacred and tradition is tradition, but it made me sad, seeing the child-goddess up there, peering out her little window, huge brown eyes, stone-faced serious, penetrating stare. I'd been blessed. I thought I might cry.

"How much you think whiteys pay for city tour like I show you?" Krishna wanted to know. He was sitting on the cement floor of our room counting rupees. I wasn't sure they'd pay him anything. A German guy had already scolded me for having anything to do with the kid. "He's a little con man."

"And you're not?" I'd mumbled.

A little con man.

On a dull Wednesday morning in the low-ceilinged café, two fat Swedish girls cried at their table and an Australian guy moaned. Their wallets were missing. Krishna jumped at the news: "I go police! I find your wallet!"

The foreigners looked at me like I could vouch for the kid, but I just shrugged, slurped up a spoonful of corn flakes as he ran off.

He reappeared half an hour later, three wallets in hand.

The travelers patted his head, cooed over his beauty, paid him cash rewards as he charmed them with his toothy smile. "Mother in village! I come Kathmandu sell shoes!" They bought him bottles of grape Fanta that stained his lips blue.

Then Saturday. The rain clouds held stubborn over the Kathmandu valley. Breakfast of thick bacon and soft-boiled eggs. And the same scene: a white girl in her Hard Rock Cafe sweatshirt and a French guy with beads in his dreadlocks. Krishna jumped up. "This is terrible! I go find!" And off he ran in his little khaki shirt and matching shorts. He'd re-skinned his left knee running in circles around a shrine in Durbar Square. Back up in our room in the late morning, he showed me the spoils: almost seven hundred rupees in reward money.

I glanced up at him from my book. "Listen, Krishna. That was a good scam. But don't do it again."

"Do what? I find wallets. I am good boy!" He clapped his hands in front of his nose. Of course he was a con man. With a face like his, round and expressive, how could he resist the ease with which the tourists fell for him?

"But who stole the wallets in the first place, Krishna?"

"Thief steal!" He looked like he would cry.

"And yet somehow you find them. In the whole city of Kathmandu, it only takes you half an hour to find the wallets. And nothing is missing."

"You think should take longer? Should be missing one thing?"

"I think you better cut it out, Krishna." I didn't care so much that he stole the wallets, but he was being so obvious about it. He'd get into trouble, get us kicked out of the lodge. If Krishna wanted to be a con man, he had to learn something about suave.

He stuck out his lower lip, crossed his skinny arms. "First day you laugh."

"And third day you go to jail. Just stop it."

Krishna wanted to stay in our room and pout while I went out shopping, bought silver jewelry, a wool cardigan, a used boom box and a half-dozen bootleg tapes, a book on Nepali Hinduism, a square red silk purse, tampons, colorful saris, a new pair of khaki shorts for the kid and a bright poster of the elephant god Ganesh—lord of the poets, protector of children and thieves.

From the Yak Hotel, I made an international call, left a message on my parents' new answering machine. They'd finally caught up with the technology of the early eighties. They'd probably have a microwave by the time I got home.

"I buy you one Gorkha beer," Krishna announced when we sat down to dinner. "In the morning, I go home." The smells of garlic and nag champa incense clashed in the café. We'd been on Freak Street for nearly a month.

One Gorkha beer.

I accepted, bought him an orange Fanta. "You'll be OK traveling on your own?"

He flashed me his mischief-eyed smile, patted his pocket full of rupees under the table.

"All right," I said, sipping my beer. "But first I want to take you someplace you'll like."

Krishna's great brown eyes widened. "Someplace I like?"

I led Krishna through the streets and alleys he still knew better than I did, across squares and over footbridges. The sun was setting, turning the clouded sky the color of ripped flesh.

"Coke, hashish, brown sugar, change money?" a skinny Nepali kid with burn marks on his face called out as we passed.

"No, thanks."

I wondered what would become of Krishna when he lost his baby face. "Why don't you go to school?" I wanted to know.

But Krishna didn't answer me.

"Shoes are a good business," I told him.

At the little movie theater downtown, I bought tickets to ¡Three Amigos! dubbed in Nepali. We ate stale candied popcorn. And Krishna laughed until he cried.

"I love cinema," he sighed as we walked home through the autumn night. "I love cinema and I love shoes."

In the morning, he folded up his almost-empty pack.

I gave him a trinket statue of Ganesh.

"And I love *you*, sister," he called out as his bus pulled away.

It was high noon before I realized my combat boots were missing.

Zero Mass Theorem

I n Basantapur Square, I bought a baseball-sized round of hash from a kid with a Shiva tattoo. I made curtains for my room out of my fuchsia and gold saris. I taped the bright poster of Ganesh to the wall, set a vase of flowers at his feet, played bootleg Grateful Dead tapes on my new-to-me boom box. "Truckin'" and "Sing Me Back Home" and "Goin' Down the Road Feelin' Bad" and whatnot.

I hung out in my room, mostly. On the rare sunny day, I stretched out on the damp cement roof of the lodge, smoked, practiced writing Chinese characters in my journal, read my book on Hinduism. Most of the other travelers in the Namaste Lodge café annoyed me. I preferred the company of Brahma, the supreme creator who had built the world of our awareness out of *maya*, the maternal void; Shiva, the mad creator-destroyer whose trident-carrying devotees still wandered the streets of Kathmandu; and Vishnu, the great preserver-protector who slept his eternal sleep, to be awakened only a total of ten times in human history, called upon to save our sorry asses from certain doom. Vishnu, with his many arms and indomitable spirit, had already roused himself nine times—when called upon again, he'd show up in a black chariot and destroy everything in his path. Buddha, it turned out, was just the ninth, most recent, avatar of Vishnu.

❧

Journal entry #107

27°42'N 85°12'E

Fall, 1987

attachment to places, land, geography
what if "home" referred to the soles of my feet?

I would have been happy to read, wander the city barefoot, eat alone, sit on the roof in the fog or the sunshine, watch dusk fall over the hazy skyline of brick buildings. I liked my solitude. But without a cave, the world won't leave you alone for long.

Her name was Violette. She smoked MS cigarettes left-handed, carried a super-8 movie camera. She wore silver rings on every finger, three silver hoops in each ear, a diamond stud through her nose, a knit cap over her dark curls. Her fine features reminded me of Saskia. She pulled up a chair, set down a bottle of Gorkha beer in front of me. "Violette," she said. "After Violette Leduc."

She claimed I'd been staring at her.

I hadn't realized.

Old, maybe twenty-nine, she talked too fast, had the faintest Italian lilt, bit her nails ragged. American, but she grew up in Milan. She'd just flunked out of a physics program at Stanford University, said she was in Kathmandu to make her first movie.

I sipped the beer. I was thinking about *Vagabond*. "You know the Varda film?"

She didn't.

I tried to explain, but I kept getting tongue-tied and even when she nodded, I knew she wasn't getting it. She wanted to make a movie about an Italian girl and a Nepali girl, about passion and culture clashes and secret rendezvous and the inevitable scandal when the Nepali girl's family found out she wasn't going to marry her fiancé, that she planned instead to run away to Venice with her sweet-tough white girl.

"My working title is *Maya*," Violette said. "It means love, but also illusion."

I lit a cigarette, nodded. *Maya*, the maternal void. I suspected Violette was a Varda. One lover would end up dead. Or they both would. Like a girl version of *Romeo and Juliet* set on Freak Street in Kathmandu, autumn, 1987.

Violette already had a real actress lined up to play the Nepali girl. The real actress wasn't really Nepali, she was Indian-British, a Londoner, but who would know? And was I an actress? I looked Italian enough. Maybe I could play the sweet-tough white girl who believed in love.

I wasn't sure I believed in love, but I said, "All right. If you want me to."

"I can't pay you anything," Violette admitted.

"Well. I can't act."

"Wonderful—that makes us even." And she handed me a copy of the handwritten script, minus the last three pages. "I think you will find it compelling. We begin shooting next week. No rehearsals."

I read on the rooftop, hoping for a late autumn tan. The script was all stage directions and soundtrack notes and fadeouts. I was the co-star, but I didn't have any lines. The real actress didn't have any lines, either. The shopkeepers and the hotel doormen had lines. The Nepali family members had lines. The fiancé had lines. The beggars had lines. But the lovers were silent.

I thought to rush downstairs and tell Violette that it couldn't work that way—that you couldn't have a consummated love affair without words and without rail yards. There were no trains in Kathmandu. But I rolled a joint instead, kept reading. This was Violette's movie, after all, and who really cared about realism? I just had to be the silent Italian girl who believed in love. I'd shop on Freak Street and in the open market, drink sweet brandy and bitter beer. I'd laugh in the square, stare longingly off rooftops as the locals hung their laundry out to dry. I'd sit at the feet of Hindu statues, smoke hand-rolled cigarettes, kiss the real actress.

"How long you been traveling?" Violette wanted to know. She was stretched out on Krishna's old bed, smoking.

"Almost a year."

"And what is it you're searching for?"

Searching for? I lit a cigarette, shrugged. "I don't know—traveling—it's just an experiment, really. The world is vast. My world in California got too small. In Palo Alto. Small town."

"Palo Alto is hell," Violette said matter-of-factly. "But it must be nice coming from a place like that. At least then you know it can't get any worse. I come from Milan, which isn't bad, but I'm looking for the promised land. Haven't found it yet. Kathmandu is a great movie set, but it isn't paradise. I'll find it, though—paradise. I mean, theoretically, it can exist. So why wouldn't it?"

"Send me a postcard when you find it?"

When she stood up to hand me her joint, I noticed how tall she was. Built like a fashion model. "You want to know a secret?"

I took a drag, didn't answer.

She peeled off her knit cap. "The world—the universe, really—it doesn't matter." She lay down on her belly, stared at me across the space between the beds.

"How do you mean?"

She smiled. "You've got an electron, which is really just a

field of possibility with a particle dancing around in the middle of it, right?"

I nodded. I knew what an electron was, had a vague idea anyway, but I also knew she was about to lose me. Like maybe I'd missed the high-school year when they got into the whole field of possibility.

"You can put the electron in a box, and you can contain the particle. It can't get out, right? So it bounces around in there. But the field of possibility is nonmatter—it's not a thing, right? It has no density. So, slowly, the field of possibility starts to seep out of the box. Because you can't contain nonmatter. So this field of possibility is seeping out—it's seeping out because it can—and then, as soon as more than half the field of possibility is outside the box, *bam*!" she snapped her fingers, sat up. "The particle jumps out. If more than half the field of possibility is outside the box, then the particle, by definition, is outside the box, too. So you can't contain a particle after all. You can't contain an electron. You can't contain matter. Period. The field of possibility seeps, and then the actual matter jumps out of the box. Do you know what that means, Ghost Girl?"

I shook my head.

"It means that the box doesn't matter—because if it can't contain anything, it doesn't really exist. And if the box is the universe, then the universe doesn't matter, either. It can't contain anything, right? The universe is just a box that can't contain anything. So it's not even a box." She waved her smoking hand in the air. "It's nothing."

On Monday, Violette moved into my room. She didn't ask permission, but I didn't protest. My room was a box. It didn't exist. So what did it matter? By twilight, her video equipment and ashtrays were piled on the table and strewn across

Krishna's old bed. I pulled out Martine's camping stove, boiled up some stale coffee. I was nervous about the movie, but Violette just picked up her wooden pipe, inhaled deeply. "Don't worry about it. You'll be perfect." She wore a short-sleeved black T-shirt and jeans. She pointed with her chin at my poster of Ganesh. "What's with the elephant god?"

"Protector of children and thieves," I said. "Lord of the poets."

Violette nodded. She was sitting at the foot of my bed, drawing spirals on a blank page in my journal. "Do you know the Zero Mass Theorem?"

"What you were talking about the other day?"

She had that same crazy gleam in her eye. "Yes and no," she said, then jotted an equation down for me. "You see—" she turned the page around to show me: $m = E(0)/c$, underlined the equation with her index finger like a schoolteacher. "Mass equals energy times zero divided by the velocity of light."

I nodded.

"Or!" She grabbed the pen again: $m = 0$. "Mass equals zero. Get it?"

I picked up the wooden pipe. The algebra made sense enough.

"Zero!" she said.

"That's cool." I poured the coffee into Sierra cups, handed one to Violette. I said, "Freedom means free, right, and free means zero, like something you don't have to pay for? It's from the Old English "frēon," *to love*. So free equals love. Love equals zero, like in tennis, right? Freedom equals free equals frēon equals love equals zero." I passed her the pipe.

"Love. Frēon. Free. Freedom. Zero—" she whispered the words to herself slowly, like she was trying to work out the equation in her head. "Love. Freedom. Free. Frēon. Zero—holy shit!" she spat out her coffee. "That's fucking *it*, Ghost Girl.

Maya equals love equals illusion. Love equals illusion. Love equals zero. Mass equals maya. Maya equals zero. It's *everything*, Ghost Girl. Everything equals zero. Nothing matters!"

"But if everything equals zero," I said softly, "then zero equals everything, too. And everything matters."

Violette set down the pipe, covered her face with one hand. She had little razor slash scars all the way down her olive forearm. "Holy shit," she whispered. "Everything matters?"

"Yeah, I think so—by the same theorem."

From Saffron and Dirt

The real actress showed up in the low-ceilinged café on a damp Saturday. She wore a white tank top and black miniskirt, had these amazing cheekbones. Her rough hands looked like they were made for hard work and callused from doing it. She sat down at our table without saying hello. I couldn't tell if she was high. Almost all the travelers in Kathmandu were high, but with Beatrice it was hard telling. High or not, she made me nervous.

Violette fluttered her hands, talked about scenes and schedules.

What was I thinking? A movie? I'd always played the narrator in elementary-school and junior-high productions because I couldn't act. But I tried to reassure myself: All I had to do was pretend.

For the camera, I bought silk and tobacco in an underground mall. I handed out rupees like candy to the Freak Street beggars. I crouched under stone statues and floral altars, smoked hand-rolled cigarettes. I gazed hungrily after Beatrice, who finally caught my shoulders in a dusty alley and kissed me.

"Cut!" Violette shouted. "Beautiful, girls. It's just beautiful."

Back at the Namaste Lodge, I took a cold shower.

Violette wanted me to wrap a thin towel around my head like a turban. "You have gorgeous curls, Ghost Girl," she said. "This is how you set them: Let your hair dry in the towel. Half an hour. Then use just a touch of gel. Egg whites if you have no gel. We should do this tomorrow before the shoot. And maybe a little makeup to even out your skin tone."

"All right," I agreed. "If you want me to." I was thinking of Beatrice's soft mouth.

That night in dream, she led me into a dark underground bar. We drank rice wine and laughed about the movie, laughed because Violette didn't know we were in love for real. All around us, travelers were turning into owls and white leopards, rising up into the air.

Violette woke me early. "Hair and makeup for you!"

But I could already feel the dream following me into the day, the day following me into the movie.

Beatrice met us in a downtown square. I crouched between a shrine to the goddess Parvati and a curry stall, watched drug deals and quaint dramas unfold in the chaos as Beatrice and Violette talked about scenes I wouldn't be a part of.

But the afternoon was all about us. Me and Beatrice. In the square. In alleys. On the outskirts of town. I started pretending that our silent love affair was for real, that Violette was just tagging along with a super-8 camera. I didn't have to act, after all. I just had to look smitten, which I was. Pretty soon, I forgot Violette was there at all. Navigating the limits of reality.

We decided to film the love scenes in my bed at the Namaste Lodge because of the room's good light.

I knocked back two glasses of sweet brandy in the café. A new waiter with a pixie haircut winked at me.

Upstairs, Beatrice wore a gold sari, stood in the window like some polished bronze idol. I pushed her onto my bed, kissed her on the mouth, gripped my hand tight around her waist, worried that somehow she'd know I'd been dreaming about her.

Under the gold cloth, she wore a half-shirt fastened down the front with little metal hooks. My hands shook as I undid them, brought my tongue to her brown nipple. But she tasted sweet. And all of a sudden it was Beatrice who seemed scared.

"God—" She started to sit up. "What are we doing?"

I lifted my head, "*shhh*," kissed her salty neck. "*Shhh . . .*" I held Beatrice's shoulders and listened as her heartbeat slowed. I ran my tongue down her warm torso, tasted the musk of her belly, licked the deep scar that circled her waist.

I looked up at her—the perfect cool beauty I'd been shadowing through the alleys of Kathmandu, now all vulnerability. When Beatrice sighed, I wondered if she would travel with me, then pushed the thought from my mind. I dug my fingernails into her hips. She tasted familiar. *You're just making a movie, Ariel. Illusion. Pull yourself together*. I closed my eyes, imagined the two of us swimming in the warm surf at night. The South China Sea. Or somewhere off the coast of southern California. Soft soft skin. My throat felt tight. I glanced to the side, but Violette wasn't there. Disoriented, I mouthed the words to Beatrice: "Is this for real?" And she nodded.

How long had we been there? Fifteen minutes? Five hours? Someone whispered, "Take your shirt off."

Beatrice had stubble on her thigh. Her hip bone under me felt like granite and I wondered if I was drunk. My mind flickered on and off like a strobe light, some crazy current running through me and back into Beatrice.

I held her waist as she groaned.

"*Shhh.*"

"Beautiful, girls!" Violette's voice came out of nowhere. Beatrice jumped up, pulled on her faded jeans, refastened her sari shirt. In the last amber light through the window, her skin glowed, just a little. "See ya," she said without looking at either of us.

"See ya." I sat in the middle of my bed, a little embarrassed.

Violette smoked left-handed and played back the footage on her machine.

"This is gorgeous," she said. "Just beautiful. You have to see it, Ghost Girl."

But I didn't want to look. Had she been there all along? I put my shirt back on, watched Violette's face. She was focused on the film, and maybe on the bird tattoo on my back, when I saw the sudden flash from her dark eyes. She bit off a fingernail. "Next time," she said, "next love scene, Beatrice on top. Or maybe side by side. No. Beatrice on top. She slides down you, disappears out of the shot. The camera focuses on your face. Every viewer imagines—well, imagines Beatrice is going down on you. Your eye makeup is smeared and you're writhing in exquisite pain—you're *coming* for the camera. But then the shot widens. We see that she is tattooing something on your chest. She's marking you. Maya in Sanskrit across your heart. It could be so passionate. . . ."

As she talked too fast, I tried to picture it. Beatrice's rough hands, the ink and the blood, the needle ripping my pale skin.

Violette sighed. "C'mon, what do you think?"

I was scared, but I said, "All right. If you want me to."

Violette cocked her head to one side, ashed her cigarette onto the floor. "How old are you, Ghost Girl?"

"Nineteen," I lied. And I picked up my book on Nepali Hinduism.

The goddess Parvati was actually born a human—the daughter of the king of mountains. She meditated her way to divinity. It can happen. And then she married Lord Shiva.

One summer, when Shiva was away in battle or meditation, Parvati created a model of a beautiful boy out of saffron and the dirt from her own skin. She breathed him to life, named him Ganesh, sent him to stand guard outside her door as she bathed.

When Shiva got home and found the strange kid guarding his wife's room, he soared into a rage. In the ensuing battle, the great creator-destroyer cut off the boy's head.

Parvati heard the commotion, rushed out to see her beloved son lying dead at her husband's feet.

When Shiva realized what he'd done, he freaked—raced out to find Ganesh a new head. The first living creature he happened to run into was a baby elephant, so he beheaded the poor thing, rushed home to perform a quick transplant.

The operation was successful, but Parvati was still bummed about their ugly Dumbo son, so Shiva made her a promise: Ganesh would have the power to answer prayer. Shiva gave their boy the gift of extraordinary intelligence, made him the remover of obstacles, the protector of kids and thieves, the lord of new beginnings. As the patron of letters and learning, Ganesh transcribed the *Mahabharata*, the longest epic in world literature.

The next morning, while Beatrice and Violette were off shooting family scenes without me, I lay in bed, flipped through Violette's thick Italian *Vogue*, picked up random books, read passages.

Muriel Rukeyser, unassigned: *Breathe-in experience, breathe-out poetry.*

And Bernard Shaw, when asked if he really thought the Holy Ghost had written the Bible: *I think the Holy Ghost has written not only the Bible, but all books.*

And from the *Mahabharata*, Book Eighteen: *What is found in this epic may be elsewhere; What is not found in this epic is nowhere else.*

My co-star and director reappeared in the early afternoon.

Beatrice looked tired. But Violette bounced up and down, invigorated. I wondered if these two would ever be my friends for real. Did they like me? Or was I just the only one they could find to play the Italian girl?

Oh, grow to know me.

They wanted to start shooting.

I took my clothes off, but this time it was all skin and faking in the good light of my room. Beatrice was cool again and when she kissed me she didn't lick my teeth and when she grabbed me she didn't dig her nails into my skin, and when she sighed it meant nothing. Violette circled my bed, whispering, "More passion. More passion, girls."

With a safety pin and black ink, Beatrice left her mark on me. Messy Sanskrit text. And I knew the expression on my face exposed more pain than pleasure.

Pretty soon, it was over. Beatrice pulled on her jeans.

I pulled on my Chinese army pants and dropped a chunk of hash into the pipe. Marked for life now. "Illusion" in Sanskrit across my chest. Or did it mean love? Long months chasing sanity.

The three of us smoked in silence, then crept downstairs for shots of brandy and peach pie.

Violette licked her fork. "Now," she said, "for the missing scene." She wore a long-sleeved T-shirt. I was thinking about the slash marks on her arms when she handed us the final pages of her hand-written script.

Here was the way things would end: A monsoon of rose petals. Beatrice and I kissing in a square. Beatrice's father appears out of nowhere, curses, shouts. She cries bitterly. The fiancé appears. He and the father argue. Blame circles, refuses to land. Someone is screaming at Beatrice. Suddenly the fiancé is holding a knife that gleams in the dull afternoon sun. He raises it over his head, stabs Beatrice. He stabs her amid the rose petals and wafting incense. She falls. Silence. My tears. I'm holding her. I'm holding her in a pool of blood. I'm holding her and then I'm running. I'm running through an open market. I'm running down streets spiraled like seashells. I'm running under a bridge, through an alley, cobblestones dissolving under my feet. I'm running past Kumari Bahal where the virgin goddess gazes out of her box, expressionless. I'm inconsolable. I'm running. Me and my fucked-up broken heart, me and my fucked-up tattoo.

When we were finished shooting, Beatrice shook my hand and said, "Nice working with you."

Violette thanked me, too, said, "Heart and guts, *bella*, that's, all you've got and that's all you need." She moved out of our room, promised to send a copy of the final video to me poste restante in Kowloon.

I believed her. I believed her like I believed "I'll be back soon." And I sat there in the middle of my bed in the golden light of late afternoon, smoking a hash-laced cigarette, fingering my scabbed tattoo, and feeling weirdly dumped by the both of them.

Tacky little movie.

From the Mahabharata, Book Sixteen: *Tell me what is good for me. I am a wanderer with a hollow heart.*

New travelers showed up at the lodge every day. More left. Christmas was coming. People were heading home. *Christmas*. It had been the most excellent time of the year when I was a kid. My posada parties and the piñatas, my mother's mulled wine and all those horrible songs, the lights along Christmas Tree Lane and the dull California winter, John's church services bright and early Christmas morning after stockings full of chocolate and cheap beautiful Cost Plus toys. Most excellent. But I wasn't a kid anymore, was I? I didn't want to go home.

For the travelers staying in Kathmandu, a Christmas Eve potluck at a café a few doors down from the Namaste Lodge. Everyone was invited. I wanted to make mulled wine, so I bought cloves, cinnamon sticks, nutmeg, cardamom pods, lemons and oranges at the street market. I spent a small fortune on two bottles of burgundy wine and a fifth of aquavit from the fancy shop for Westerners near the grand Yak Hotel. On my way up to the register, I grabbed a six-pack of Pabst Blue Ribbon. Some people didn't like wine, after all. And the Pabst cans looked festive enough with their silver-lined blue ribbons and red stripe.

In my room, I mixed the spices with the wine, heated it up on Martine's old camping stove, let it cool and mull overnight.

Christmas Eve afternoon and all I had to do was sweeten it, heat it up again.

In the kitchen downstairs, I asked the cook if I could borrow a bigger pot, some sugar. He handed me a tin pot, pointed me to a shelf of spices and condiments. I grabbed a half-pound plastic bag of white granules, trudged back up to my room. It smelled like Christmas. I heated the wine in the big tin pot, poured the granules from the bag into my hand without measuring, dumped them into my brew, licked my hand.

Uk! I spat on the cement floor. *Salt!*

I grabbed the pot from the camping stove, burning my hand, quickly tried to pour the wine back in its bottles, spilled half of it on the floor. Maybe the salt hadn't been fully absorbed yet. I rushed downstairs, grabbed a pound bag of sugar. The young cook laughed at me as I ran. Back upstairs, I rinsed the salty pot in the bathroom sink, poured what was left of the wine back in, added handfuls of sugar. But it was hopeless. I tasted it, gagged. And you can't add potatoes to mulled wine.

I curled up on my bed, covered my face. *How stupid could I be?* In my world, salt came in a round, blue, cardboard container. The little girl with her umbrella on the label. *How could it not have occurred to me that it might not be sugar in that plastic bag covered with Sanskrit writing?* As the sun set, I headed downstairs with my six-pack of Pabst, hoped the cook wouldn't see me.

As I approached the party café, two girls with bobbed brown hair and hiking boots chatted or gossiped. "Oh. My. God." One of them gasped when she saw me coming. I was wearing jeans and my Wuhan Punk T-shirt. "*Look* at that girl. She's bringing *Pabst Blue Ribbon* to the party."

"No. Way." The other one turned to look.

I laughed nervously as I passed them. I circled the block, crept back upstairs to my room. I filled my pipe, cleaned up the wreck of my Christmas, opened a bottle of the piss beer, doodled hearts in my journal.

Just before the kitchen closed, I headed downstairs, ordered tandoori chicken and apple pie. "Not enough to eat at the party?" the waiter wanted to know.

I didn't answer him. I took the food up to my room, slept through Christmas morning.

Under the spell of the wicked Witch of the East, the Tin Woodman of Oz lost first his legs, then his arms, then his head, then his torso. Reconstructed completely of hollow tin, and without any organs at all, his heart was the only thing he missed.

After that, I stayed in bed mostly. Ordered room service. The waiter with pixie hair didn't wink at me anymore. I'd had enough of Kathmandu. My perfect, ridiculous replica of home.

I dug through my money belt. I'd already cashed my last traveler's check. I flipped through my passport, admired all the pretty visas. Maybe it was because I was high, but when the little red piece of paper fluttered to the floor, I took it as a message from the gods: Mr. Wong's phone number in black ink.

Who was that girl in Hong Kong who'd given it to me? June? No, Djuna.

I picked it up, turned it over in my hand. The little red piece of paper. Djuna. Mr. Wong. Surely they were messengers of Vishnu, the great preserver-protector.

I headed down to the Yak Hotel, made the international call, set up a smuggling run. A ticket back to Hong Kong would be waiting for me at the airline counter. I settled my bill at the Namaste Lodge. Maybe I'd be back and maybe I wouldn't. I smoked a last joint on Freak Street, packed two hash cookies from the health food store, slept soundly.

Off to the airport in the back of an old bicycle rickshaw in the first pale glow of morning, the streets already full of shouting chaos and reverence at the sacred altars. I had my passport. I had my body. Two things of value. I felt raw, hopeful.

Where We Can Be Ourselves

U p, up, up, the dry air, the safe airplane, the tiny trays of salty food. I concocted a plan: After this first smuggling run, I'd set up a little home base at the abandoned scout camp on Lamma Island. I'd work for Mr. Wong. I'd travel a little here and there on my own, leave Hong Kong often enough to keep my visa current. But mostly I'd save my money. I could do one smuggling run a month through the rest of the winter, spring and summer. I'd save up a few thousand dollars, go back to China. Maybe I'd meet up with Vincent in Shanghai after all, give a life with the heart doctor another try. Or I'd go to the Cold War Café, play mahjong in my underground city.

I spun through Hong Kong's neons, its familiar smells of fish, pollution and sweat. A dorm bed on C-block. A meeting in a stark high-rise office with Mr. Wong. He had a smooth face, a mole on his cheek, was younger than I'd imagined him. Thirty, maybe. He checked my passport, handed me a red suitcase and a round-trip ticket to Seoul.

"You have clean clothes to wear?"

"Yes."

My instructions: Take the suitcase to the airport in Kowloon, check it, claim it in Seoul, get it through customs, wait for a driver, who would identify himself to me. My accommodations would be taken care of. On the plane back to Hong Kong, another man would meet me, pay me five hundred U.S. in three different Asian currencies.

"All right," I agreed.

"No funny business."

I shook my head. "No funny business."

Up, up, up, the dry air, the safe airplane, the tiny trays of salty food. Through customs. Nothing to declare. A Korean official whose pants were too big made a cursory search of my suitcase, but he didn't rip the lining. Home free. A Chinese man in sunglasses called me by name, put my suitcase in his trunk, drove me to a hotel.

Seoul, South Korea. Like Shanghai meets San Francisco, but everyone drove a Hyundai and I was passing through so quickly it hardly mattered where I was and whether or not the war was over. I took a long nap between crisp sheets in my private room, woke up as night fell.

Near the hotel where all the smugglers stayed, a cheap all-night restaurant-bar on a low sloping hill overlooked some north-south train tracks. I spotted a white woman alone at the bar. She wore a blue-green business suit. I sat down next to her, said something to the effect of "Mind if I join you?"

Exhaustion. Strange city. We ate spicy cabbage kimchee that smelled rancid and tasted divine, drank Japanese beer and shots of Korean rice wine. I felt like we were in Beijing, warm and safe from the unrelenting cold outside. Or in Palo Alto, waiting in an all-night diner for a dose of psychedelic mushrooms to kick in. We talked, didn't mention the smuggling, both knew what the other was doing in Seoul. Quick money and getting off, just a little, on the danger of it all. I'd heard that a white guy had been sentenced to life in prison for doing what we'd done, but I wasn't afraid.

"I'm not going to tell you my name," the white woman said. "If that's going to upset you, leave now. And I don't want to know your name, either. This way, we can be friends forever." She kept opening and closing her purse.

"Fair enough," I said

"This way, we can relate to each other in real time. Here and now. Names are about the past." She looked like she'd make a nice PTA president and that's just what a smuggler should look like. Fat and gorgeous in her blue-green suit. And I wasn't surprised when she said she was from Cleveland. Gorgeous. Of course she was gorgeous. Maybe it had to do with my age, or all the drinking, but everyone looked so beautiful to me then. She told me she had an American husband on a military base in Okinawa, that she'd just left a lover in Thailand. "The love of my life, really," she said, her green eyes wet with tears. "But it was the wrong time."

"Isn't it always?"

"Maybe." A blond corkscrew curl fell across her forehead. "Maybe it is." She finished off her rice wine with a noisy gulp, rested her head on the bar and stared up at me.

"Sometimes I wonder how anyone could love me at all," she said. "My lover—he was an activist. Okinawan. He wanted the U.S. troops out of Japan. And how does the government get rid of a good activist? Gets him hooked on junk, that's what the government does. . . ." She trailed off. A long freight train barreled past. Her lover, the Okinawan junkie. She said, "I'll tell you something. You don't get happiness in this life. You get heartbreak, survival."

It made me feel so empty to see a woman like that—older than I was by a dozen years, just a normal military housewife from Cleveland, and I could tell by the curve of her spine and the curl of her lip that she hadn't figured out a damn thing more than I had about keeping her spirit in her body. About love and illusion. If I'd met her in the States, we wouldn't have exchanged a second glance. But here in an all-night bar in Seoul she spoke as if we'd known each other forever and would surely meet again.

"This is the kind of bar I come to when I'm trying to decide which world I want to live in. But I think I've already made up my mind." Her blue-green suit. Her army husband. Understated makeup. Salon-styled blond hair. Or her lover in Thailand. Her Okinawan junkie. U.S. out of Japan. Her smuggling run. A cracked barstool in Seoul.

I took a bite of kimchee, washed it down with rice wine. The staccato Korean conversation and American torch songs on the boom box behind the bar faded into the background. Spotlight on the Nameless Woman and me sitting at the bar. The whole rest of the world muttering in languages I would never learn. *Trying to decide which world I want to live in.*

"It's because I'm a Libra," she said. "I have to choose."

I took one of her Benson and Hedges cigarettes from its creamy brown box without asking. "I'm no Libra," I told her. "But I know what you mean."

"Two worlds. They're not good and evil like they tried to teach you, or right and wrong. They're more like day and night, maybe—"

"Or streets and tunnels?"

"Yeah," she looked out the window, then back in my general direction, lit another cigarette off her last.

"Down here we can be ourselves," I said. "There are no secrets. Everything's cut open. The weird thing is, from the street you can't see the tunnels. But from down here there are plenty of views up. You can see it all. You're in a tunnel with a one-way glass ceiling. You start to think that maybe they're happier up there. They make beautiful meals and plant gardens and go to work and have simple sex and so much more hope. Up there the world feels safer, but what if it's just a fantasy they have? What if we're made to feel things for real and go numb and come back and hurt and cry and love and wreck everything? What if all that up there is just bullshit?" Maybe I was drunk, but it all felt true. And even as I babbled on to her, I felt totally betrayed by both worlds.

The heart chakra encompasses both the heart and the lungs. It's associated with the color green, with love and hatred, resentment and forgiveness, hope and trust and the Catholic sacrament of marriage. Just above the heart is the throat chakra, associated with personal expression, will power, the color blue and the Catholic sacrament of confession. I will tell you everything.

The Nameless Woman was silent. A tear rolled down her cheek.

I wanted to cheer her up. "Maybe," I tried, "maybe we don't have to choose. Maybe there's a way to live in both worlds. Maybe we can have both streets and tunnels, like every city does."

But she just buried her face in her hands. "No. I have to decide. I have to climb back up. I love my husband. We have a beautiful home. And safety is safety. Even if it's a lie. Everyone wants a husband they love, who loves them. Everyone wants a beautiful home. Who am I to say I want more? Do I think I'm better than everyone else? Should I get happiness? You don't get happiness. You survive. That's all. You get survival or you get death. You don't get happiness."

We walked back to the hotel under neon signs that flashed in the cold Korean night, hugged a quick goodbye in the red wallpapered lobby.

You don't get happiness.

In my room, I flipped through TV channels, watched *Cat on a Hot Tin Roof* dubbed in Korean. I turned on the air conditioner and the heater. I wasn't hot or cold, just tripping on all the appliances I suddenly had at my disposal. My own private bathroom. And the thick mattress and crisp white sheets and soft red blankets. I'd been sleeping on cots and calling them beds for so long, I'd forgotten what it was like to lie down naked on a real mattress. I snuggled between the fitted and top sheets, drifted into blissful drunken half-sleep. I was dreaming of a Chinese man with gold teeth when I heard the knock. I opened my eyes, not sure where I was. The TV still on. I wrapped a blanket around myself, cracked the door. And here was the Nameless Woman, eyes red like she'd been crying, her blond curls a frizzy mess. "Can I sleep with you?" she asked, then blushed. "I mean sleep. With you. Not *sleep with* you."

We lay between the crisp sheets. Her head felt heavy on my chest, her breaths shallow. She fell asleep quickly. I wrapped my arms around her thick, soft waist, whispered, "It'll be OK." We were both leaving Seoul in the morning with dreams of brightly colored Monopoly money, no suitcases and no gold.

And If I Forget

As the plane took off, cool gust of relief. And I hadn't even realized that I'd been scared. My lids felt warm, heavy. The middleman had to wake me. A mainland Chinese kid, I was sure of it. Uneven bowl haircut. Clothes one step out of fashion: collar just a centimeter too long, sleeves just a centimeter too short. He'd never pass for a Hong Konger at the Lido. I wondered how he'd ever gotten out of China, thanked him for the cash, put my head back down on my tray, closed my eyes. And when I woke up, he was gone.

Maybe I'd finally found my calling: master gold smuggler.

I got a bus from the airport to Chungking Mansions, picked up the backpack I'd left on C-block, bought a new pair of combat boots in a basement store. I headed down Nathan Road toward the Star Ferry terminal, smiling to myself because no one knew how bad ass I was.

The boat pushed across the water toward Lamma Island. The salty cold wind on my face felt like home. I'd get dinner somewhere in the village near the dock, find a place to crash for the night. And in the sweet topaz light of morning, I'd make my way to the abandoned scout camp on the hill above the beach.

I headed up the cement path from the dock. A table full of travelers glowed rosy at the first café. People talking, drinking, singing. I smiled in their direction as I approached, but I didn't recognize Djuna until she jumped up: "Ghost Girl! What the fuck?" She was fatter than I remembered, her dreadlocks gone now, hair short and black. She hugged me.

"Shit—you're still in Hong Kong?"

She held my shoulders. "Obviously! What are you doing? You look like hell."

"Thanks a lot—I ran out of cash, so—"

"That's right! So you came home to Hong Kong for the Year of the Dragon! All the travelers come home to Hong Kong."

I'd met Djuna—what? Once before? A few nights in Chungking Mansions. I might not have even remembered her name if she hadn't been the one to hook me up with Mr. Wong, but she pulled me into the drinking crowd like we were childhood friends, saying, "Listen, everybody. This is Ghost Girl. She's been on the road longer than any of you lot, so don't give her any shit."

Nods all around. A few hellos. And then back to the traveler's tales. Callused hands slapped the wooden table. Heads thrown back in drunken laughter. Once-true stories of smuggling runs and massacres and endless roads spun into fantasy. I ordered a Dragon beer.

The cook skipped toward the door, smoking. He paused at our table, glanced around and laughed. "Before, I want to go to England or America or Australia," he said. "And then I ask myself, 'Why?' All the Brits and Americans and Australians want to come to Hong Kong!" The sky glowed red, reflecting the city across the water. "Ring of fire," the cook said. "You kids watch out." He crushed his cigarette on the cement, marched inside.

Djuna nudged me. "Where you staying?"

"I was thinking about that scout camp up from the beach."

Djuna sipped her seltzer water. "Well. Tonight you stay with me, all right? I've got a flat up the hill."

Year of the Dragon: an electric time of extreme ups and downs.

○○○

Djuna played Bob Dylan incessantly in her dorm room-sized flat, gave me the tour to the soundtrack of *Nashville Skyline*: A main room with a telephone stand, a round table and two chairs. Slick brown tile floors. A closet-sized kitchen. Empty mini-fridge. In the bathroom, a small water heater and shower head installed over the toilet. A drain on the tiled floor. To bathe, you had to sit down on the toilet.

Djuna's double futon mattress barely fit in her bedroom. She peeled off her purple leggings. "Aren't you going to ask me when I'm due?"

I set my pack at the corner of the mattress. "Due?"

She whipped off her black sweatshirt. "Yeah. Due."

"Djuna! I didn't even notice."

"Yep," she smiled. "Bun in the oven."

"Shit. Congratulations. Or . . .? When *are* you due?"

"I'm almost six months along, silly. Are you serious? You just thought I'd fattened right up?"

"That's so cool."

"Well." She sat down on the futon/floor, rested both hands on her belly. "Actually," she said, "it's a bloody disaster. Tonight's the night I planned to call my mum and tell her, but it can wait until tomorrow, you know?"

She'd meant to get an abortion at the clinic on Hong Kong Island, but suddenly it was too late.

"I'm looking into adoption," she said. "I'm thinking a Canadian couple." She looked up at the only window.

"The dad's not in Hong Kong anymore?"

She fiddled with her bellybutton. "He's here all right. But I haven't told him. Bloody banker. I was in the mime troupe in Kowloon for a few months, you know? He asked me out. I wanted to go to the rotating restaurant, you know? Maybe I had a little too much to drink. Anyway. I ended up at his place. I didn't really want him, but I didn't feel like arguing, you know? So finally I just said, 'fuck it.' So he fucked it. I missed a pill." Djuna looked more annoyed than anything else. Layers of fiery pissed-off concealed her flesh-toned hurt. A Canadian couple. Soon it would be too late for that, too. I already knew she'd keep the baby. "It's gonna be a mutt," she said. "He's black and Vietnamese. I'm all Welsh and Russian. You smoking these days?" She rolled a joint, dragged on it with a husky thirst, passed it to me across her silk-cased pillow. "So, you're finally smuggling?"

"Yeah, just did my first run," I beamed.

"It went OK?"

"Without a hitch."

"The alchemists thought gold represented the imperishable spirit." She sighed, pointed to her swollen belly: pale, freckled, stretch-marked. "I lost my job for this shit," she said. "Mr. Wong won't send a pregnant girl out. But enough about all that. . . ."

I passed the joint back to her, but she waved it away.

"I shouldn't smoke that shit. And, you know, Ghost Girl? That scout camp's been torn down."

I stayed with Djuna on her lime-green futon for six weeks, flew to Thailand, looped back through northern India.

In Calcutta, I took a job with a street doctor, sat on an empty gas can every day from sunrise until mid-afternoon, cleaned leper sores with cotton swabs and hydrogen peroxide. On a dusty cold morning, a greasy-haired man of indeterminate age sat in front of me. I looked him up and down.

He pointed to his bare foot. A beautiful, woundless foot the color of red clay.

I raised an eyebrow. "What's wrong?"

He pressed his index finger into his soft skin, lifted it. The dent remained for a full minute.

∽✥∾

When I got home to Hong Kong, I did another run to Korea for Mr. Wong, filled Djuna's mini-fridge with pork, oranges, pride, bok choi, soymilk, and EGO preserved mangoes with chilies.

Djuna said she wouldn't be able to travel much after the baby was born, so we got a hovercraft to Guangzhou, a ship to Hainan Island. "Ten years I'm going to be tied down to this thing," she said, then threw up over the ship's railing. "Fuck. I haven't been ill since the beginning."

"You think any more about telling the banker?" The wind off the South China Sea felt like silk on my cheeks.

Djuna shrugged. "You mean the wanker? I suppose I could get some Hong Kong dollars off of him. Pay the bills anyway, eh?"

Through the pink evening haze, I thought I could make out the coast of Vietnam in the distance. Paul Simon sang "Diamonds on the Soles of her Shoes" through the speakers on deck.

We docked at a gray port in the early morning. A gray-blue bus to a village near Sanya. Then a motorcycle tuk-tuk. Djuna held her belly.

On a sandy beach where ancient faces were carved into the red cliffs, we watched the fishermen drag in their nets. Unmistakably pregnant now, Djuna had ballooned to almost three times her original size. We ate boiled lobster with garlic butter at a deserted café. "Life is good," she said.

We were the only white travelers in Sanya. I felt so far away from everywhere and everything, the February wind warm and foreign. "You call your mom yet?"

"Well. I wrote." She sucked the meat from a claw. "You fuck men, Ghost Girl?"

"Sometimes."

"Then get on the Pill. And don't miss one."

Those tiny pink pills made me fat and crazy. "OK," I lied. But she saw right through me.

"*This* is what makes you fat and crazy," she said, pointing to her belly.

In our room at Chairman Mao's old summer palace, Djuna stretched out on the mosquito-netted double bed. "Those communists sure knew how to live."

A gecko scurried across the white wall.

I took my shirt off.

She slipped a Dylan tape into my boom box, played "Lay Lady Lay." "That's a fucked-up tattoo," she said, pointing to my chest. She'd seen it a dozen times before, never mentioned it. "Safety pin?"

I nodded.

"Want to mark me? In commemoration of life without a baby?" She lifted her wraparound skirt, drew a dragon on her dimpled thigh with a purple pen. "Just follow the lines. I don't care if it's fucked up."

I fingered it. "I don't know, hon. Looks kind of complicated."

"Well," she shifted her weight, licked her finger and rubbed the sketch to a blur. "How about infinity?" She drew the horizontal figure eight. "Forever young."

On the full moon in April, when the smell of the sea held heavy in the thick Hong Kong air and cotton dresses clung to sweat-drenched skin, Djuna went into labor.

I offered to take her to the hospital, had always assumed I would take her to the hospital. By ferry and taxi.

But she just moaned. "Call that fucking wanker." We were in the main room of her tiny apartment, window open. She dialed the number from memory, handed me the bitter red phone.

"What should I say?"

"Tell him to go fuck himself. Tell him next time he wants to fuck something to go fuck himself." She walked into the kitchen, then back out into the main room, then into her bedroom, and back. She paced.

"Hello?" came a man's voice.

She grabbed the phone from me, sat down at the round table cluttered with unread pregnancy books, old soymilk boxes and half-empty packs of 555 cigarettes. "Yes, this is Djuna. Remember me?"

—

"I'm in labor. How are you?"

—

"Yes."

—

"Well."

—

"It's yours."

—

"Of course I'm sure, you bastard fuck."

—

"Well. You can either count back nine months and believe me, or I'll send you a picture in the morning and you can tell me what other wanker in Hong Kong could have given me a mutt." She stood up, walked across the room, hand on her back. She replaced the phone, didn't look up at me. "Wanker." She pushed play on her Sony boom box. As far as Djuna was concerned, there was no occasion that didn't call for Dylan.

In the kitchen, I filled a plastic Minnie Mouse cup with ice, poured some soda. "You need anything else, Djuna?"

From the speakers, Dylan wanted to know how it felt.

"No."

To be on our own.

The knock came so soon, I figured it couldn't be the banker. The complete unknown.

But when Djuna opened the door, she looked him up and down. "What took you so long?"

Sometimes you need more than a compass to find a direction home.

The banker wasn't any older than Djuna was. Maybe twenty-five. Clean cut. Sexy in a nervous lost kind of way. He wore black suit pants, a white T-shirt, just stood there expressionless.

I'd laughed when Djuna bitched about him over the weeks and months, but now I felt kind of sorry for the guy. Father-to-be in the doorway. Hands in his pockets. Looking at his shoes, then at Djuna, then at his shoes. "The thing is," he said softly, "I just got married."

Djuna walked back down the short tiled hallway, one hand on her belly, the other holding the small of her back.

He followed her, glanced at me.

"I don't have any money," Djuna was saying as I slipped into the bedroom.

I opened the window, lit a cigarette, started flipping through Djuna's copy of *The Little Prince*. I was thinking about the Zero Mass Theorem.

Antoine de Saint-Exupéry, unassigned: *For I do not want any one to read my book carelessly. I have suffered too much grief in setting down these memories. Six years have already passed since my friend went away from me, with his sheep. If I try to describe him here, it is to make sure that I shall not forget him. To forget a friend is sad. Not everyone has had a friend. And if I forget him, I may become like the grown-ups who are no longer interested in anything but figures. . . .*

Soft knock on the bedroom door. "We'll be going to the hospital, then," was all the banker said.

I looked at Djuna sitting there at her table, head in her hands, red-brown roots showing under the black dye job. "You sure you don't want me to come with?"

"Don't worry about it, Ghost Girl." Djuna moaned, then looked up, half-smiled. "You'll be here if I need to call you?"

"Yeah," I promised. "If you need anything—"

The baby was born lithe, with bluish skin like some Hindu goddess. A full head of dark locks. "That thing's my baby," Djuna said, pointing.

I peered into the little wooden crib next to Djuna's bed. "She's beautiful." Not even a day old. I handed Djuna a can of Guinness and a chocolate bar I'd bought at the Star Ferry terminal. "Have you named her?"

"Peggy Day." She popped the beer, took a sip, frowned. "What the fuck am I going to do, Ghost Girl?"

I didn't know. "I'm doing another smuggling run," I offered. "I can work until you can. Get groceries, pay the rent. And you can just rest, you know? Take care of the baby? Work whatever out with the banker? Or, you know, think about whether or not you want to go home?"

The banker showed up at noon with pink cotton infant clothes and a blanket made of Australian wool.

"Thanks," Djuna said without looking at him.

"I'm sorry," was all he kept saying.

The baby whimpered in her wooden crib.

Djuna picked her up awkwardly, forgetting to hold the head. She lifted her greenish hospital gown, pushed Peggy Day to her tit. "Listen," she finally said. "I know I should have called you sooner, OK?"

He looked down at his shoes. "Thanks for calling when you did."

I wanted to disappear.

"Listen," he said. "I can't take the baby. Whatever you need, just tell me. But I can't take the baby."

Djuna didn't look at him. She stared at the spiral of hair on Peggy Day's head, then smiled. "Don't worry about it, wanker."

And he smiled, too, placed his large hand on Peggy Day's tiny back. "I should go home now. You girls will be all right?"

"Yeah," Djuna said. "Get the fuck out of here."

I spent the balance of the spring and summer drifting, floating. Through other people's lives, through other people's countries. In and out of Hong Kong. In and out of Korea. In and out of mainland China. In and out of Southeast Asia. Across borders on foot. And buses. And planes. And boats. And hovercrafts. And trains. So many trains. Sometimes I was smuggling, other times I traveled without assignment. On the day I should have graduated from Palo Alto High School, I lay in a hammock on Koh Samet, smoking a joint, staring out over the Gulf of Thailand. Blue and more blue. Djuna's place was home for a time. We changed diapers, warmed bottles, cooed at Peggy Day. But mother and child were packing up now, heading home to England.

There was me and there was circumstance. There was me and there was geography. And then there was this sadness. It followed me. Or maybe it didn't follow me, exactly. Maybe it was a part of me. Or maybe it wasn't a part of just me. Maybe it was a part of everyone. Everywhere. In everything. Air, water, blood, pollution, salt, dirt, sadness.

Part IV

Heartburn

The symptoms of major cardiac diseases are few: pain, difficulty breathing, fatigue, lightheadedness, palpitations, weakness. Overall heart size is often unequivocally normal despite severe heart conditions. Close attention must be paid to subtle variations.

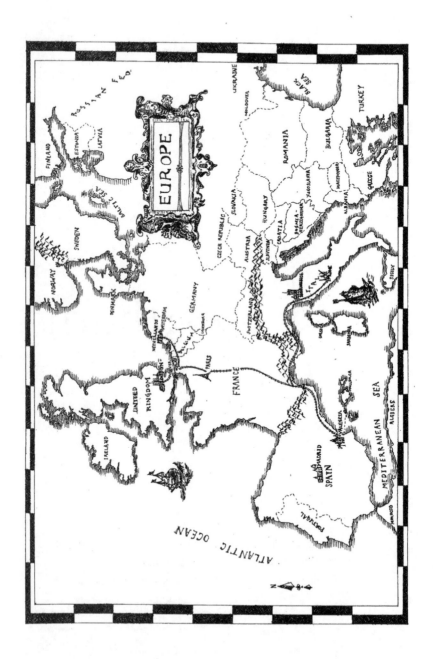

Choose Your Own Adventure

JOURNAL ENTRY #181
52°23'N 4°55'E
SUMMER, 1988

with the lights of a new city
i flash between panic and faith

A smuggling run gone slightly wrong landed me in Amsterdam with neither compass nor map. No money. No ticket to anywhere. My silver jewelry from Lhasa and Kathmandu spread out in front of me. Selling my travels in the square for some food and some hash.

My assignment had been simple enough: Take Mr. Wong's bags from Hong Kong to New Delhi, drop them off with a man named Singh, pick up a bag of gems, fly to Amsterdam, drop those off with a man named Steve, fly home to Hong Kong. Pass go. Collect one thousand dollars. Simple.

I made the run from Hong Kong to New Delhi without incident.

Singh was fat, bought me brandy and Lucky Strike cigarettes in the airport bar, warned me that Europe could be dangerous.

"New Delhi can be dangerous, too," I offered, and he nodded his fat head.

My mind spun tipsy as I left Singh, but that's no excuse. I was stoned, too, having smuggled a joint in my bra and smoked it in the air-conditioned bathroom. I checked the bag at the Aeroflot counter. A 747 routed through Moscow. Five-hour layover in a cold, stark airport. *What's the point of being a superpower if there's nothing to eat but cabbage stew?* Then on to Amsterdam. From my window seat, the world spun below. An argument with the blond steward about cutlery: I'd pocketed the airline's stainless steel fork, spoon and butter knife. He said I couldn't deplane. He knew I'd stolen them. He stood in the middle of the aisle, hand extended. "Do you want me to call the police?" I gave in. Of course I gave in. I handed him the fork, the spoon and then, reluctantly, the butter knife. I was the last passenger off the plane.

Midnight at Schiphol airport. Watching as the suitcases and backpacks and boxes circled the belt. I just stood there. Watching. Waiting. Watching. Waiting until there were no bags at all. Sinking disbelief at my own stupidity. *I checked the bag of diamonds and emeralds and rubies through Cold War Moscow. I checked the bag of diamonds and emeralds and rubies. I. Checked. The. Bag.*

I sat down on the thinly carpeted floor next to the now-empty conveyor belt, buried my face in my hands. My cheeks felt hot against my palms. *Master gold smuggler. How could I be so stupid?*

Hong Kong to Seoul we were supposed to check the bags. Hard suitcases with gold in the lining. Hong Kong to New Delhi we were supposed to check the bags. Hard suitcases with god-knows-what in the lining. But Singh had handed me a neon green duffel bag. Carry-on size. I'd stuffed my own things into it, checked everything but the clothes on my back, the jewelry on my body, the passport and wallet and trinkets and journal and Wilhelm translation of the *I Ching* in my red silk purse from Kathmandu. Singh hadn't mentioned that I was supposed to keep the duffel with me. *Probably because only a complete idiot would check a bag full of diamonds and emeralds and rubies through Cold War Moscow.*

I sat there until the conveyor belt stopped moving.

A thin, freckled woman wearing a creased blue airline uniform appeared next to me. "You are waiting for a bag?"

I stood up, wiped my eyes.

She had Cyndi Lauper hair and the face of somebody's mother, mascara smudged on one side. "Don't worry, honey," she whispered, placing a hand on my shoulder. "Surely your luggage is only temporarily lost. Perhaps someone else has picked it up? Many bags look alike. They will return it. Or perhaps it will come through on the next flight?"

But even if it turned up, I knew I wouldn't be able to claim it. I wanted to call Mr. Wong. Or Singh. Surely there was some way to get the gems back. I couldn't believe I hadn't asked either of them a single "what-if." I couldn't believe they'd sent me off without any advice. *How much were the gems worth? Would I have to pay for them now?* Maybe there were drugs in the bag, too. Maybe the woman with Cyndi Lauper hair was waiting for me to describe my bag to her, to claim it. I wondered if I'd go to jail in Amsterdam or be sent back to Moscow, to New Delhi, to Hong Kong. I would refuse to leave Amsterdam. I could handle a Dutch jail. My connection would be waiting for me outside customs. Steve. *Could I meet him? Tell him what happened? He'd say I had to go back, claim the bag. He'd say I owed him thousands of dollars. He'd have sharpened gold teeth, and a three-day beard. I'd try to explain myself— he wouldn't care. He'd kill me, dump my body in a canal, take my passport.* I wanted to call Djuna. *How well did she know Mr. Wong?* I stood up.

"Honey?" the airline woman whispered.

"I'm sorry," was all I said. "I guess I forgot to check a bag. I didn't bring anything."

She cocked her head to one side.

"I'm sorry." I turned toward a glowing customs sign.

I counted my breaths as I walked past the uniformed officials, nothing to declare. I still had two hundred dollars U.S. in my wallet, traded it all for guilders at Thomas Cooke. I kept my head bowed as I stepped through the glass doors into the cool night. Either my middleman would approach me or he wouldn't. Either he'd be looking for a neon green duffel bag or he'd be looking for me. I took small comfort in the fact that I didn't stand out in Amsterdam. Dark hair, pale skin. I could be French. Or Russian. Even Dutch.

No one approached me.

I hailed a taxi into town, took a bed in the first hostel I saw. Single bunks with pink, fitted sheets. I must have fallen asleep, because next thing I was running through the long fluorescent-lit hallways of the Moscow airport. I held the duffel bag tight at my side. I could hear footfalls close behind me. I thought I was running from Steve, from Singh, from Mr. Wong. But when I tripped on a thick, coiled rope and turned to face my pursuer, a bejeweled Teacher Fu from the Beijing Language Institute stood over me. I clutched the green bag. "We're not going to the Lido," was all I said. I had to find the underground tunnel out of Moscow.

I woke up early, my inner clock still set to the Asian sun.

In the dull August light seeping through venetian blinds, the other kids in the room looked like orphans. Tattered sleep shirts. Dirty military backpacks at their feet. Neglected punk hairdos—natural roots under messy blue or blond or red or black dye jobs. They clutched their money belts even as they slept. I focused on a girl in the bottom bunk across from me. Thick black hair. Bleach job at least six months old. Her wide face acne-scarred. She looked Korean. Or northern

Chinese. But by her silver and turquoise earrings, I guessed she was American. I watched her as she slept. Her blanketed chest rose and fell. She felt my stare, maybe, opened her eyes, turned sleepily toward me, squinted, then focused: "Were you there when I went to sleep?"

"No. Got in late."

"I'm not hallucinating you, am I?" Her lips hardly moved when she spoke.

"Not unless I'm dreaming you, too."

She closed her eyes, took a slow breath, opened them again. "You ever actually *wake up* stoned?"

"I don't think so."

"It sucks, man. This is the only city in the world where I actually *wake up* stoned. I keep thinking I'm going crazy. But then I remember I'm just stoned." She lit a roach from the ashtray under her bed, took a hit, then held it out for me.

I finished it off.

"Careful," she mumbled as she dozed off. "That shit's a train wreck." She had an orange copy of *On the Road* next to her pillow.

I climbed out of bed, still dressed in my Chinese army pants and gray sweatshirt. I'd slept with my red silk purse on my chest. I laced up my boots, slung the purse over my shoulder, headed out into the morning to find a cup of coffee.

I'd forgotten how pretty a city Amsterdam was. Overcast skies forever threatening to weep. Endless circles of canals. Three- and four- and five-story buildings huddled together as if to stay warm. Brick streets and cobblestone alleyways. One-speed bicycles and yellow tramcars. Artists and buskers setting up on every corner. I passed a Chinese herb shop, a Parisian shoe store, an Italian restaurant, ducked into a café with a tangerine ceiling. The only waiter, a pale goateed kid with a silver ring through his nose, spoke English, said, "Business is slow. You would like to fuck?"

"No, thanks."

"I have a room in back." He gestured with his head, raised a thin eyebrow.

"No, really."

I sipped cappuccino and nibbled a hash cookie at my corner table. I had stuff to figure out, like: *How was I going to get back to Hong Kong?* And: *Where could I get a cheap bottle of conditioner?* I needed a new backpack, too. Maybe a change of clothes. I lit a cigarette.

Another girl stumbled into the café. Her black sweater fell over one shoulder revealing a pale purple bra strap. She sat down near the front window, dropped her oversized plastic handbag onto the hardwood floor. The goateed kid approached her, said something. She picked up her bag and followed him into the back. He shot me an arrogant glance as they passed.

I left without paying.

You just go around in your own little world and you don't know where you are.

Outside, I headed down the main road toward Central Station. As I neared it, a youngish man approached me. Maybe twenty-five, he reminded me of Guy. Smooth skin. Sweet smile. "You lost?"

"Not really. Just trying to figure out where I can find a drugstore."

"Oh, yeah," he nodded. "There's one around the corner. You got a cigarette? I can take you."

I gave him a Lucky Strike, followed him through an alleyway. He scratched his nose, asked where I'd come from.

"I fucking lost my luggage on the way in," I was saying when I felt someone's warm breath at the back of my neck.

As I turned, she whispered, "That's too bad, because now I'm going to take your money." She had a knife pressed against my throat. Dark skin, pretty face. No one I'd ever think to be afraid of.

I glanced back at the man, somehow thinking he'd help me. But he had my red purse open.

Disoriented, I said, "OK, but can I keep my passport?"

"Take the passport," the woman hissed, pressing her cold blade against my skin.

He rifled through my wallet, grabbing at the guilders, held my dark blue passport in his palm.

I said, "Oh man, come on."

And he smiled his Guy-smile, winked at me. "Yeah—let's let the girl keep her passport."

"Hurry it up," the woman seethed, screwing up her pretty face.

Just then an old man on a black one-speed bicycle bumped around a curve in the alleyway.

"Shit—" They took off running. As they rounded the corner, the man dropped my passport onto the cobblestones.

I picked up the worn booklet, leafed through the pages of visas and travel permits, looked at the old picture of myself— fourteen years old in my red *Flashdance* sweatshirt.

Well, fuck, I thought.

I didn't get any conditioner. I didn't go back to the hostel. I didn't call Djuna. I didn't call Mr. Wong. I stayed in Amsterdam, spread out my silver jewelry and Hindu trinkets in Leidseplein. Selling my travels in the square. I felt alone and alive in the best kind of way. All the knife-wielding thieves and gold-smuggling recruiters and language institute spies and date-rapists in the whole world could really just go fuck themselves. They didn't know where I was now. I bought an ash-colored woolen cap, a used Rilke book and a copy of *Sassafrass, Cypress and Indigo* by Ntozake Shange. I ate the free food the Hare Krishnas served near the waterfront behind Central Station, slept in a covered doorway on Van Ostadestraat until a dreadlocked white kid nudged me with his boot one morning. I looked up at him from the sidewalk, the blue sky brilliant behind his wild hair.

"I don't know why you sleep out here," he said. His accent was British, but I couldn't place it any more specifically than that. "We have free rent practically right downstairs."

We Are Here to Ruin Ourselves

The squat on Van Ostadestraat was accessible via a ground-level window in an alley a quarter of a block down from my covered doorway. The dreadlocked kid introduced himself as Monk, opened the black-silled window for me. "You just squiggle on in there."

So in I went, feet first, landed solidly on a wooden chair propped there under the window to catch the entrants. Monk followed me down into the brick-walled basement. Half a dozen sleeping kids lined up on mattresses across a red concrete floor. A table was piled with books and a boom box under the only other window.

"I was just on my way out," Monk whispered. "I have to go, but you can sleep over there." He pointed to an empty blue mattress, then climbed onto the chair and hoisted himself out again. He stuck his head back in through the window. "I didn't get your name."

"Ghost Girl."

He winked at me. "This is a shit hole. But I'm sure you'll be more comfortable than you were on the street."

Almost all of the squatters on Van Ostadestraat spoke English. They were white. They came from Sweden or Finland or Ohio or Germany or England or Wales. Most nights, a half-dozen kids slept on the red cement floor in the main room that was connected by a dark hallway to a bathroom and a windowless back room decorated with silk-screened communist propaganda posters.

Mornings, I watched the travelers from my bed. I could tell by the way each of them moved through the space whether they considered the place home, or just a transitory crash pad. Bobby McFerrin sang "Don't Worry, Be Happy" from the boom box on the table. And Bono wailed "I Still Haven't Found What I'm Looking For."

We were allowed to invite anyone we liked to come and live rent-free in the basement squat, but we could get eighty-sixed for bringing in an "asshole." The rules—and the determinations regarding who was an asshole—were said to be made by consensus, but the system functioned more like a stockholder's meeting favoring tenants with seniority and voice-volume. As far as I could tell, a drunk Londoner named Lance who slept in the back room with his skinny-boy sidekick from Liverpool had the seniority thing wrapped up. And Flower, a hippie chick with tremendous red-blond hair, had voice enough to move and propose and veto and vote for all those absent or silent. I never cast a ballot.

I sat on my mattress, mostly, read my books, wrote in my journal, smoked fat joints, hoisted myself out the window in the afternoons to wander the narrow Amsterdam streets counting elms and ginkgos and London plane trees.

Rilke, in unassigned reading: *Often a star was waiting for you to notice it. A wave rolled towards you out of the distant past, or as you walked under an open window, a violin yielded itself to your hearing. All this was a mission. But could you accomplish it?*

I set the book down on my blue mattress, worried: *What if it all had been a mission? What if I'd accomplished nothing?* I tried to push the questions out of my mind, rolled another joint instead. As I lit it, I thought, *This wouldn't be such a bad way to spend my whole life, would it? Outgrowing shells, searching for new ones. Tide pool hermit crab. Ebbing and flowing with the tide.* I held the smoke in my lungs for as long as I could, exhaled with a cough.

The cool thing about smoking pot was that it lent a certain profundity to total inaction. Come to think of it, it lent a certain profundity to *everything*. With a joint in hand, I wasn't a complete idiot who'd gone and lost a duffel bag full of diamonds and emeralds and rubies in Cold War Moscow, then managed to get mugged in broad daylight. No. *Destiny* had brought me to Amsterdam. *Providence* had found me a bed. This was what life was all about. Riding possibilities. I wasn't some lost broke traveler girl sleeping among strangers in the basement of a condemned building, queen of unaccomplished missions. No! I was a Taoist warrior. I knew the wisdom of not-doing. My life was a riverbed. And I was the water—rushing trusting, not knowing where I was going, because the water isn't *supposed* to know where it's going. The water just flows. Sometimes my stream would cross someone else's stream. We'd meet, mingle, and then we'd flow on— alone. Water. Riverbed. I was water and life was a riverbed. *I am water and life is a riverbed!* I wrote this down in my journal so as never to forget what a deep thought I'd once had.

I'd been coming up with damp and profound metaphors like this for a couple of weeks the morning Monk brought in the stoned girl with silver and turquoise earrings I recognized immediately from my first night in town. *Nikki.* She introduced herself in a whisper, took the empty mattress next to mine, stacked her collection of Kerouac books against the wall, went right to sleep.

She never woke up before noon.

By then blue-eyed American Joey was usually awake, too,

crying at the table because his grandmother had broken his heart. Sometimes, when he drank whiskey or sweet imported Southern Comfort, he talked about it, talked about her. "I miss her so much," he'd say.

And his shaven-headed German boyfriend would wrap his arms around him and rock him, just a little.

Joey whimpered, "She used to say she'd always love me, you know? And now it's like I can't even visit her anymore. She's beautiful, my grandma, you know? Smells like jasmine soap. I miss watching her put on her makeup in the morning."

His boyfriend rocked him and whispered, "You really ought to call her, Joe Joe."

But Joey shook his head. "She don't love me no more. Sixteen years I lived in her house. But she says we're sinners now."

"Do you wanna go get something to eat at the Krishna place?" I asked Nikki when she opened her eyes and sparked up her first joint of the day. "All right," she said. "Smoke out first?"

I took a single hit off her tobacco-hash joint, closed my eyes.

In Amsterdam, everything felt hazy, expansive. The air held water. The bricks held water. The concrete held water. It was a wonder the whole city didn't just dissolve into liquid nothingness. Just the opposite: The city felt solid. Water solid.

At the Krishna place, orange-clad monks dished up bowls of thick purple borscht. They offered chunks of whole grain bread—dry, but heavy. I thought the texture alone could surely sustain me.

"This food is fucking good," Nikki said. She wore a black sweatshirt, black army pants, black boots.

I wondered what it might taste like if we weren't so high.

We walked under the tram wires in the waning gray afternoon. The smells of cigarette smoke and patchouli mixed uneasily with the dampness along the crowded brick streets. "You're from the States?"

"Yeah." Nikki looked down as we walked, her eyes only half-open. Her grin made me think she'd just told herself a good joke. "California."

"Bay Area?"

"Yeah."

"Me, too."

"San Jose."

"Palo Alto."

"So where'd you get a name like Ghost Girl?"

"China."

"Figures," she said. "All my grandparents were from there. But I've never been."

I lit a cigarette.

"Listen," Nikki said. "I actually have some guilders. Do you wanna see a movie?"

My face must have lit up, because she didn't wait for me to answer. She giggled, pulled me into the red-carpeted lobby of a theater I hadn't noticed we were passing. *"Moonstruck?"*

"In Dutch?"

"No, English."

I hadn't seen a movie since *¡Three Amigos!* in Kathmandu. How long ago? Ten months? And before that? *Vagabond?* I couldn't remember the last movie I'd seen in English.

The dark theater smelled salty, like home. Onscreen, Cher fell for Nicolas Cage. I felt like such a sap, drawn into the whole Beauty and the Beast plot line. *"I love you,"* Nicolas Cage pleaded with Cher in a snowy moonlit alley. *"Not like they told you love is, and I didn't know this either, but love don't make things nice—it ruins everything. It breaks your heart. It makes things a mess. . . . We aren't here to make things perfect. The snowflakes are perfect. The stars are perfect. Not us. Not us! We are here to ruin ourselves and to break our hearts and love the wrong people and die. . . ."*

I glanced over at Nikki. Tears streamed down her pale cheeks. *Relief*. Two homeless suckers for Hollywood aren't nearly so lonely as one.

We left the theater holding hands. "That was the best fucking movie," Nikki sighed, looking down at her boots. Her glossy black hair glinted under the street lamp. "Listen, I have to work tonight. See you back on Van Ostadestraat?"

Wide-eyed: "You have a job?"

"Of course." She raised her eyebrows, like, *You don't?* Then she let go of my hand. "Have you been to the red-light district yet?"

"No."

"Well. Maybe I'll take you one day." She winked at me, turned.

I'd seen Lance shouting epithets from the street corner and squiggling in and out of the squat window with his skinny-boy sidekick, but I'd never actually spoken to him before. Some of the other kids avoided him.

"Watch out for that one," Monk had warned me. "Bit of a temper."

But on a candle-lit night, Lance sat down on a carpet remnant near the foot of my bed. He had a cloth bag full of stolen groceries, offered me a piece of his baguette and half the sardines in tomato sauce from his oval tin. He pointed to my silver Ganesh pendant, the last of my Kathmandu jewelry, said, "You're a Hindu, then?"

I sat up. "No. I'm a poet."

He wore Levi's, Doc Marten boots. A blue T-shirt silk-screened with the word "Tramp" peeked out from under his beat-up biker jacket. "You can't be a Hindu poet, then?"

I shrugged. "I'm sure you can be, but I'm not." I chewed on my salty fish sandwich.

"You write poetry, then?"

"No. I just believe in it."

"You can't very well be a poet if you don't write poetry, can you?"

I said, "Sure I can. To me it's not a profession. It's more like a faith. You asked me if I was a Hindu, so I figured you were asking about my faith."

He finished off his sandwich, thought about that, said, "*I'm* a poet, but only because I write poetry."

I studied his face in the flickering light. Wide features, sunburned and slightly bloated. Natural brown hair fell over half his face. His short beard had been bleached and dyed a midnight blue. I watched his eyes, dark brown and clouded. I said, "Well, maybe I'm not a poet. Maybe I'm more like a poetist, OK? It's just my religion."

"Religion is a crutch." He handed me his open bottle of port.

The rain against the window sounded like an oncoming train. I looked up at the dark ceiling beams. "So is shelter."

He smiled without showing his teeth. "Read me a story, then, will you? Or a poem?"

I leaned back onto a pile of jeans and black cotton clothes that didn't seem to belong to anyone in particular. I didn't want to read Lance a story. But I didn't want him to leave the foot of my bed, either. Something about him made me uneasy, but his presence felt weirdly familiar, too, like maybe I'd dreamed him before. "All right," I said. "If you'll roll me a joint."

From his jacket pocket, he produced a blue packet of Rizla papers.

I paged through *Sassafrass, Cypress and Indigo* as he mixed the tobacco with hash in his palm, rolled it, lit a black candle, then lit the joint and passed it to me.

I smoked, read from the first chapter until he held up his

hand to stop me. He ashed the joint onto the floor. "Tell me a story of your own. Tell me a true story."

I closed the book. "I don't remember any true stories."

He leaned back against the brick wall. "Right, then. Means you won't remember me."

"No," I promised. "I won't remember you."

"I'll read you one of *my* poems, then," he offered. And he recited lines from memory, in rhyming meter, something about greening fields, knights and damsels.

If the poem had a narrative line, I couldn't follow it. But the rhythm alone lulled me like a narcotic.

"It's not polished," he said.

As I smoked, he rambled on about this and that. Life, travels. He'd come to Amsterdam by way of Spain and Greece, tried to make some money performing magic tricks in Leidseplein, but the disappearing acts he promised in grandiose introductions were beyond his skill, and by day's end he never had more than a few guilders in his hat. "I'm a Renaissance man," he sighed. "Born in the wrong century."

I laughed even though I wasn't sure if he was kidding.

Lance carried three passports, each with his own picture and a different, fictitious name. He drank whiskey in the daytime, red wine at night. He never worked, shoplifted what he needed. As far as he was concerned, all the groceries in the store were rightfully his. And all the liquor on the shelves, overpriced. Even if the ethical person might pay for it, the hyperethical among us were duty-bound to shove it under our shirts and walk out the door.

"What if you get caught?" I wanted to know.

He shrugged. "This is Europe. The nicks are nicer than the squats." He tilted his head back and poured more wine down his throat. "This world is fucked for people like us. You don't even know yet. I'm thirty-six years old. I can tell you, it's fucked. You get on a train and immediately a conductor starts hassling you for a bloody ticket."

"Thirty-six?" I'd had Lance pegged at twenty-five. Maybe thirty. "How'd you get to be thirty-six?"

He set the bottle down between us. "What kind of bloody question is that?"

Lance was missing his skinny-boy sidekick that night, and I was missing Nikki. I didn't realize the two were out together until they squiggled back through the window in the first light of morning, damp and smiling, one behind the other.

"Hi," I whispered when Nikki climbed into bed next to me.

"Hey, Ghost Girl."

And we both fell asleep.

That night I dreamed I found a secret door under my blue mattress. I climbed down a metal ladder, could hear a river flowing below. Darkness. I couldn't see down or up. I felt each rung of the ladder with my bare feet, climbed down. The sound of the river got louder. A waterfall? I climbed down.

Nikki woke up before I did, pinched my arm. "I have a new boyfriend!" she squealed as she sparked up her breakfast joint. "He's Dean Moriarty!"

Her new boyfriend had longish blond sideburns, bowlegs. He was no Dean Moriarty, but I think his name might have been Dean. Until he'd hooked up with Nikki, he'd followed Lance in and out of the squat like a puppy dog. His wide, expectant smile made him look younger than the twenty-five he said he was. In the back room, he strummed his guitar, tried to sing "Beast of Burden." Now he would move between Lance and Nikki, watching and smiling, nodding his blond head.

"We should all go out some time," Nikki said. "The four of us."

ikki had money, but Lance insisted on talking his way into free slices of space cake and cappuccinos in a Pink Floyd–themed coffeeshop near Vondelpark. We were travel writers, he told the

The Four of Us

N green-haired woman behind the counter. We'd rec-
ommend the place in a book we were all collabo-
rating on. She squinted her eyes in disbelief, but he
just barreled along, ignoring her doubt, until he'd all but con-
vinced himself.

I sat on a tall vinyl upholstered stool between Nikki and
Lance at the bar, "Wish You Were Here" playing softly on a
stereo near the espresso maker. The hash-laced chocolate cake
tasted like blood and sugar. I wished we really could recom-
mend the place in a starred review.

"Have you read the Ten Commandments?" Lance wanted
to know.

The Ten Commandments? I wracked my brain. I knew I'd read
them at some point, but I couldn't remember where or when.
Maybe the space cake had already started shifting things
around in my mind, making memories hard to locate.

Nikki leaned over me. "The Ten Commandments?"

"Right," Lance said. "They've got 'Thou shalt not kill,' 'Thou
shalt not commit adultery,' a bunch of stuff, but nowhere in
the Ten Commandments does it say anything like 'Thou shalt
not lie.'"

I laughed. Surely Lance wasn't about to make a case for
his own Christian morality. "I think 'Thou shalt not steal' is
in there."

"You think I *steal*?" Lance sputtered, indignant. "Nah, I

don't steal. I *reclaim.*" He took another bite of cake, smacked his lips. "Not bad."

Dean nodded. "We *reclaim.*"

Under a streetlight a block away from the coffee shop, my companions looked so strange, their lost and eager little faces red against the wind. I could tell the space cake was hitting my bloodstream because I couldn't feel my feet.

Lance stopped in front of a corner store with a tattered green awning. "This is reclaiming," he said. And Dean followed him inside.

Nikki and I watched through the window as they blatantly pocketed red apples from a wooden crate, plastic sealed packets of smoked mackerel, French rolls.

They emerged, proud and stupid. "Reclaiming," Dean clucked.

"Do you like Lance?" Nikki wanted to know. "I mean *like him* like him?" We were sitting on a stone bridge watching the sun set eggplant behind a huddle of brick buildings, our feet dangling over the water. *Did I like Lance?* I took a cigarette from my pocket. He reminded me of someone, but I couldn't pinpoint whom. I wasn't sure I trusted him, but I scolded myself for the thought. He was a nice guy—sharing his reclaimed food and wine with me. And funny—yelling insults at passers-by just because he didn't like the corporate look of them. What had gotten me this far, anyway? Blind confidence in strangers. This was no time to become unnecessarily distrustful. "Yeah," I admitted as I ashed my cigarette into the canal. "I like him."

Nikki nodded. "I thought so." She rubbed her hands together, then rubbed her face. She had to work that night. "Walk me there?"

I followed Nikki through cobblestone alleys in the September night. A light drizzle. We talked about Kerouac, about the way traveling starts out as this grand adventure and then it just seems to settle into daily routines until pretty soon you're not thinking about adventure anymore, you're just looking for a hot shower, your next meal, a little bit of money. She said, "Traveling doesn't change you. It just changes the setting you're fucking up in. But going home now, it would be like surrender, you know?"

Behind the Old Church, we turned onto a narrow street lined with red glowing picture windows. Behind each pane of glass, illuminated in the rosy light, women in lingerie posed and gestured and curled their fingers: *Come here.* Frat boys and businessmen and tourists and guys in overcoats shuffled along, blowing kisses to the ladies, catcalling, or looking at their own feet.

"You stand in a window?" I couldn't picture Nikki vogueing like that for anyone.

"Yeah," she laughed. "You haven't told Dean, have you?"

I lit a cigarette, shook my head. "I hardly ever even talk to him."

"It's not like I'm ashamed or anything, but don't tell anyone, OK? I mean, Monk knows, but he's hardly ever around. It's not like he's going to tell anybody."

"You make a lot of money?"

She reached for my cigarette, and I handed it to her. She dragged hard, blew an impressive cloud of smoke. "Used to, when I worked full-time, but now I just fill in a few shifts a week. It's pocket money, anyway. I first came out here to write a paper on the girls, you know? I was going to the New School in New York. But I got, like, halfway through my paper and I thought, What the fuck am I doing? I'm paying to go to college and these girls are making a couple hundred dollars a night.

That's how I got into it. But it's hard work. I did it for a year. Now I'm on sabbatical. Or maybe I'm in semiretirement." She stopped at a stone stairway that led down to a red-lit doorway, crushed the cigarette with her boot. "I gotta go," she said, and kissed me on the cheek.

I walked home alone, retracing the path I'd taken with Nikki.

Outside on the curb, Dean strummed his guitar and tried to sing "Me and Bobby McGee."

Only Lance and Flower were inside the brick-walled basement. They sat facing each other at the table, candlelight illuminating their unwashed faces. The Clash sang "Should I Stay or Should I Go?" from the boom box.

I tried to ignore them, changed into a pair of black sweatpants from the pile near my mattress, lit a joint.

"Fuck you, Lance," was all I heard Flower say before she climbed up onto the chair and hoisted herself out the window.

"Ghost Girl." Lance stood up, took the boom box from the table. "Come and have some wine?" He motioned toward the back room. "I've a present for you."

"A present?" I followed him down the dark hallway, felt around with my bare feet for his mattress, sat down.

He lit three candles, opened his wine by jamming a Swiss Army blade into the cork and forcing it into the bottle, turned the volume down on the boom box. "You don't mind The Clash, do you?" From his cloth bag, he produced a faded pair of black Levi's, a Joan Jett T-shirt and a yellow parka. "I thought you might like to have another outfit," he said. "Had to guess at your size."

"Thanks." I had to figure out how to make some more money.

"You know, I fancy you," Lance whispered.

I nodded. I was thinking about those red-lit windows, Nikki with some stranger.

Lance slipped his hand under my shirt, felt my belly, then inched down the front of my sweats. In the candlelight, his face seemed soft.

I reached over, felt his blue beard, whispered, "Don't you kiss a girl before you try and get down her pants?"

And he pushed me back onto his blankets, kissed me hard. Under his weight, my pulse quickened, breath shallowed. The smell of burning wax, spilled whiskey, damp brick.

The damaged heart cannot pump efficiently. It is susceptible to blood clots, cardiomyopathy, and strange rhythms. Heavy drinking can increase these risks.

In the anvil of Indian summer, I gave up my own mattress to sleep with Lance on olive sheets in the back room. He tasted like Jack Daniel's and vanilla sweat, made me laugh when he described night dreams of run-ins with the police, vivid chases, flag-burning riots.

Cold blue afternoons with Nikki and Dean, we marched alongside squatters carrying black flags and demanding a garage sale of reforms: expanded housing rights, healthcare for foreigners, demolition of the prison system, secession from NATO, full divestment from South Africa and freedom for Nelson Mandela.

Lance kicked in shop windows as hippie boys pleaded with him to keep the demonstrations peaceful. "We're not here to vandalize small businesses," they reasoned. He ignored them. Of course he ignored them.

"No justice, no peace!" Dean shouted, then took a swig from the bottle.

On the equinox, when the Amsterdam summer finally surren-
dered to the northern chill and all the Indo-European gods
abducted their spring maidens in preparation for a winter in
the underworld, Nikki, Dean and Lance came to me. I was sitting under the street lamp on the curb outside the squat on Van
Ostadestraat, wrapped in a gray blanket, smoking, studying the
pattern of the bricks that paved the street. "What's up?"

Dean spoke first: "Amsterdam's fucked. We three were talking
just now and we agreed. It's fucked, you know? We can't get
work here, none of us. So we were thinking let's go back to
London. We'll get some work. Lance has a nice big squat there.
It'll be easy. We'll just go back to London."

I shrugged. No one had ever asked me permission to leave
a place before.

Lance: "You'll come along, then?"

"Me?"

"Fuck, yeah," Nikki laughed. "We're a team, right? We four?"

A team. It had never occurred to me that we would travel
together, but the thought made my heart swell. They wanted
me to come with them. I wasn't ready to leave Amsterdam,
didn't think it was so fucked. I still vaguely dreamed of finding
a way back to Asia. But the idea seemed so rare, precious: to
cross a border with friends.

Lance knelt down beside me. "Right then, you'll come?"

London. I crushed my cigarette in the gutter. "Maybe."

He smiled a sad smile, looked like a little boy. He gazed
down at the bricks in front of us. "It's just this place," he said.
"It's fucked up my head, being here. Getting hammered every
day, you know? I have to get back to England, get my shit
together. I want you to come along. I need you with us, Ghost
Girl. You make me want to sort myself out, you know? Me and
Dean, we've got some business to take care of on the east side,
and Nikki has some girls she wants to say goodbye to. But

meet us at Central Station at dawn, all right? It'll mean the world to us."

Nikki winked at me. "The world."

When you leave a place, it's best if it's raining. Not pouring, but not just drizzling either. You want fat drops that fall on your cheeks like tears. It's best if it's early, too, the tail lights and porch lights and streetlights and station lights all begging you to stay just one more day.

When you leave a place, it's best if you're hungry. A girl should never travel on a full stomach. It's best if you're tired, too, still wrapped in the dreams of sleep, oblivious to gravity and the heaviness of your own body.

When you leave a place, it's best to take as little as possible— ideally a single change of clothes, the jewelry on your body, the money in your pockets, memories safely stowed in your secure imagination. Never pack more than you can comfortably carry across the Himalayas on foot, because you never know where a road will take you. It's best not to bring along anything you care about, either. You'll lose it, anyway. Give it away before you go.

And when you leave a place, it's best not to cry. If everything is as it should be, the sky will do your crying for you.

Wandering or Withering?

Have you seen that movie, *Vagabond*?"

Nikki and I were out on deck. A boat crossing the English Channel. Lance and Dean drunk at the bow. Gannets and gulls barely visible through the sea fog.

"Yeah," she said. "I saw it a couple of years ago. I think it was playing at that theater in Palo Alto."

"Uh huh. So what do you think's the difference between wandering and withering?"

She kept her eyes fixed on a distant lighthouse across the gray water. "I don't know. More like what's the similarity? You ask funny questions." She fished a pre-rolled joint from her jacket pocket. "We should smoke this before we cross the border."

At the Dover port, Nikki and I made our way through foreign immigration with a bullshit story about a friend in Liverpool. The pale official eyed us suspiciously, but then waved his hand dismissively, stamped our passports.

We met Lance and Dean on the other side, slept for a few hours in the terminal. Then a night train. As dawn broke through the storm-streaked windows, we sped past greening banks and brick row houses, glimpsed bridges over a warehouse-lined river. We arrived at Victoria Station in the shrouded morning.

Nikki still had some money, so we ordered tea and white toast in a station café, waited while the boys went to check on Lance's old squat and apply for the dole.

"It's weird being the *girls*," Nikki said. "Like we just have to wait around for our boyfriends to find us shelter and money."

"It's kind of nice, though," I admitted, sipping my Earl Grey.

"Yeah," she laughed. "Feminism is really such a crock of shit. Like, *Thanks a lot for burning that bra, Mom. Now I have to support myself. . . .*"

We paid fifty pence each to take showers in the station washroom. Under the steady stream of hot water, I tried to count back through the spiral of months since the last time I'd been through Victoria Station: twenty-six. They curved through my mind like a string of boxcars making their way up a steep mountain track.

A constant drizzle behind the sound of trains arriving and departing. Inaudibly loud announcements about platforms and destinations. Dense crowds of travelers clicking their heels across a white and brick-red patterned floor. Midafternoon and the boys finally reappeared: Lance had a black eye, clutched his shoulder. Dean's face was pink and swollen from crying.

"What happened to you guys?"

Lance moaned, "My whole squat's been taken over by these fucking skinheads."

Dean nodded. "Taken *over*."

"There's fucking swarms of them in there," Lance said.

And Dean nodded. "*Swarms.*"

"I'm telling you, they've *demolished* the place," Lance said. "I could have kicked their bloody heads in, but who'd want that shit hole now?"

And Dean: "It's *demolished.*"

A train departing from platform three. The commuters' *clip-clop chatter-blah*.

"But listen. Here's the deal." Lance pushed his hair out of

his face. "We've found a new place. It's little, all right? It's nice. It's like a flat."

"*Like* a flat?" Nikki crossed her arms, not amused.

But I felt kind of sorry for the boys, standing there, spattered with blood and city rain.

"Like a flat," Lance said. "And we've got our first week's dole." He held up a wad of five- and ten-pound notes, pleased-defeated, his biker jacket bunched up under his arm.

Like a flat. It was more like the landing on a stairwell between the first and second floors of a fourplex on All Saints Road in Notting Hill. But it had its own window. Lance dropped his blankets onto the floor. Dean set down his guitar. And then the two of them headed out into the evening to spend their dole money.

"Get some dope, will you?" Nikki called down the stairs after them. She was sitting cross-legged on the brown-carpeted landing. When we heard the heavy wooden door shut behind them, she turned to me. "Do you believe a word about that other squat swarming with skinheads?"

"What do you mean?" I was arranging Lance's blankets into a bed.

"I mean there never was another squat," she said gravely, then cracked her knuckles. "I mean, I don't care whether or not he had one. And I don't care if we have to sleep here or whatever. But I don't like being lied to, you know? They brought us to London saying Lance had this big squat, and then all of a sudden we had to wait at the station, right? And then they come back with this crock of shit about skinheads, figuring, like, *She's Chinese, she'll be scared of skinheads, she won't question it.*"

I said, "C'mon, Nikki. They're trying to take care of us. They suck at it, but don't you think it's kind of cute?" I held out a cigarette, and Nikki took it from me. "Anyway. It's not like Lance would have given *himself* a black eye. Do you think?"

Nikki pursed her thin lips, lit the cigarette. "I think Lance gets into trouble," she said. "I think he could've gotten a black eye from anyone. Like somebody got pissed off when he called them a corporate wanker. Or when he tried to steal their shit. And then it went along with the skinhead story, you know? I mean, maybe you're right, but I don't believe a word of it." She riffled through her small pack. "Why the fuck didn't I just bring some hash over the border? They didn't check a thing."

The boys came home late, carrying a case of Red Stripe beer, four foil-wrapped baked potatoes with melted cheese and sour cream, two cans of baked beans and a pea-sized round of hash. We devoured the food.

Lance opened four beers, passed them around. "To our new home," he said.

Cheers.

Nikki held the hash in her palm. "Please don't tell me you paid more than a quid for this." She crumbled the whole thing into a single joint.

"We're in England now," Dean offered, then sucked down his beer.

With hydrogen peroxide and a cotton swab from Nikki's little first-aid kit, I cleaned Lance's bruised eye and an open wound on his shoulder. "You poor thing," I whispered.

Dean picked up the plastic box that held Nikki's Band-Aids and condoms, turned it over. "Aren't these the kits they pass out to the prostitutes in the red-light district?"

"How the fuck would I know?" Nikki snapped.

I thought she was kind of cute when she got grumpy, but it made me nervous. We were a team, we four. I didn't want everything to go to shit. Not yet.

Listless morning. From under Lance's warm blankets, I watched my traveling companions as they slept. A pigeon landed on the windowsill outside, then flew away. A patch of blue sky peeked through the clouds. And then the sound of a door opening, closing, being locked. I nudged Lance.

A Caribbean-looking guy with short dreadlocks shuffled down the stairs, whistling. He stopped abruptly a few steps above us. "What the bloody hell are you lot doing sleeping on my landing?"

Lance sat up. "Hey, sorry, man. We were looking for a squat, you know? I got beat up trying to defend my girlfriend here," he pointed to me. "I'm really sorry. We reckoned the building was empty."

The guy crossed his arms, checked me out. "Looks like that one could defend herself," he said, then shook his head. "Well. It must be your lucky day. You give me the rest of that Red Stripe, I give you a squat. Lucky day."

Lance didn't hesitate, scrambled out from under the blankets in his black boxer shorts, handed over the beer.

"Name's Winston," the man said. He led Lance upstairs, opened a padlock on a white wooden door, pushed it open. "There's your lucky squat, then. But you listen to me. I'm living across the hall here with my woman and my boy, either of them have any trouble with you lot and I'll have you thrown out of here faster 'n you can say 'Drink up.'"

Lance nodded. "Thanks, man. Thanks. You won't have any trouble with us at all."

Our lucky squat. Two bedrooms. White walls. A living room. Hardwood floors. A blue-tiled bathroom. A yellow linoleum and Formica kitchen. Cold running water. Picture windows. A council flat.

Lance beamed. "Didn't I tell you I'd find us a nice big squat, eh?"

Nikki and Dean took the smaller bedroom.

I set up the blankets on the floor under a window that led to a fire escape, folded my few clothes in a pile in the closet. I could imagine a tattered couch in the living room. An oak coffee table. Mattresses on the bedroom floors. Soft cotton sheets. Red checkered curtains in the kitchen. But I pushed the fantasy out of my head. Even empty, it was a nice squat.

We spent the next few days settling in, scrubbing the floors. Nikki said she sensed a ghost in the bathroom, so we pored over *Sassafrass, Cypress and Indigo* in search of a cleansing spell, ended up just sprinkling salt in all the corners of the flat, then tossing it out the windows. I read Nikki's orange copy of *On the Road* and it reminded me that a good beatnik girl's place was in the kitchen, making something edible from the raw vegetables and meat the boys stole from the big grocery store in Kensington. I asked Lance to pick me up a camping stove the next time he itched to steal something bulky, so he did, brought it home from the Saturday market like a trophy.

Dean procured the Chinese bowls and copper cooking pot.

Nikki begged spices from a Sri Lankan restaurant.

I made curried beef stew.

Nikki set four places in a circle on the living-room floor, lit a red candle in the middle, smoked a wooden pipe full of hash. "You wouldn't believe what this little piece of dope cost me," she said before she passed it around.

I set the cooking pot on the floor, opened four beers, served up the spicy stew using my own bowl as a ladle. I sipped mine first. Hot. Delicious.

Lance frowned when he tasted his. "What are you, a bleedin' Paki? This is hot as fuck!"

"Just drink your beer between mouthfuls," Nikki laughed, rolled her eyes.

Every poor person in the world should know to make dinner as spicy as possible. The peppers trick your stomach into thinking you're full.

We ate and drank. Drank some more. Lance smiled at me, then winked at Dean. "It's like a family," he said.

"Like a family," Dean hummed. He had a sad strange look in his eye.

Lance and Dean didn't find work, didn't look for it. But they left the house in the afternoons to shoplift and rush through the slick autumn streets in their mad quest for who-knows-what. They came home at dinnertime. I tried to turn whatever they brought into a meal. Drunk and full, they'd head out again in search of cheap hash and trouble. "See you girls later. . . ."

Nikki and I drank Red Stripe beer, painted each other's fingernails.

"Have you ever been with a woman?" Nikki asked me one night.

"Not really," I admitted. I was thinking of Beatrice and Violette in Kathmandu.

"Too bad we have these boyfriends," she said, wiggling her freshly painted nails. "We'd make a cute couple, you and me."

I tried to picture it, hanging out with Nikki. No boys. We'd sleep together under the wool blankets, cuddle in the morning. Our days would be sweet and easy. But who would do the shoplifting?

"I thought you liked Dean a lot."

She blushed, bit her lip. "I love him. He's so cute. Shy. You know, sometimes, when we're alone, he just gets this really naïve look on his face, talks about all the places he wants to travel."

That night I dreamed of a bus station: Paul McCartney

and Lance in some crazed brawling fistfight. Commuters gathered to watch. The men swung at each other, bloodying lips and temples. I woke up suddenly, sharp pain in my side. I opened my eyes, opened my mouth to yell, but only managed a low moan. In the dim light from the street lamp outside, I could make out Lance's silhouette above me.

"Wakeupyouslag!" He slurred his words together, kicked me again.

I sat up, disoriented, pulled the blankets around me, scrambled back toward the corner, away from his boot. "Lance?"

"Isaidwakeupyoucow—" And then he stumbled, fell awkwardly to his knees. I could just make out his face in the strange yellow light. "Oh god," he said slowly. "I'm so sorry." He passed out on the floor at my feet.

In the morning, I thought maybe I'd dreamed the whole thing.

Nikki sat crouched in the kitchen window, smoking her breakfast joint, feet dangling outside.

"Nikki? Did you hear some commotion from my room last night when the boys came home?" I slipped a Tina Turner tape into the boom box and pressed play so Lance wouldn't hear me if he woke up.

"No." She turned to climb back inside. "What commotion?"

"I don't know—I think I woke up and Lance was kicking me."

"What? No way—that's fucked up."

I rinsed the curry pot out in the sink, put some water to heat on the camping stove. "I don't know," I said. I lifted my T-shirt, inspected my waist and ribs. "It's not like I have a bruise or anything. It's weird. I must have dreamed it."

Nikki stared at me.

My muscles ached. Roses heavy on the bush. "I feel fucked up. Life here is just kind of spinning, you know? I can't think right." I took off my T-shirt, dunked a rag into the warm water on the stove and started scrubbing my belly. I looked up at her in the gray light, and all of a sudden, like a kick in the ribs middream, it occurred to me: I loved her. Her wide face, blond-tipped black hair. She was luminous. I inhaled quickly. Worse: I loved Lance. His beard that only showed a faint trace of blue dye now. His dark brown and clouded eyes. When he fucked me, everything else in the world faded away until my whole body shook and I cried from the chaos of us and it. It occurred to me then, too, that I even loved Dean, the bow-legged little fellow who strummed his guitar, couldn't sing his way out of a bucket. We were a team. We four. And even though it was only a week old, there was something warm and everyday about the family we were making. Or maybe it was just the fancy of having a family at all. Four expectant travelers in a world that had banished all that was spine-tingling and kind and painful and real. Maybe I'd been on the road too long, but I didn't want Lance's nighttime freak-out to be true. I willed it out of my mind. If it had happened, it was only because he was drunk. If it had happened, it was only because he loved me. And love is confusing and scary like a first autumn storm. And love, it ruins everything.

"Never mind," I said. "I just had a fucked-up dream."

wan·der *v.* 1. To move about without a definite destination or purpose. 2. To go by an indirect route or at no set pace; amble. 3. To proceed in an irregular course; meander. 4. To go astray. 5. To lose clarity or coherence of thought or expression. 6. To be sexually unfaithful to one's partner. 7. A trailing plant.

with·er *v.* 1. To dry up or shrivel from or as if from loss of moisture. 2. To lose freshness; droop. *v. tr.* 1. To cause to shrivel or fade. 2. To render speechless or incapable of action; stun.

I thought of the Buddhist refuge vow—the acknowledgment that there is no need for home or ground. Did uprooting myself again and again really make me free? Or would it, eventually, just cause me to shrivel from loss of moisture, from lack of a life source?

A Sorry Dear

JOURNAL ENTRY #227
51°30'N 0°10'W
FALL, 1988

> *roads flow over bridges*
> *i am here (i am not there anymore)*
> *imagine the rickety confused stories i would tell*
> *if i grew up and wrote a book*

We'd been in our lucky new squat less than two weeks the night Lance and Dean didn't come home. I woke up every hour with a start, thought I saw Lance standing over me, drunk and pissed off.

In the first glassy gray light of morning, I finally fell into a steady sleep. When I opened my eyes, I could hear "Stairway to Heaven" from the boom box in the kitchen. "Oh, man, Nikki," I shouted. "Anything but that."

There wasn't a half-pence in the house, and nothing to eat, so that evening we guzzled the last of the whiskey, smoked a joint, headed up to Notting Hill Gate. We panhandled meekly outside the tube station. Most of the commuters and tourists and pub hoppers turned up their collars and looked down at their shoes as they passed us, but a few handed us coins without comment. A short, olive-skinned man wearing a blue sweater stopped in front of us. He emptied his pockets, stared at Nikki. "I know you, miss," he said in a singsongy Indian accent. "Amsterdam this time last year, no? That's a lovely little gem you've got between your legs. I remember it well."

She fixed her gaze on him. "You must have me confused with someone else."

He shrugged. "In any case, I do have the evening free." He pointed to the change in our manicured hands, looked Nikki up and down, then me. "Wouldn't you rather have a fifty-quid note?" He had a strange, four-pronged scar on his brow like someone had tried to gouge out his eye with a fork, but missed.

Nikki pulled me a few steps down into the tube station, out of his earshot. "He wants one of us to fuck him," she whispered. "You up for it?"

My mind went blank. I felt tipsy, but not drunk. It seemed easy enough, only mildly repulsive. I took a deep breath, exhaled slowly.

"Because if you don't want to—" she started.

"No." I'd been happy enough to spend Nikki's guilders with her in Amsterdam. I had to start pulling my weight. What was I hanging on to at this point, anyway? "I can do it."

I let the little man lead me down Portobello Road, then into an alley. I was afraid I'd have to fuck him on the rain-wet cement, but he pointed to a brown hatchback. "I'll take you to the country," he said.

"I—I'd rather stay in town," I stuttered. I was thinking this might be what a serial killer looked like, but I climbed into the passenger's seat.

"You don't have to be afraid of me, miss," he offered as he turned the key in the ignition. "I'm a family man."

A *family man*.

The car smelled of cherry air freshener. We drove in silence for a long time. "What's your name, miss?"

I started to say Ghost, then hesitated. *I should make something up.* "Gh-Gina."

"Gagina? After your lovely vagina?"

I closed my eyes. I could not believe I was having this conversation. "Gina," I said. "Just call me Gina, OK?"

"Well then, Gina," he chuckled. "My name is Vishnu, you can call me Vishnu."

I watched the lights from bridges and bars out the window as we sputtered out of the city. *Vishnu.* This was what the great preserver-protector had been reduced to? It seemed high time the Hindu god roused himself to save our sorry human asses from certain doom.

We drove.

At a quaint bed-and-breakfast inn that seemed like a nice Mother's Day destination, I stripped down to my bra and panties, lit a cigarette.

"You are lovely," Vishnu whined. He was sitting on the edge of the double bed, arms stiff at his sides, still dressed in his blue sweater and brown slacks. He peeled them off slowly, asked me to turn around.

I turned, showing him the pale geography of my body.

"Is that Sanskrit on your heart?" he wanted to know.

I didn't answer him.

"Come and lie down, then," he said.

I closed my eyes under his weight, tried to meditate, count my breaths, tried to remember the weird wind sound Martine and her nun made in their desert cave.

Vishnu reeked of cigars, emitted the foulest dust-grease-and-cum odor I'd ever inhaled. I felt nauseous as the bed squeaked and Vishnu moaned, "Gi-na, Gi-na."

In the pink and yellow wallpapered bathroom, I leaned over the toilet bowl, threw up a little whiskey, dry-heaved. Under the hot stream of the shower, I washed until the little bar of complementary lavender soap had completely melted. I thought of Lance and Dean, the way the narrative of my life seemed to be dissolving between my fingers. I thought of Violette and Beatrice in Kathmandu, the way a movie could feel more true than reality.

I wrapped a clean white towel around my body, another around my head like a turban. *"You have gorgeous curls,"* Violette had said. *"This is how you set them."* I brushed my teeth with a dab of complementary toothpaste on my index finder. And when I finally emerged, Vishnu was gone. One hundred quid in ten-pound notes stacked neatly on the pillow.

The bed still reeked a little, but I fell asleep easily between the soft sheets, dreamed a fire raging through a forest of lodgepole pines, a great red Sierra mountain exploding into smoke and ash.

Midmorning. I padded down the pink-carpeted stairs.

"There you are, dear," the fat proprietor cooed. "Your husband won't be joining you for breakfast?" When she stood up, I noticed she had a wooden leg under her house dress.

I shook my head. "Do you know where I am?"

She widened her tunnel-dark eyes. Maybe she said, "You're in Surrey, dear!" But I heard her clearly: "You're a sorry dear!" Then she let out a strange, high-pitched sigh. "Well. Everyone else has eaten and gone, but you sit down." She pointed to an antique chair at a round dining-room table, adjusted her ruffled apron. "Sit, sit, dear."

I ran my finger along the forget-me-not flower motif of the cotton tablecloth.

The woman wobbled into the kitchen, returned with a steaming white plate of fried eggs and sausage, a side dish of scones and clotted cream.

"Thank you," I said softly. I pricked the yolks with my fork and watched the bright yellow ooze to the rim of the plate.

"Choices, choices," the proprietor chirped as she turned and left me to my breakfast. "You always have choices."

I pocketed the scone.

"You fucking got a hundred quid off that guy?" Nikki beamed when I finally made my way back to All Saints Road and showed her the spoils. "You must have been *good*." She was sitting on the floor in the room she'd shared with Dean.

I sat next to her, studied the grain of the hardwood. "I think he felt sorry for me, actually," I admitted. "It wasn't worth it."

"Oh, shit," she said, changing her tone. "I'm sorry." She put her hand on my shoulder. "The first time is always shit. It gets better. Or you get used to it. But—you know—no. Don't do it anymore if you don't want to. I should've gone with him."

I wanted to cry, but I sucked it up. *What kind of a wimp was I?*

That night, Nikki slept next to me. "You smell like lavender," she whispered, pushing my hair out of my face.

I let a single tear fall, and she licked it from my cheek. "It'll be OK, sweetie." She half-smiled, then kissed me on the mouth, slipped her tongue between my lips.

She fell asleep with her hand at my bare waist.

I woke up alone, called out for Nikki, but she was gone. I didn't get up. I looked out the window, imagined that if I stared into the gray for long enough, it would mystically transform itself into something else.

Nikki came home shivering, crazy. "Lance is in jail."

I sat up. "Figures."

"Fuck," Nikki said, her wide face dirty and tear-streaked. She spun around suddenly, kicked the closet door with her boot, "fuck," then composed herself. "He's gonna be gone for a long time," she said. "Pile of warrants for that one." She cracked her knuckles, stared at me.

I said: "That sucks. But where did you think he'd be?" I was surprised to see her taking it so hard. "Dean, too?"

She arched her back a little, yelled up at the ceiling, "Fuck!"

"Calm down, Nikki. Do you want a cigarette?"

"Apparently Dean's with some kind of youth authority."

"Youth authority?" I slipped on Lance's old blue silk-screened "Tramp" T-shirt. The word has a slightly different connotation when worn by a girl.

"Yeah." Nikki smoked furiously. "Turns out my *boyfriend* isn't a day over sixteen. Do you know what that makes me?"

"Pissed off?" I tried.

"It makes me a child molester." She dropped her cigarette into a half-empty beer bottle on the floor. "How old are *you*, Ghost Girl?" A jackdaw hopped from the fire escape onto the windowsill outside, cocked its head like it was watching us, wondering what was going on.

"Eighteen."

"*Jesus*—what the fuck is this?" She covered her face, her red nail polish chipped now. "Is this some kind of high-school exchange student program? Is this, like, a *field trip* for you?"

"I'm really sorry," I whispered. "You never asked how old I was. And I figured—well I figured you were my age. You said you were in college."

Nikki shook her head. "You know what, honey? I'm gonna tell you this and you're gonna say, 'Whatever.' I would've rolled my eyes when I was eighteen, too. But there's a big fucking difference between being eighteen and being twenty-two. And between being sixteen and being twenty-two—I don't even want to think about it, OK? It's not just you. He's fucking *sixteen*. This is weird. It's just really *weird* here, OK? I've gotta go back to Amsterdam for a while. Or someplace. This might be a field trip for you, Ghost Girl, but this is my *life*."

I offered Nikki a joint, but she didn't want to smoke out. I got dressed, washed my face, took one of my ten-pound notes down the hill to Portobello Road, bought two packages of fish and chips wrapped in newspaper, dosed them with salt and vinegar, inched home.

I couldn't sleep that night. I stared up at the white ceiling in the window-filtered moonlight. What did Nikki mean, a *field trip*? Wasn't this my life, too?

In the morning, she apologized, said she was just tripped out about Dean, said that when she was sixteen, a grown man had fucked her, too, drawn her into his world, that she'd never recovered. "Victims become predators," she said. "That's what happens." And she handed me her wooden pipe.

"You're not really a predator if you didn't know," I offered.

She shook her head. "You're sweet. But listen. I have to get out of here for a while. I'm losing my shit. And you don't need that, you know? Anyway. You'll be OK?"

"Yeah," I promised.

When she hoisted her little black daypack over her shoulder, she said: "I'll be back soon."

The Chinese acupuncture point known as "ghost heart" is located in the middle of the inner wrist, between the tendons. It can be needled or pressured to calm the spirit, to treat insomnia and to clear heat from the heart.

Drinking had always relaxed me, loosened my tongue, made it easier for me to speak. Drinking had drawn me out of myself. But in London it led me further inside. My heart contracted, things didn't smell good. I went quiet, covered my belly, willed my shell to grow thicker, harder.

I was a lousy beggar, so I took a job washing dishes at a dark pub on Portobello Road from midnight to 3 A.M., slept until noon every day, passed time at the Kensington and Chelsea branch of the library reading every volume of Maya Angelou's autobiography. I ate tasteless meat and potatoes at the Salvation Army, dropped the occasional postcard in the mail, guzzled cheap Gilbey's gin to warm me into sleep. It's no wonder the British are such colonists—with shit for food and shit for weather, I wondered who, given half a chance to escape, would stay on this cold cold island.

Browsing through a used-clothing store near Notting Hill Gate, I spotted a thin, dirty girl in a yellow jacket. Hair a mess. Pale, pale skin. She looked like a ghost, stared back at me with icy blue eyes. She scared me a little bit, but my heart flooded with a sudden compassion for her. I didn't have any change in my pockets, but I wanted to offer her my help. Maybe Nikki's old room in the squat. Or directions to the Salvation Army. I took a step toward her, opened my mouth to speak, but our faces flushed crimson when I realized I was standing in front of a mirrored wall.

November 15, 1988

Tiniest!

We were so excited to get your postcard! What on earth are you doing in London? You give us no news, just this address! Please call. You know we're home every Sunday night from 7-8 P.M. watching 60 Minutes. *Why don't you call right after eight sometime so we don't miss Andy Rooney?*

All is well here. Leslie is living in Berkeley and working as a nanny. John took some wonderful trips to the Sierras over the summer. He's back working at the bookstore now, of course.

I'm working in my studio more and more, particularly on a series of acrylic paintings inspired by the myth of the Handless Maiden.

Enclosed is a Polaroid picture of Gabriel and me. He's the cutest of my old students at San Quentin. I visit him every Wednesday and Friday to work on his screenplay.

As I'm sure you've heard, that bastard George Bush will succeed the ever-in-denial Reagan.

Like I said, do call, Tiniest! Collect if you have to. And know we'll be jealous, thinking of your beautiful English Christmas.

Love, Mom

In December, a train wreck in south London killed dozens of rush-hour commuters. And nine days later, a Pan Am flight crashed over Lockerbie, Scotland. No survivors. The pub buzzed with news of death and rumors of more to come.

Lance had left a bottle of Valium in the bathroom, so I took a few with my gin every night. I saved my wages in a Mason jar under the kitchen sink. I wanted to get back to Hong Kong, dreamed of flying to the Mascarene Islands, imagined finding a magical door that would lead me into an underground city made of gold. But every time I poured my change and multi-colored notes onto the hardwood floor and counted them, the squat felt a little smaller, the water that separated the British Isles from the rest of the world felt wider. Two quid an hour under the table doesn't add up so very fast. I was a failed smuggler and a failed whore in a world that didn't seem to value anything else I might have to sell. My worthless passport. My worthless body. I thought of calling my mother on a Sunday after Andy Rooney, asking her to send me a ticket home. But the Palo Alto in my mind didn't beckon. *What would I do when I got there? Go back to high school?* I was too old now. The idea rang through my mind like a joke. Like surrender. Like grasping at a faraway past. I missed Beijing a little, that unrelenting gray winter seemed cozy in my memory compared to the freezing rain of London, the darkness that fell only a few hours after I'd opened my eyes, the icy grass under my boots as I wandered through Hyde Park. I closed my eyes, imagined flying away—the relief that comes with height and distance from the earth. But all I could bring to mind were movie-vivid images of every stupid thing I had ever said, ever done.

Nights when it wasn't raining too hard, I took a meandering route home from work, lingered outside the Gypsy encampment under the Westway. I spoke to no one, and no one spoke to me. In my room, I read aloud to myself by candlelight so as not to forget the sound of my own voice. I licked my lips, wanted to memorize the brassy taste of emptiness. And every night in dream, I was shipwrecked on the Dover shore, cold under my useless blankets, those white cliffs looming like walls. It's no coincidence or groundless habit that has poets forever associating hope with light. I was marooned on an island devoid of both. The spiritual ends of the earth. In times of famine in ancient Britain, the women and children all walked to the nearest sea cliff and threw themselves down into the waves. I didn't think of suicide, but the days all begged the question: *What's so special about survival?* And those days became weeks. Then months. I thought the winter might never end. Navigating isolation.

Patient Is Unable to Give a Clear Account of Her Origin or Destination

On a ridiculously cold night in March, I got off work early, headed home through the miserable rain, arrived soaked and dreading the hours I'd shiver under my wool blankets, alone in my stupid lucky squat on this rotten vast globe. I opened the door, thought I smelled whiskey and burning wax. "Hello?" A flickering tangerine glow from my bedroom. "Is someone in here?" I was half-scared, half-hopeful.

Lance sat on our bed, flowers and cigarettes and bottles of Jack Daniel's and plastic-wrapped sandwiches and an old leather jacket spread out around him like gifts under a tree. "Ghost Girl—I reckoned you'd never come home. I reckoned you'd left me."

I raced to his side, knelt to hug him. "Oh my god—when did you get out? Nikki made it sound like you'd be away for years, with a stack of warrants. . . ."

He tilted his head to one side. "Wasn't all that. This is England. They give you a short sharp shock and send you on your way. But five months isn't nothing. Seemed like a bloody long time from my side of things. That beak had it in for me. I should have got thirty days, max."

"It's really nice to see you," I whispered. And it was. I could feel the blue smoke from his cigarette enveloping me. I lay down, rested my head on his lap. His face was clean-shaven.

"I got you this biker jacket," he said, holding it up.

We shared the whiskey, and when he kissed me, I licked his teeth.

He slipped off my army pants easily.

I unbuttoned my shirt.

"Wait," he whispered, then put a Clash tape in the boom box. "I missed you so."

Under the wool blankets, I dissolved into smoke. He inhaled me.

Lance didn't want me to work, so I quit my job. We spent his dole money and my savings in a brilliant dusk-tinted rush through Notting Hill and Camden Market and Soho, bought new black clothes and wine and Southern Comfort and imported mangoes and rich coffee and Sex Pistols tapes.

We slept even later into the steel gray days now, fucked and laughed into the nights. I followed him through the streets he still knew better than I did, and when we ran out of money, I stuffed a pillow under my sweatshirt and we stood outside the Notting Hill tube station, Lance telling passers-by stupid sorry stories about why he and his pregnant wife were broke. They filled our palms with golden pound coins. We bought baked potatoes and packs of Drum tobacco. He stole the whiskey and the port.

With his fake passports, Lance trotted from neighborhood doctor to neighborhood doctor collecting prescriptions for Valium. "It takes the edge off the alcohol," he said.

And I knew it did. I downed handfuls with my wine. Days sputtered and swirled past. Lance told me I was getting fat, and I agreed with him. I weighed just over ninety-five pounds. As we walked home down Lancaster Road toward All Saints one night, he told me he'd come out of jail inspired to get his life together, but my dark energy pulled him down.

Confused, I said, "You know, Lance, you can be a real asshole sometimes."

He spun around, slapped me hard across the face.

My cheek stung, more from the shock than the pain. "What was that for?"

Under the yellow light of the street lamp, he stared at his hand for a moment, then at me. "You just called me a bloody arsehole!"

I apologized.

When we got home, Lance said, "You know, if you don't like me, why don't you just go home to L.A.?"

I took a handful of valium, gagged when I downed the pills with whiskey. "Because I'm not from L.A." As I fell asleep, Lance's face looked so strange. I felt claustrophobic. I breathed unevenly, couldn't get enough air on the intake.

"Jesus, Ghost Girl. You're not crying now, are you?"

"No."

The last thing I remember that winter: walking dim-eyed with Lance along a frigid dreary street somewhere in south London. Late afternoon. As Lance babbled on about something, his voice seemed to stretch itself out like a tape playing on low batteries. The passing traffic slowed. I started to cry, covered my face.

"What's the matter with you?" Lance seemed half-concerned, half-annoyed.

I doubled over suddenly, fell onto an icy patch of green-brown grass. My heart hurt. I tried to move my arms, to get myself up, but I managed only to curl myself into a ball. Lance stood over me. I could hear his voice: "Get up—what the bloody hell are you doing?"

"I . . . can't . . ." is all I managed to say.

His voice came closer, quieter. "Are you ill?"

I didn't move. It seemed to me that I could get up if I wanted to, but when I willed my limbs to aid me, they just shivered. I woke up between crisp sheets in the softest bed I'd ever felt under me. I blinked. Warmth. I didn't want the dream to end. A woman's voice asked me questions: *Name? Age? Where are you from?* I didn't answer, slipped back into the blessed blankness. And when I came to again, I was back in our cold squat, huddled under the brown wool blanket on the floor.

"About time you woke up," Lance said. He offered me a lukewarm cup of milky sweet coffee in a Styrofoam cup.

"Where have I been?"

He rolled his eyes. "You're lucky I got you out of there, anyway."

I downed the coffee, went back to sleep.

"Jesus Christ, Lance, what did you do to her?" It was Nikki's voice.

I opened my eyes, focused on her silver and turquoise earrings, smiled dumbly.

She wore black kohl eyeliner.

"I've been looking after her," Lance whined from the other side of the room. "I came out of lock-up and she was all by herself here having a fucking nervous breakdown. *You're* the one who left her alone."

Nikki leaned down, whispered in my ear, "What the fuck happened to you?"

"I don't really know," I admitted. "I think I wanted to go to bed, but we were outside."

She turned back to Lance. "Why the fuck didn't you leave her in the hospital, you idiot? There's something *wrong* with her."

"They were drugging her up in there," he said, more agitated now. "I had to break her out. Have a look at this rubbish." He handed Nikki a white piece of paper. "They might have a whole file on her in there. This is all I could get."

Nikki read it aloud: "'Sex: F. Color: W. Legal status at admission:

Voluntary. Patient is unable to give a clear account of her origin or destination, or indeed her personal identity. Suffering from dissociation, depression, anemia, headaches, exhaustion, dehydration, malnutrition and bouts of weeping. There is evidence that the patient travels widely and compulsively. Wandering behavior suggestive of hysterical fugues.' What is this shit?" Nikki slapped the paper down on the floor. "It says 'voluntary admission,' Lance. You didn't have to break her out of anywhere. You are so full of shit." Nikki pressed three fingers against my forehead. "What did he do to you?"

"Nothing. I just got super tired. I don't really remember."

She leaned in. "Are you sure he didn't do anything to you?"

"Yeah. I'm sure."

"Sit up," she said softly.

I sat up just enough to let her pour cold water down my desert-dry throat. My whole body ached. "I guess this is rock bottom," I tried to say, but it came out in a whisper.

"Never say that," Nikki scolded me. "There's a bottom below."

Lance stood over us now, arms crossed.

Nikki said, "OK, man. I'm sorry. But I walk in here and she's all fucked up and you're the one standing over her. You would've thought the same thing. I was just worried, OK?"

I looked out the window, squinted my eyes. Surely I was hallucinating now: a perfect square of brilliant blue sky behind a fire escape. "Holy shit, where are we?"

Nikki stared at me, answered slowly: "We're in London, honey."

"Is it summertime?"

"Jesus, Ghost Girl. It's March."

I fell back asleep.

When I woke up, Nikki had my things packed in a black

drawstring bag. "Drink some water. We're getting the fuck out of England. You OK to travel?" She held out my leather jacket.

"Sure." I drank from her cup, put the jacket on. "Is Lance coming with us?"

"Yeah," she said. "He's an idiot, but he's all right."

The three of us left England by bullet train and boat, my hair in a tight braid for the journey. From Calais, we hitchhiked south toward Paris with a cardboard sign. I'd decided I shouldn't drink so much anymore, so I mixed my whiskey with water in a plastic Evian bottle, but Lance drank his straight with handfuls of pills. He was bug-eyed drunk by the time we got into the city. He kept falling down in Montparnasse and stealing things we didn't need, so Nikki and I ditched him near Gare du Nord.

We sat on smooth red plastic chairs then, in something like a McDonald's, sharing something like a Happy Meal. We'd already finished the greasy cheeseburger when Lance flung open the glass doors and stumbled inside the—maybe it *was* a McDonald's. He threw back his head and flung his arms into the fluorescent-lit air. "I'm Superman!"

Nikki dropped her little paper bag of fries. "I've had it with him." She licked the salt from her fingers.

Outside, it had started to rain. Fat drops fell on the nape of my neck and trickled down my spine.

Nikki and Lance stood in the pink glow of a neon sign between the fast-food joint and a boarding bus. "You're going back to Holland now," she told him matter-of-factly, then shoved him up the steps of the pale blue bus bound for Amsterdam. The doors closed behind him. The coach pulled away. Nikki turned to me and smiled. And just then I remembered why I loved her. Such a weird-looking girl. With her smudged eyeliner. Pure Chinese. And so obviously Californian. I wanted to snip the blond ends from her hair. "That was easy enough," she said, brushing off her leather jacket. But her face froze when we heard the bus stop abruptly a few yards away.

We turned in unison. The bus doors opened, spitting out a red-faced drunken Lance. He staggered towards us, eyes bloodshot and vacant.

Nikki's dangling silver earrings glinted under the neon. She screwed up her face, let out a sudden howl, dove toward him. A tall woman in a white suit grabbed her leashed poodle, stood back. "I'm fucking sick of you," Nikki screamed as she pushed Lance onto the cobblestones of the narrow street.

Someone shoved me from behind, craned her neck to see what was happening. Someone shouted in French. I watched from the sidewalk, mouth half-open, as a Paris taxi knocked Lance down and mowed over his thick body. My hand moved instinctively to cover my chest as the driver reversed, ran back over him with a thud, yelled something out his open window, sped away.

Nikki took a step back, grabbed my arm. "Holy shit."

I could feel the half-moons of her nails as they dug into my flesh.

Lance lay there on the wet cobblestones in his ripped black Levi's.

Two Arab men in jeans stood over him.

Was he dead?

The neon hummed above us. I stared with the crowd.

And all of a sudden, like some elastic cartoon character, Lance stood up. He brushed himself off and laughed, threw back his head and lifted his arms into the night sky: "I *am* Superman!"

"Oh. My. God." Nikki whispered. "He's Rasputin."

We woke in a covered doorway that smelled of gasoline.

Lance wanted to know why his legs hurt so bad.

I could see the Eiffel Tower from where I lay, but didn't mention it.

Nikki said, "You got in a fight with a taxicab, Lance." Left it at that.

In a train station café, we sipped espresso and nibbled on plain croissants.

Onward.

Why You Go Back

A drunken train-hopping swirl through Lyon, Marseille, Barcelona. I hardly noticed the scenery as it morphed from verdant French greens to dusty Spanish browns. We slept in rail yards and bombed-out buildings, a transient shelter and a Moorish underground city.

It was early April when we tumbled into the coastal village outside Valencia. An anachist kid with a Japanese tattoo on his neck had told us we'd get work there, picking oranges next to the abandoned tracks. Instead, we found jobs in a dry potato field, digging spuds out of the dirt, and set up camp in the farmer's barn.

"*Dónde vives?*" Nikki asked the jewelry maker who sold his silver wares near the beach.

"*En la calle,*" he said. "*Como tú. Como todos.*"

White spray-painted graffiti outside the soup kitchen read, "*¿Y los Americanos, en la luna?*"

I wished I hadn't been writing social studies papers during high-school Spanish class. I could understand the language well enough, had heard it all my life in California. But speaking it was another proposition altogether. *Vivo. Vives. Vive. Viven. Vivimos?* I tried to remember how to conjugate a regular verb.

When the round-faced potato farmer found us sleeping in the barn, he shook his head, led us to a sparsely furnished apartment in a condemned building that smelled of death. "You can sleep here," he said. "I'll try to find you some blankets." Our new squat: everything dust-covered, floor littered with bottles and yellowing newspapers, stone tiles crumbling into the shop below. The iron-barred window looked out on the town plaza: a statue of Franco, an old church. I thought of the civil war. Spaniards killing Spaniards.

Under the hot spring sun, we crawled through the dry field, piled potatoes into a crate, got paid by the kilo. When we couldn't find any more potatoes, the farmer told us to go home and wait. He'd come for us when the oranges were ripe. We walked away toward the plaza then, tired and dirty.

He never came for us.

On a Friday—I know it was a Friday because the soup kitchen was closed—two excessively clean Mormon missionaries appeared at our door. Nikki told them we were too hungry to talk, so they left, returned half an hour later with five egg sandwiches. We sat on the stone floor of the living room then, chatting about this and that. They'd come from Salt Lake City. The taller one missed his fiancée. They wanted to tell us all about their Lord and Savior, Jesus Christ, but Lance said he'd slit their throats if they did.

I guess they didn't know whether or not he was kidding, because they scrambled to gather up their Holy Bibles and their Books of Mormon and scampered out the door.

"That was mean, Lance," Nikki laughed, then lit her wooden pipe. "I didn't even get a chance to offer them a drink."

Lance opened a bottle of Southern Comfort. "All the more for us."

The first page of an eighteenth-century Huguenot booklet titled Le

Coeur Humain *pictures a human heart "enslaved to sin and dom-*
inated by Satan." The heart contains seven beasts: a proud peacock,
an impure goat, a ravenous pig, a lazy turtle, an angry tiger, a
greedy frog, a jealous snake, a lying eye and a winged devil.
According to the booklet, a person with a heart full of beasts only
appears to be alive.

I headed across the plaza—flagstones hot under my bare feet.
From the gray pay phone in the bar, I placed a collect call to
my parents. I didn't know what time it was in California.
Answering machine. The operator left my message. "Collect
call from Ariel. Is anyone home?"

I lingered in the bar for a while. I wasn't sure what I wanted
to talk to my parents about. Maybe nothing. I hoped someone
would buy me a beer. But I was dirty and I smelled like death.

When I got back to our squat, Lance was throwing chairs
against the walls, burning the legs in the kitchen hearth. I
approached him warily. "Hey," I whispered. I reached out to
put my hand on his shoulder. "What's the matter?"

I thought I would calm him, but he sneered at me. "You
don't *love* me."

"C'mon, Lance. You're acting crazy."

He pulled back from me, clenched his fist, swung furious at
my jaw, then my eye. I spun around, shielded my face with my
arms, felt his fist hit my shoulder, then the back of my ribs,
and again. The thud of his blows vibrated through my chest. I
coughed a breath, fell to the floor, made a sound like weeping.

Nikki screamed from the doorway.

Lance lunged toward her. "Shut up," was all he kept saying.

So I shut up. And then, so did Nikki. The house went quiet.
And Lance staggered out the door and down the stairs.

I stood up slowly, crept into the living room. My whole face
pulsed with a dull pain.

Nikki didn't want to talk. She didn't want to smoke.

I sat on the floor while she cleaned a back room. She called to me only when she discovered that one of the walls was made of cardboard, not stone like the rest. She pushed through it. On the other side: a secret room, empty except for a rotting mattress and the thing next to it. Lying with its jaw wide open in some silent scream, the bones and skin of a black cat. "I fucking knew this house was possessed," she whispered.

She never looked directly at me as we peeled the cat's brittle bones from the flagstones and carried them out to the dumpster at the edge of the plaza. We sprinkled salt in the corners of the secret room, then in all the corners of the flat, thinking somehow we could remove the evil from the place.

I ran my fingers along my brow and cheekbone as it swelled, wiped the blood from my lip. And then the strangest emotion flooded my body, so unexpected it took me a full minute to recognize it: *relief*. My bruises were on the outside now, where they belonged. I didn't have to tell anyone what had happened. They could see for themselves. I didn't have to question what was going on, wonder if I'd dreamed it. I had the proof in brilliant plum across my face.

A beating of wings, a bird trapped in the bell tower of the old church. A beating in my chest, rib dislocated but not cracked. My heart still somewhat protected. Everyone imagines themselves a phoenix, but when the time came for me to rise, I curled up in the ashes and went to sleep. The morning was a glare.

Lance knelt next to the mattress, whispered sorries. "I don't know what's happening to me," he cried. "I've never been like this before. All those months inside, you know. They must have really fucked me up."

"They've been screwed by the system," my mother used to

say when she talked about her students at San Quentin. *Screwed by the system.*

I stared up at the ceiling beams. I was supposed to be the director of my own life-movie. And it wasn't supposed to be some long-suffering tragedy: scenes that didn't flow into one another, a plot lunge into some dark chasm that left you empty—feeling nauseous from too much Diet Coke sipped through a Red Vines straw.

I slipped on a black T-shirt and skirt, padded down the stairs from our apartment to the plaza, past the statue of Franco and into the old church. An old woman sat in one of the pews, counting the ebony beads of her rosary. In this cave of worship, I knelt down in front of the Black Madonna and prayed for a whole new life.

Back in the farmer's condemned flat, I threw up in the sink.

JOURNAL ENTRY #263
39°28'N 0°22'W
SPRING, 1989

> *a free fall*
> *a brick wall*
> *i found an empty bottle of lithium in the garbage today*
> *the prescription sticker had nikki's name on it*
> *a pharmacy in new york*
> *she's on the mattress in her room now,*
> *doesn't want to get up*
> *i feel paralyzed*
> *i want a drink*
> *potato season is already over, and we have no money*
> *¿y los americanos, en la luna?*

Nikki seldom spoke now. She stayed in her room, smoking.

We passed each other in the hallway, the kitchen, stumbling in and out of the tiny bathroom.

I said, "Are you upset about something?"

And she laughed bitterly. "What's there to be upset about?" she deadpanned. "I'm having the time of my life here with you and your Superman. Always dreamed of vacationing on the Mediterranean."

No air in the hallway. I felt lightheaded. "I'm sorry, Nikki."

But she just shook her head. "Don't be sorry. You don't owe me anything, Ghost Girl. But maybe you ought to take a look around here sometime, you know? This isn't a field trip anymore. This is your life."

Bright morning in early June. I already knew I was pregnant.

I sat at the bar, nursing a *cafe con leche* and my second black eye in as many weeks, vaguely watching the soccer game on a television mounted near the ceiling.

When CNN cut into the sportscast, the portrait of Chairman Mao grabbed my attention. It took me a moment to focus on the pictures, on the words, some in English, some in Chinese. Spanish subtitles. Tanks rolled through Tian'anmen Square. Students wearing headbands and white shirts chanted, fists raised, as they marched down the Avenue of Heavenly Peace. I blinked, thought I recognized Kuan on the screen: uneven bowl haircut, her face anguished and naïve. I squinted, the TV camera jolted back, then focused in again. The girl fell to the ground, her white shirt bloodstained. The camera jolted away. A newscaster. Soldiers. Students. Screams. More tanks. I picked up my coffee and moved to a table closer to the TV, watched numbly as the chaos exploded in front of me. I kept my eyes glued to the screen. I wanted to feel surprise, but I didn't have it in me. My heart felt like it had turned to granite.

I ordered a glass of mineral water. My mind reeled. Was it

Kuan who fell to the ground on that tiny TV, shot in the back on the Avenue of Heavenly Peace? Maybe not. But when I saw her face, blurry and strange, to me it was Kuan.

When we'd talked on the cold, cold green at Beijing Language Institute, she never said she wanted social reform, but I knew she did. I also knew that she wasn't lying when she said, "I want to live. I want to study hard and help the motherland move forward. I want to get married and have a son."

I wondered if she knew she could be killed for marching on Tian'anmen Square that day, decided that she did. She knew. She knew and she had no idea.

I watched report after report from Beijing, looking for Kuan's face. News footage. Commentary. More footage. More commentary. But no Kuan.

What seemed to mystify the journalists was that even after hundreds of protesters had been shot and the square had been cleared, the students came back. More were killed, the square cleared. And still they came back. Again and again. The body count unknown. Thousands. And they kept coming back.

When the bartender finally turned off the TV, I walked home under the stars.

"Where the hell have you been?" Lance wanted to know when I opened the door. The veins in his neck looked like vines that could strangle him.

"At the bar," I said. "Watching the news."

"Nobody watches the news for four hours," he snapped.

In my room, I lit a candle, rummaged through my black drawstring bag looking for my passport, asked Lance if he'd seen it.

"Where are you going?" he wanted to know.

"I'm not going anywhere."

"Then why do you need your passport?"

"I don't need it," I said. "I just want to know where it is."

He shook his head. "You're always making some secret

plan, aren't you? If you want to know, then, I have your fucking passport. I have it for safe keeping. You'd fucking lose it the state you're in."

I said, "I want it back."

But he just stomped out of the room, slammed the wooden door behind him.

I got into bed with my clothes on, thought about those journalists and their baffled commentary. In my mind's eye, I sat on the edge of the Great Wall. The journalists didn't understand about civil wars. You go back. The journalists understood about foreign enemies: We're all taught to fear strangers, build walls. But brothers and fathers and mothers and sisters and lovers and friends and friends of friends and members of the People's Liberation Army? You go back because you can't believe it. It doesn't add up. You don't want it to be true, so you will it out of your mind. You go back because where else are you going to go? You go back because you can only endure the swirling gray paranoia for so long, can only listen to so many lies, so many promises, can only suck up so many insults before you snap. The center doesn't hold. The paranoia breaks. And all your fears, all your misgivings, all your intuitions—they were right on. Of course they were. You knew it. And you can't believe it. You start cursing in a dozen languages. You rush back into the square, hysterical now, heartbroken. You're screaming: *Kill me, then.* Because what does it matter now? If everyone is basically an asshole? If everyone is the enemy? What does it matter?

That night I dreamed the news footage playing backward. I dreamed Kuan alive. I dreamed her all dressed up in my black jeans and T-shirt, purple lipstick and Great Lash mascara, the queen of Hong Kong. She circled me on the dance floor, singing "White Heat" and shaking her fist in the air. In the dream, I didn't have a black eye. We danced like Chinese, stopped the world right then and there under the flashing disco lights. And in the dream, the man in brown never came for her. And me, I never went home to Lance.

In the morning, I lay in bed, bathing in my own salty tears. I thought about the baby growing in my belly. It didn't seem real. But maybe she was the answer to my silent prayer to the Black Madonna. Through the walls, I could hear Lance yelling at Nikki. And something like a baby's cry. The front door slammed and I pictured Nikki walking her slow walk out to the edge of the dusty village, across the abandoned tracks, into the orchard. And the cry again.

"Lance? What is that?"

"Nikki fucking bought this Siamese cat," he yelled from the living room.

Nikki. She was the only thing that softened my dull pulsing silent grief. Just watching her. We hardly spoke, but she was still with me. We milled around bars and soup kitchens, drinking bitter cheap wine. She was still with me—sad and high and way too skinny now, but still with me.

A gentle knock at my bedroom door that night. "I need to talk to you," Nikki said.

I nodded. "I need to talk to you, too."

She carried the crying kitten under her jacket as we headed toward the bar where the Gypsy men sang and drank. We ordered amber beer and dry sandwiches. She didn't look directly at my face when she talked. She looked down into her glass instead, petted her tiny cat. "I'm sorry. I just can't stand to look at your face like that."

"It's OK," I told her, even though it wasn't.

A fat man with a gray beard danced passed our table, snapping his fingers. He smiled down at us, a glint in his eye, blew a kiss to the kitten in Nikki's lap, muttered something about "*el corazón azul.*"

I said: "I'm pregnant."

Nikki stared at the wall somewhere behind me. "I know." She lit a cigarette. "If you want to get out of here, I'll take you to Paris."

I sipped my beer.

Nikki was luminous, sitting there on the other side of our white plastic table.

I hummed. Dry abstract grief.

It's a fucked-up night when you look at someone across a white plastic table and you realize that you'll love her until the day you die, and in a nervous quick heartbeat you realize that she'll love you, too, almost like in the fairytales. But only almost. Because in real life—here now in the dense world where you're pregnant and you've got a black eye and you already know you'll puke up your beer and dry sandwich in the street—in real life this love that's sisterly and passionate and strong, in real life it won't be enough. You won't stay together through thick and thin. You won't live happily ever after. You won't make each other feel adored, or even safe.

Nikki left. Of course she left. I turned nineteen and she left. She asked me to take care of her cat and she left. *What was she supposed to do?*

On the station platform, she rummaged through her backpack, fished out a joint and a small handful of multicolored Monopoly money. "Lire," she said, handing me the bills. "I was saving them for next time I was in Italy. It's not much, but you should take it. Exchange it for pesetas."

She dragged hard on her tobacco-hash joint, looked me squarely in the eye. "I want you to remember one thing," she said.

I nodded, waiting for her to say something deep.

But she just winked at me: "Pooh Bear is god."

On my way home from the station, I stopped at the bar, made another collect call to my parents from the gray pay phone.

John answered this time, accepted the charges. His voice sounded so close. My mother wasn't home.

"I have news." I pictured John sitting at his desk in the living room, sun streaming in through the French doors that led to the patio. "I'm pregnant."

Silence. Then: "You know we'll support you whatever your decision is, Ariel."

And I said, "I know."

We didn't talk for long: *Did I want to keep the baby?* Yes. *Should he tell my mother?* Yes. *Was I all right?* Yes. *Was I coming home?* No.

On my way out, I asked the bartender for some sandwich scraps for the kitten.

In the crumbling apartment, I found Lance sitting on our bed. "I'm gonna have a baby," I told him. "If you don't want it, you should tell me now."

A smile crept across his sunburned face. He took my hand, said, "If you had my baby, I'd worship the ground you walked on."

But later that night, the kitten cowered in Nikki's old room as Lance raged through the house, knocking over candles. He found me crying in the kitchen. "What's the matter with you now?"

I didn't answer.

"Say something!" he screamed this time. He swung his fist hastily, missed. Then swung again.

I jumped back, watched his fist hit my stomach. But no pain bloomed through my body.

He slouched over, stepped back and buried his face in his hands, whispered, "What the fuck is the matter?"

The kitten cried like a newborn.

Say something. But what? I wanted to tell him he was an ass-hole. I wanted to say "I'm leaving," pack up my shit and run away on some glorious lacquered yellow train. But more than that, I wanted to take a hot shower and go to bed. I wanted to wake up in the platinum light of morning. Lance would kiss me on the cheek and ask me how I felt. "Fine," I'd say. And we'd get dressed in clean Levi's and T-shirts, head out to find an English-language bookstore where we could buy a copy of *What to Expect When You're Expecting*. We'd stop somewhere for breakfast, then walk hand in hand through the street market, shopping for a pair of hand-knit baby booties, soft and pink.

A pretty watercolor arrived in the mail from my old high school friend, Veda. Orange peonies and swirling calligraphy: "You Create Your Own Reality." From the postmark, I knew Veda was in Santa Cruz. Maybe in college now. She must have gotten my address from John. I wanted to go see her, sit with her on the beach, ask her what she meant by that. *You create your own reality.* Did she mean the same thing Lance meant when he told me that the violence in our home was my own fault, that I provoked it, that I could leave if I wanted to, but that it wouldn't make any difference? That anyone who got close to me would have the same reaction?

Lance came home that night with a bouquet of freshly picked flowers. He had tears in his eyes when he gave them to me. I didn't deserve them. I who had brought the violence. But Lance had forgiven me. Couldn't I forgive him?

In *Sassafrass, Cypress and Indigo*, when the father beat the mother, she told her children, "You have to make room for the fool in everyone."

And the *I Ching* said: *The wife must always be guided by the will of the master of the house, be he father, husband, or grown son. Her place is within the house. . . . She must attend to the nourishment of her family and to the food for the sacrifice.*

"Ghost Girl," Lance said softly. "I swear on my mother's grave, nothing like this will ever happen again."

I thought I heard a windy voice whisper in my ear then,

"Just leave." *Leave.* But hadn't these past three years been all about leaving? Hadn't my whole life, really, been about leaving, giving up, running away? Maybe it took work to build a real life, a real relationship. Maybe you had to make room for the fool in everyone. Maybe running wasn't always the answer. Maybe I created my own reality. Maybe anyone who got close to me would have the same reaction. Maybe my place was within, yielding and receptive. Maybe I was the one being cruel to Lance, bringing out the worst in him, then making him beg for forgiveness. *If it ever happens again,* I promised myself, *I'll leave.* Another wave of nausea.

Lance said, "Let's just go away from here. We have to get out of Spain. This place is possessed or something. It's making me mental. And we have to get you to a doctor, you know? The jewelry maker says they have free healthcare at the Vatican hospital, even for Americans. I never should have brought you to Spain. I'm so sorry about everything. But now we have to focus on the baby, you know?" He placed his hand on my belly, closed his eyes. "Let's just go away from here, Ghost Girl."

The time and the place. There's always hoping, anyway.

"Don't call me that anymore," was all I said. "My name is Ariel."

And in the morning, I followed him onto a train without a ticket.

Part V

Heart

The brain, the skin, the lungs and the heart make up our vital organs. We are made to think and feel and breathe and love. The rest is optional.

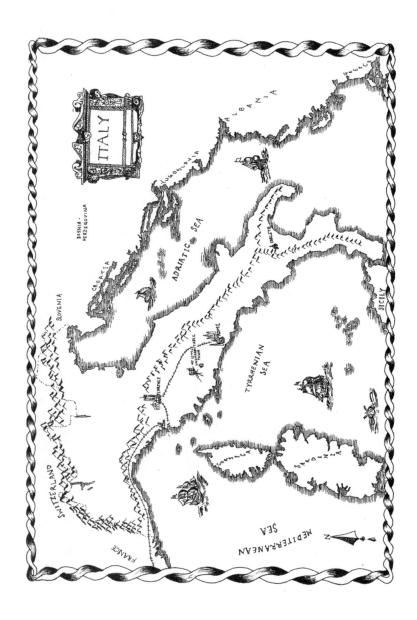

For Every Person, There Is
a Unique Tragedy

We'll call the cat Gitana," Lance said. *Gypsy.*

It took four days and three nights to round the Mediterranean—getting escorted off the train every few stops by a uniformed conductor wanting a ticket. Barcelona, Perpignan, Montpellier. The spirited chatter of a thousand tanned Eurail-pass tourists speaking Spanish, Italian, English, Greek, Japanese.

I carried Gitana under my leather jacket.

On a crowded platform in France, where the salty July breeze lapped across my face, an old woman dressed all in black wanted to sell me a small glass bottle of holy water.

I told her I didn't have any francs.

She spoke French, said something to the effect of: *But you need this.*

I turned out my pockets: *For real, I'm broke.* I pointed to my bag. "Lire?"

She shook her head, twisted the rose-shaped cap from the bottle, dabbed some of the holiness onto her callused fingers.

I stood statue-still as she reached up to rub the water on my forehead.

She placed the bottle in my palm then, curled my fingers around it.

"*Merci.*" I thanked her. Blessed and exhausted. Another train.

We arrived in Rome too late in the evening to find a squat, so we headed west on foot from Termini Station, walked for what seemed like hours. We passed the Pantheon, circled Piazza Navona, finally unrolled our blankets at the edge of Campo dei Fiori.

I fell asleep easily on the cobblestones, let the dreams spin through my mind like so many movie trailers: I was in labor in San Francisco, crisscrossing the city in a yellow taxicab, looking for a place to have the baby, but all the hospitals were closed or under construction. Then a mirror on a white-sand Mediterranean beach. I scanned the cobalt waters. It was the Gulf of Thailand. I squinted my eyes. It was the Pacific Ocean. I reached in through the glass of the mirror, removed my hand, reached in again. I looked around, cautious as a suspect, but there was no one in sight. I stepped through the mirror into a dark, windowless space. An electric blue lava lamp glowed from the center. Red light bulbs flickered overhead. My eyes adjusted slowly to the lack of light. Wall-to-wall black carpeting. Vinyl booths on either side of me. A dozen bleach-blond and Mohawked Chinese kids leaned over tables, playing mahjong. All at once, I recognized the Joes. The Cold War Café. I sighed, relieved. Maybe I'd dreamed all of Europe. The bartender smiled up at me: *Fuckin' long time no see.* I said: *Are you a ghost?* And he let out a throaty chuckle: *We're all ghosts, don't you know?*

I felt something wet on my cheek, opened my eyes to Gitana's charcoal and ivory face. My back hurt like hell. I sat up, dizzy, managed not to puke.

In soft sunrise light, vendors hummed, set up their stalls, arranged their goods. The marketplace materialized around us: herbs and spices in bulk, bright T-shirts and pastel linens, roses and daffodils, snapdragons and Dutch irises, hyacinths and potted hydrangeas, cherries and golden apples, provolone and giant sausages, tomatoes and lush salad greens. I brushed off the back of my jacket, could

smell panini fresh out of an oven somewhere. I was famished. I elbowed Lance awake.

"Fuck," he mumbled. "I was dreaming of Greece."

We spent Nikki's lire on salty bread and sweet cappuccino
at a tiny café. Italian pop songs on the radio. Lance wanted to
visit an old acquaintance somewhere in town, but I already
had my mind fixed on the Hospital of the Holy Spirit. "I don't
know what your rush is," he said. "But I'll take Gitana. Meet
me back here at noon."

Which way to the Vatican? Follow the gaze of the dark statue
of Giordano Bruno—poor sucker who was burned in the piazza
in 1600 for suggesting that the earth moved around the sun.

The hospital waiting room smelled of must and garlic
sweat. I sat in a corner, barefoot and my bra already too tight.
I closed my eyes, tried to imagine the baby. In a little house
with white walls and huge picture windows, I held her close at
my breast, rocked her into sleep. Life had been messed up in
England and Spain, but I still believed in magic—in all the
magics. Everything would turn out all right in the end.
Wouldn't it?

In the cement-floor exam room, a solemn nun sat me down
on the table, made a downward scooping gesture with one
hand: *"Aborto?"*

Who knew they offered abortions at the Vatican? I laughed
out loud. I would have gone to Paris for that. "No." I pointed
to my chest: "Mama." Then to my belly, "Baby OK?"

She took my pulse and blood pressure, frowned. Slow and
low. She pressed a cold stethoscope to my chest, pressed three
fingers into my belly, sent me on my way with a shrug of
bewildered reassurance: "Baby OK."

In my mind's eye, the baby had fallen asleep in my arms. I
carried her through the little house with white walls and huge
picture windows, tucked her into a wooden crib. *Baby OK.*

That night in a cheap restaurant, we twirled spaghetti around forks, chatted with a gaunt thirty-something woman name Vittoria who Lance had found begging in Piazza Navona. They'd shared a cigarette at the fountain, compared sad stories. And, strange beggar, she'd ended up giving *him* a handful of lire.

Vittoria had stringy black hair, the laugh of a schoolgirl and the eyes of a grandmother. She spoke English with a thick and rhythmic accent, told us she was sick with AIDS. "For every person, there is a unique tragedy," she said. "Mine is no more grievous than yours or anyone else's."

We stayed with her in a charmless apartment on the outskirts of Rome for two weeks. A three-room mess of self-help books and healing crystals.

In the cracked bathroom mirror, I studied my face. The bruises from our last fight in Spain had faded into pretty sunset colors: mustard-seed yellow, avocado green, pale pale purple.

Vittoria said, "Will you mind if I touch you? Even with the AIDS?"

I shook my head. "I'm not afraid of you."

She traced a circle around my eye, her index finger cold as snow. "One can meditate in order to heal with greater velocity," she said. "But one cannot avoid one's fate."

To pass the days, she led us through the city on buses and on foot, pointed out dirty needles in the street everywhere we went, in and out of cafés and bars, *her* Rome. We scarcely caught glimpses of the monuments and fountains of the tourist maps. Instead, she instructed us on how to beg in Italian, said she felt tired all the time, warned us that there were bad people in the world and never to bathe our cat.

"I have a little house out in Tuscany," she told me one morning over stale anchovy pizza in her cluttered kitchen.

"You can live there. I think it will be good for you and your baby. A small village in the country. *Bellissima.*" She giggled awkwardly, then gasped, steadied her breath, smiled, embarrassed. From a basket on the Formica table, she produced a giant iron key that looked like it would open a castle and a ragged hand-drawn map to the little house that "needed work." She lit a cigarette, coughed violently. "I have not been out there in years," she managed. "However, I hope to retire there when I am old."

I wondered if Vittoria would ever grow old.

We hitchhiked north that night, slept in an open field. As the sun rose, Lance built a fire with twigs and a Danielle Steel paperback he'd been carrying around. I fingered the giant key in my pocket, thought of our luck: a little house in Tuscany. Maybe it would have white walls and huge picture windows. The baby would grow up bilingual in the Italian countryside.

At a stone monastery at the edge of a village, we begged a loaf of bread and a can of salmon from a fat Capuchin monk. Lance couldn't understand why the monk didn't have any coffee for us. "Cappuccino," he kept saying. But the monk just rolled his eyes and shut the heavy wooden door.

We made sandwiches on the gravelly bank of Lake Bolsena, fed Gitana chunks of fish from the can. "Have you ever seen that Fellini movie, *La Strada*?" I was thinking of the poor blond clown girl beating her drum, announcing the arrival of the brute Zampano. I was wishing we had a covered circus wagon to travel in.

But Lance ignored my question. He watched the hooded crows over the water. "Italy agrees with me," he said.

And it seemed true enough. He drank grappa now and then, but he didn't fall down in the squares, didn't steal things from the shops, didn't kick me as I slept. Almost three weeks of peace.

"This could be a whole new life for us," he said. "It all depends on you—on whether or not you intend to dwell on the past."

To dwell on the past. Maybe Lance hoped my memory would fade like the bruises into pretty sunset colors. But memories don't fade. Forgetting is a deliberate act. We cut and splice the footage of our lives, keeping what we think we need, discarding scenes, rewriting lines, smoothing over transitions, representing whole seasons with montages or jump cuts, editing out characters and complexities at will.

We hitched another ride with a German hippie whose VW bus smelled like tobacco and hash. He bobbed his head up and down—Queen on the cassette player—babbled to Lance in the front seat.

I stared out the window. Vast glistening fields. A lone black cypress on a hill. Cloudless sky. "We're in northern California, now," I laughed, but Lance and the hippie didn't hear me. Miles of rolling hills blanketed by silvery olive groves and dense brilliant vineyards. Our destination rose up from the landscape like a fairytale castle—a medieval hill-town made of stone. We thanked the hippie, climbed out into the piazza. The air tasted sweet and clear, like a Sierra wind. I closed my eyes. Only the sound of the Volkswagen leaving us, laughter from an outside café table. I hoped Vittoria's place had a shower where I could wash the smog-grime of Rome from my skin.

In the bar, Lance ordered a dark beer. I picked up a cheaply produced tourist brochure in English.

Housewives in drab smocks stared as I trudged into the little market. My muddy boots. My torn Chinese army pants. I bought prosciutto and cheese. Back outside, I studied Vittoria's ragged map. "It looks like we go down there." I pointed toward an archway and cobblestone alley that led into a cluster of green-shuttered houses.

Lance took the map from me and I followed him down the narrow stone road marked Via Roma. He stopped, scratched his head, turned down a steep tunneled stairway, then onto a dirt path and past a rusted sign: *Pericoloso*. Dangerous.

I looked out over the row of ash-colored ruined houses that barely clung to the overgrown hillside. Below, a steep drop into a ravine. "It can't be down here—" Lance shook his head, pointed to a wooden door with a chipped tile sign: 405. The address on the map.

I stepped in front of him, touched the sign with my index finger, hoped I was dreaming. I took the iron key from my pocket. Maybe it wouldn't fit the giant lock. Maybe we'd turned off the cobblestone alley too soon.

Ch-click. I pushed open the door to the roofless half-house. Three walls and a cliff where the fourth might have been. A crumbling stone floor. A broken mirror. A wooden chair. A hearth built into the corner. A waist-high wall separating the main room from a cracked toilet and a marble bathtub filled with dirt and fennel plants. And who needs any windows when you're missing a ceiling and wall? I swallowed hard.

Lance looked like he might cry, but he managed a smile. "Maybe we can fix it up, you know? Make it nice?"

I dropped my bag onto the dirt-covered floor, nodded. "Maybe." But my disappointment tasted like dry coffee grounds. Expectation in overdrive. Everything fails.

"Listen," Lance said. "You get settled in, then. All right? I have to go and find these farmer friends of Vittoria's. She said they'd have work for me. She said their olive orchard needs tending."

Gitana dug around in the marble bathtub as I watched the sun set persimmon behind golden hills on the other side of the gorge. I scanned the tourist brochure that waxed poetic about the little town "off the beaten path" in southern Tuscany, set on a bluff of soft volcanic tufo stone above the Lente River, dominated by two massive castles. It described the valley below: a honeycomb of Etruscan cave-tombs. And the town itself: tiny roads, steep and crooked; a labyrinth of stairs and tunnels— "full of the medieval charm that makes it so enticing to the visitor."

A postscript, set in slightly smaller type, was more illuminating: *Pieces of the town have been sliding off the cliff for centuries. In 1929, after a particularly ruinous slide, Italian legislators declared the town uninhabitable. However, the town's residents refused to leave. Their houses had been sliding away for years. They were used to it.*

It's funny, the way you can get used to just about anything.

I wondered if Vittoria knew the state her house was in when she'd handed me the iron key. I wondered if she thought we could fix it up, make it inhabitable. More likely she hadn't seen it in years. And none of her few friends in town had the heart to tell a dying woman that her retirement home had fallen away.

But the view was gorgeous. An Egyptian vulture circled a near hill.

I'd arranged our blankets on the stone floor next to the hearth and was trying to get comfortable when Lance finally stumbled in, high and tipsy. He climbed under the blankets next to me, rested his rough hand on my belly. The smell of red wine. "There's no work up there. Just a couple of drunken potheads. But the woman Norma, she wants to know if you can make brownies."

"Brownies?"

"Yeah—she reckons Americans can make brownies."

I stared up at the indigo heavens. A blanket of silver stars all doing what stars do. When a single glimmer fell across the sky, I made a wish: *the antonym of numb.*

That night in dream, I climbed down the hill from our new stone house, into the ravine. I walked against the current of the Lente River, but when I looked down, it was milk, not water, flowing under my feet. A tiny opening appeared in a mound of volcanic stone on the riverbank. I climbed inside the cave-tomb and slept soundly.

If I Had Three Coins

JOURNAL ENTRY #349
42°41′N 11°43′E
SUMMER, 1989

what am i doing in this uninhabitable town?
if i had three coins, i would ask the i ching

Knock knock. I closed my journal as the door swung open. The woman, Norma, stood and stared. Her short, black hair was spiked in front. "You are Ariel?" She wore black jeans and a Che Guevara T-shirt, glanced around our cave-tomb of a house.

"Yeah."

She nodded slowly. "And you intend to live here?"

I stood up. "I guess we'll have to find another place, huh?"

She raised an eyebrow. "No comment. Anyway. Come on. Your boyfriend told me you could make brownies."

I followed Norma back up the dirt path that led through the stone tunnel and into the cobblestone alley.

A middle-aged woman with two large pink curlers in her hair stared down at us as she hung laundry from a second-story window.

"*Buongiorno,*" Norma called up to her.

But the woman didn't answer.

"I come from Firenze," Norma said. "No one from around

here will ever talk to you. Know that. No one except perhaps the butcher—and she is as nosey as they come."

Up through the piazza, past the fountain and the bar, up a steep, one-lane curving road, down a blackberry bush-lined driveway. I had to skip to keep up with Norma's brisk pace. "Where did you learn English?" I wanted to know. We were climbing the stairway to her giant stone farmhouse.

She laughed. "It is only Americans who cannot manage an extra language or two."

On a butcher-block table in the kitchen, Norma had flour and sugar, chocolate and eggs, baking soda and salt, butter and vanilla, bowls and pans. She lit a cigarette, covered her T-shirt and jeans with a white apron, stared at me. "What do we do with it all, Miss America?"

I scanned the ingredients, bit my lip. "I don't know," I admitted.

Hand on her hips, she said, "I thought Americans knew how to make brownies."

I sat down on a stool next to the butcher-block table. "My mother was a feminist."

A grin crept across Norma's round face. She said, "*Brava!* The summer arts festival starts tomorrow. All the tourists are coming. The brownies would sell for five thousand lire each. I finally find an American and her mother was a feminist? *Brava!*"

I felt like such an idiot. I'd seen my stepdad make brownies a hundred times. How did he do it? "I'm really sorry," I said. "You don't have a cookbook or anything?"

"No." She ran her fingers through her gelled hair, slipped off her apron, started rolling a joint. "My big plan was to find an American."

"I'm sure we can figure it out."

Norma smoked as I melted butter and chocolate, beat eggs,

stirred ingredients. I was trying to channel John, trying to remember something—*anything, really*—from seventh-grade home economics. "I think the thing with brownies is you don't need any baking soda." I stirred in a handful of flour. "Do you have walnuts?"

Norma shook her head, dragged on her joint. "Have you been to university?"

"No."

She shook her head. "If you cannot cook, you have to go to university. I do not know how to cook and I did not go to university. Good thing I do not want to leave my husband, eh?"

I nodded. "Good thing."

Some of the pans of brownies came out too dense, others cakelike. Some undercooked, some almost burnt. Norma didn't seem to mind. As the last batch cooled, she pointed me upstairs to the terra-cotta-tiled bathroom. I took a hot shower, checked out my belly. It looked like nothing more than a beer gut. Three months along now.

"I ought to take you home," Norma said after I'd dressed. "My husband will be back for his dinner soon. But I will pick you up tomorrow for the fair?"

"All right."

"And my husband, you know, he is asking around about work for your boyfriend. Maybe he will find something."

Norma beamed as she handed me my part of the profits from the summer arts fair: 110,000 lire. Just over one hundred dollars U.S. "Not bad for a feminist, eh?" Her front tooth was chipped.

From the market in the piazza, I bought wine and salad greens, salami and bread. From a traveling Moroccan vendor, I bought bootleg copies of *Like a Prayer* and Zucchero's *Oro Incenso e Birra*; books on Etruscan gods, alchemy, and Catholic saints. I carried the spoils down to the half-house where Lance sat on the wooden chair, Gitana in his lap.

He piled chunks of salami onto thick slices of bread, drank wine straight from the bottle, counted out the bills. "This will be just enough," he said. "There's a woman, Donatella, in the shop up on Via Roma. She talks to me, you know? She reckons we can rent a little place for the autumn and winter."

Donatella. Striking woman my mother's age. She'd talked to me once, too, told me the baby would be a girl. And I hadn't even said I was pregnant. She wore no wedding ring, gestured a cross in the air between us every time she saw me. Her tiny shop was full of canned goods, brooms and beans. I understood her slow dialect, enunciated just so, Latin roots perfectly recognizable under the staccato rhythm of modern Italian.

"I can go ask her about it," I offered.

But Lance wanted to be The Man. "I'll get us a house," he said, then: "Listen, Ariel. I'm going to make the money from now on. No wife of mine works, OK?"

"All right," I agreed, and off he went.

I lit a candle, opened a book. All my new paperbacks were in Italian, but if I read the words slowly aloud to myself, I could decipher more than half of them. Some were easy: *Impuro* meant impure, *mostro* meant monster, *pacificare* meant to pacify. Other words I had to filter through the Spanish file in my brain: *Mare* meant sea, *casa* meant house, *amore* meant love, not to be confused with *ammortire*, to deaden.

The Etruscans, it turned out, were expert diviners who could find subterranean water, bore wells, construct underground corridors, tunnel mountains. They imagined heaven and earth as consisting of four chambers, like a heart, quartered by an invisible cross consisting of a north-south "cardo" axis and an east-west "decumanus" line. The sun god was pictured rising from the ocean, the childbirth goddess as a young woman with black feathered wings. The Etruscans' sacred doctrine was revealed to them when an otherworldly being rose up from a newly ploughed field near the river Marta. The miraculous being had the appearance of a child, the wisdom of an old man. After revealing the "diciplina etrusca" to the priest-kings, the wise child fell dead and disappeared.

True to his word, Lance talked to Donatella, rented us a house at the foot of Via Roma between Giovanna's Pizzaria and the arched tunnel that led down to the ruined part of the city. *A house*. Actually, it was more like a two-hundred-square-foot converted wine cellar that smelled of mildew, but it had four walls and a ceiling. A sofa bed, too, and a pull-down table, a large camping stove and sink in the corner, a tiny tiled bathroom, hot running water and electricity, even a black-and-white TV. The place was ours until tourist season started up again in May. I taped posters of Santa Lucia, San Antonio and San Gennaro behind the door, an image of Our Lady of Perpetual Help next to the camping stove.

I flushed the toilet two or three times, watched the miraculous whirlpool as it circled the bowl and disappeared. This was *my* toilet. Running water is a beautiful thing.

"I really feel like I'm getting my shit together," Lance grinned, eager and pathetic. He was sitting on the orange and brown floral couch, some buxom babe chattering entertainment news on television. He'd just hung a huge world map on the back wall.

Getting himself together. It seemed true enough. Norma's husband had found him a job a few miles out of town. He stripped furniture for restoration every day until sunset. And he hadn't hit me since swearing on his mother's grave. Still, I couldn't conjure up much pride for him. Twenty thousand lire a day. I spent the money on food and wine. It was survival, nothing to get excited about. My bruises had faded, but there was still a murdered thing between us. On the rare evening when I conjured the nerve to ask after my passport, he clenched his teeth. The muscles in his neck and arms tensed, his whole body readying to fight. So I dropped it, offered him his bottle. "Never mind." If it meant all that to him, I could stay, build a life. *Why not?* The Tuscan hills were lovely. And we had four walls now.

When I stopped into Donatella's shop to thank her for the house, she shrugged. *"Di niente."* It was nothing. From a shelf behind the cash register, she produced a fist of dry twigs. *"L'erba della paura,"* she said, offering it to me.

I understood *l'erba* as herb, but *paura?*

"Lo stress," she said. With gestures and simple sentences, she instructed me to steep the leaves like tea and wash myself with the resulting tincture.

"OK," I agreed.

And she smiled. "Ariel?"

"Yes?"

"Non lo dire a tuo marito." Don't tell your husband.

"No, non lo dico," I promised. I wouldn't think of it.

Later, I asked Norma about the herbs for stress. She said, *"L'erba della paura?* The witches used to wash people with it. I think to give them courage—or reverse a hex. But you will not find any around here. There are no more *strege* in Tuscany."

As the lush and sticky heat of summer gave way to autumn rains, I spent my days between our converted wine cellar and Norma's giant stone house. I read my books in the mornings, listened to my bootleg tapes, met up with Norma in the afternoons. We canned tangy tomato sauce and pickled green beans at the foot of her driveway. Our men off working, we tooled around the countryside in her little silver hatchback. The sulfur hot springs at Saturnia smelled like rotten eggs and felt like heaven, turned my silver jewelry black. The Tarot Garden in Grosseto lodged itself in my imagination and filled my night dreams with giant sculptures of the Empress, the Fool, and the Hanged Man. I sent a postcard picturing a cave-tomb to my mother. I craved sour apples, the smell of irises, sweet brandy. In the early evenings, I bought liver and peppered sausage from the nosey butcher, red table wine and sweet onions from the market in the piazza, pasta and red sauce from Donatella's shop. On my way home, I padded into the church, set my groceries down on a pew and knelt to clear my mind before San Nicola—patron saint of children, protector of whores. I made dinner, scrubbed the tile walls of our bathroom that seemed to mildew daily. Most nights, Lance got a ride home from Norma's shy, red-haired husband just after sunset. We sat across the table from each other then, twirled spaghetti around forks, spoke of nothing much. He said I wasn't keeping the house clean enough. I said I wanted to go to Florence to buy books in English. After dinner, he headed out. He always invited me to come with him, but I preferred the company of the saints in my books and the child growing in my belly. I wrote letter-poems to her, burned them in the sink, then curled up on the hideous orange and brown flowered sofa bed to read by electric lamplight.

Santa Lucia, whose name meant light, was born to wealthy pagan Sicilians in the third century. Her teenage rebellion took the form of religious conversion. She risked persecution, carrying food to the many Christians hiding in underground tunnels. To illuminate the dark passages, she wore a wreath of candles.

Her parents didn't know what she was doing, or they ignored the problem, figured it was a passing phase. They chose a suitor, but Lucia had no plans to marry. The young man—not only a pagan, but an asshole—ratted her out to the pagan authorities, who ordered her to be taken to a brothel. If she wasn't going to marry, she'd have to be a whore. She prayed and prayed, and when it came time to move her, she staged a one-woman sit-in. The authorities decided to burn her at the stake then, but the raging flames didn't harm her. Finally, at the age of twenty-one, she was struck down, a sword to her throat.

And here I'd always imagined pagans to be land-loving hippies. At least now I knew who to pray to if I ever got hungry or lost. It's said she'll come across the water, bearing grain; it's said she'll travel into dark tunnels with her crown of light. Maybe she'd even brave my underground city. Navigating hope.

I changed into a pair of sweats Norma had given me, pulled out the sofa bed and snuggled under the blankets, kept reading.

San Gennaro, patron saint of blood and volcanic eruptions, was also plenty persecuted. Timothy, the pagan governor of Campania, feared Gennaro and had him placed in a furnace to burn. But like Santa Lucia, the flames didn't harm him. Timothy then sent him to the wild beasts, but the beasts left him alone. It was back to prison for Gennaro. But pretty soon, old Timothy needed a favor. He'd gone blind and demanded that Gennaro help him. Gennaro obliged, asking God to restore Timothy's vision. But as the governor began to see again, he ordered the poor sucker beheaded.

Over a century later, evidence surfaced that a vial of San Gennaro's blood had been dried and preserved. When brought near a statue of the saint, the blood transforms itself back into liquid and starts to bubble.

I lit two candles for Lucia and Gennaro, and a third for San Antonio—patron saint of sailors, travelers and lost articles. I figured San Antonio would protect me. Maybe he'd even help me get my passport back.

When they opened Antonio's tomb, all that remained of the holy Franciscan was his tongue—sprout of his heart.

Blessed guide of pilgrims, direct my steps.

On a frosted blue morning, as I sat sipping cappuccino outside the café, the butcher rushed out to tell me that there was a parcel waiting for me at the post office. "I think it is from your mother!"

I thanked her.

Back in our converted wine cellar, I opened the brown paper-wrapped box: loose-waisted stretch pants, another Muriel Rukeyser book, *Invisible Cities* by Italo Calvino and a thick tome on pregnancy. The newborn on the cover looked like a space alien. I read about fetal development. It seemed strange that I had two hearts in me now.

By the end of the first month of gestation, the embryo's heart, no bigger than a poppy seed, has started beating. By the end of the second month, it has divided itself into right and left chambers. By the end of the third month, all the vital organs are in place.

Mid-October. I stood washing Levi's in the bathroom sink. Lance shouted from the sofa bed: "Ariel! Have a look at this— your entire metropolitan area has been wiped out!" He sounded kind of excited about it. "Maybe your whole family is dead!"

I stared at the flickering screen: the San Francisco earthquake on the black-and-white TV. Collapsing bridges and overpasses. People running, screaming. Rubble where the Marina District of San Francisco had been, rubble where downtown Santa Cruz had been.

Norma came banging at the door, her ungelled hair a

mess. "San Francisco is finished!" she cried. "You must call your parents!" She grabbed my hand and pulled me out the door. We ran all the way up Via Roma, all the way to her giant stone house.

I dialed frantically, swept up in the hyperbole of international news that grows exponentially catastrophic as it crosses borders and oceans. *All circuits busy.* I dialed again. And again. Palo Alto was a shit hole, but I needed it to be there. I rarely called home, but when I did, I needed someone to answer. *All circuits busy.*

"Shit."

Norma's hands trembled as she rolled a joint.

It was three days before I got through. John's voice calm on the other end. The wine glasses had fallen and broken, he said. The house shook. Paintings and prints crashed to the floor— but they were all framed with Plexiglas. He and my mother held on to each other under the arch that separated the living room from the dining room. The power had been out for a time, the phone lines down. Chaos in San Francisco and Santa Cruz. But everyone we knew was all right.

"I'm so glad."

John sighed into the phone. "Well, Ariel. It's always good to hear your voice."

JOURNAL ENTRY #389
42°41'N 11°43'E
FALL, 1989

the alchemists likened fetal development to the transmutation of chaos into spiritual gold. life outside the womb was a process of destruction by fire.

i'm noticeably pregnant now.

the italians call my belly a pancia.
some of the locals talk to me now.

when the butcher realized i was expecting, she rushed out from behind her glass display case, held her wrinkled hand against my belly.

i hope it's a girl.

an old man named signore fiori who drinks in the bar brings me flowers in the late afternoons.

last night i dreamed i was wading upstream in the yangtze river with lance. he sat down on a limestone rock to rest, and all of a sudden, he turned into a toad.

To Save Me

You are living like an old Italian woman in the South who has no possibilities," Norma said. She leaned against the stone wall of her house, gazed out over her acres of olive trees. "Not like an intelligent American woman who has been all over the world."

I rubbed my eyes. "I don't have any energy," I whined. "And it's so pretty here. Everything will turn out all right, you'll see. Everything always turns out all right in the end."

She laughed, dragged on her MS cigarette. "*Madonna mia,* you honestly believe that?"

"Sure, haven't you ever seen an American movie?"

She stabbed her cigarette out in a green metal ashtray, started rolling a joint. "Everything always turns out OK in the end of the American movie because the writer *makes* it turn out OK. But it is easier to write a tragedy. The natural flow of everything is down." She suddenly dropped her joint into the ashtray, jumped to her feet and leapt off the porch. She half-ran, half-stumbled down the grassy hill into her orchard, fell to the ground with a thud.

I scrambled down the stone steps after her, careful not to slip in the dirt.

She lay in a heap on the ground.

"What the fuck are you doing, Norma? Get up." I held my hand out to her.

She laughed. "A miracle is going to get me up!"

I tugged at her arm. "C'mon Norma, what are you doing?"

She said, "Everything always turns out OK in the end."

I sat down next to her. "That's a stupid metaphor, Norma."

She sat up slowly. "No it is not. You want to go tumbling down a hill and you think God will send you a miracle because you are too lazy to get up? If you have already tried everything else and you cannot get up yourself, then maybe God will send a miracle. You see these olive trees? We never tend them."

I looked out over the acres of heavy branches. "So?"

"So! Nothing will ever come of them. Dreams mean work."

In the blue evening, I headed up Norma's driveway toward the piazza.

From his table outside the bar, Signore Fiori waved to me and laughed.

Lance would be home from work by now. And I hadn't made dinner or cleaned the house. I hummed as I headed down Via Roma.

Sure enough: Lance sat hunched on the pull-out sofa bed, drinking from a liter bottle of red wine. He looked up when I opened the door. "You really are a crazy bitch," he said matter-of-factly.

"What?"

"You're bloody insane." He waved my cork-covered journal over his head. "You can't even write. This is a load of rubbish."

I felt something hot in the center of my chest, like I'd been punched, only this time I could feel it. Three short inhales, but I couldn't get a good breath. "What are you doing with that?"

He smiled. "I work all day, but I suppose my girlfriend has better things to do than to make me a bit of supper."

The calm in his voice scared me.

"There wasn't anything to eat, so I started looking around

for something to read. Turns out I shouldn't have bothered. This isn't worth the paper it's written on." He opened the book, read out loud: *"Moon faced, pale / eyes like mood rings: gray or blue or green / dark circles / strong legs / too fat for the pages of a magazine, too thin to survive a month in the desert . . ."* He laughed, riffled through the pages. "Not too thin now, are you, you fucking cow? And how about this 'I love Nikki' shit. What are you, a lesbian?"

I just stood there, speechless. My whole body ached. I could feel my throat tighten. And still the heat trapped in my chest. A beating of wings. I stared at my journal in Lance's sunburned hands. He closed it, ran his index finger across the cork, poured some wine down his throat, nodded. "You really are a crazy bitch."

I boiled water in silence, bent the spaghetti into the pot and watched it as it softened. I looked down at the Wuhan Punk shirt stretched tight across my belly. In my mind's eye, our white walls were smeared with blood and ink.

Muriel Rukeyser in unassigned reading: *Slave and slaveholder they are chained together / And one is ancestor and one is child. / Escape the birthplace: walk into the world / Refusing to be either slave or slaveholder.*

Refusing, but how? My head hurt. I collected some laundry I'd hung from the bathroom window.

That night in a dream, I crept across a field of human bones. A yellow school bus appeared. The old woman in the driver's seat stuck her head out the window. I picked up a handful of bone fragments, held it up toward her: *Who died here?* I wanted to know. *His women before you,* she hummed.

In the morning, I pretended to be asleep while Lance readied for work. When I heard the door shut behind him, I climbed out of bed, boiled the fist of herbs Donatella had given me. In the bathroom, I washed my whole body. I found my journal under Lance's pillow, slipped it into a shopping bag with a translucent red lighter, a blue linen rag, the small bottle of holy water with the rose-shaped cap.

From Donatella's shop on Via Roma, I bought a box of white candles.

I climbed down the narrow dirt path to the ruined part of the city then, past the sign that said *Pericoloso*, and to the wooden door with the chipped tile address: 405. I took the iron key from my pocket—*ch-click*—and I pushed open the door to the roofless half-house. I was thinking about the Cold War Café. *Be yourself or die.*

I cleared the ashes and dirt from the hearth, set my journal inside. Next to it, I lit a candle and watched the flame as it sputtered and burned. I dabbed some of the holy water on my forehead, then placed the bottle in the hearth with my journal and the candle.

The only security that matters is the security of the imagination.

I thought of Vincent at the rail yard on the outskirts of Beijing, tried to remember his happiness exercise. I faced the western hills, stretched my arms out—palms flat—and held them like a tai chi pose. "We are alive," he'd said. "You and me— and so many others!" I flexed my hands into the shape of talons, took a deep breath, then raised both arms over my head and held them there, exhaled as I brought them back down to my sides. "I curse when I am angry and cry when I am grieving," he'd said. "And then I breathe and I am happy again."

Maybe Vittoria had known everything when she handed me her iron key. *It will be good for you and your baby.* An underground tunnel with a view to the sky. *Down here where we can be ourselves.*

On my way home, I ducked into Giovanna's Pizzaria. The tiny woman who ran the place was the only employee. A mop of black hair. Her two front teeth were made of gold. She smiled tired from behind the bar, spoke English: "I can help you?"

"I was just wondering. I mean, if you ever need anyone to wash dishes or anything?"

She nodded slowly. "Evenings?"

"Oh—it would have to be daytimes," I said dumbly. "My boyfriend doesn't want me to work. Actually, never mind. I'm sorry." I turned, took a few steps.

Giovanna cleared her throat. "It is all right," she said. "Come when you can. We will see how it goes."

Grazie, I thanked her.

When the Berlin Wall came down, I wanted to go there, but I was seven months pregnant and I had to clean the house. I had to wash the lunch dishes at Giovanna's Pizzaria, too. I didn't think she needed me, but she paid me ten thousand lire a day. I hid the money inside my journal in the hearth of my little cave-tomb house in the ruined part of the city.

Signore Fiori didn't bring me flowers that day. He stood in my doorway, empty-handed, wept as he told me. "They have smashed the wall." But he wasn't thinking of the wall. He said, "The British captured me. I worked on a potato farm for five long years. It is why I speak the English. All because I fought on the side of the damned Germans." He wiped his eyes. "Germany is back. Germany!"

I offered him Earl Grey tea without thinking. He sat on the floral sofa bed, sipping slowly as I scrubbed the tile walls of the bathroom.

"All that," he said. "And nothing."

"Well, they're happy, aren't they?" I offered. "On TV they're dancing in the streets."

"Happy!" Signore Fiori laughed. "And *I* am happy. Italy has been on the wrong side of every war in history and I am happy. I will die in this village full of lunatics—I am here with them because of potatoes, and they are lighting new fires in the streets of Berlin." His hands shook so much, the milky tea spilled on the couch.

I wondered if Signore Fiori had killed anyone, but I didn't ask. I told him to wait for me while I went out to buy more cleaner.

As I turned, I thought I heard him whisper, "Couldn't *something* have outlived me?"

Outside, I climbed Via Roma. The stone road seemed to get steeper every week. By the time I got to Donatella's shop, I couldn't remember the word for what I wanted. She pressed her hand against my *pancia* as if expecting to feel a kick.

Hush, baby, I said silently, *I will breathe for you now, but one day you will breathe in a world with no walls at all.*

Donatella smiled. "What do you need?"

"Lysol?" I tried. "Disinfectant? *Disinfectanto?*"

She shook her head. Then, "Ah—*disinfettante?*"

As I left the shop, Signore Fiori headed up Via Roma toward the piazza. He didn't look up as he passed me. "*Madonna mia,*" he mumbled.

The door to my converted wine cellar was ajar. I pushed it open. Standing in the middle of the room like a hallucination in her green Patagonia snowsuit: my mother.

"Mom? What are you doing here?"

She smiled, wide and strange. "I wanted to take you shopping for a layette."

I set down my bottle of *disinfettante*. "What's a layette?"

"Things for the baby," she chirped.

I slipped *Like a Prayer* into the boom box and sat down. "How did you find the house?"

She laughed. "I took a very long taxi ride from the airport to the piazza. Then I asked around: *Dov'é l'americana?* The butcher brought me right to your door."

My mother.

Donatella knew of an apartment we could rent by the week—like a bed-and-breakfast without the breakfast. So after she closed her shop that evening, she brought us the keys. From the doorway, we must have been a pretty picture.

Lance was home from work. I kicked him under the table. "Carry my mother's bags," I growled, hardly moving my lips.

My mother smiled a peculiar cocktail-party smile.

Lance paused, then jumped to his feet, confused, picked up the bags.

Donatella shook her head. "*Auguri,*" she said as she left us. Good luck.

I'd never been to the trattoria at the top of Via Roma before, but my mother's wallet was full. She wanted a giant plate of pasta. "We had to sell the netsuke collection for me to come here," she admitted.

I nodded. "You could have sent a layette in the mail. Why are you here?"

"There were cheap tickets advertised in the paper," she smiled, but then her face fell.

Silence.

She cleared her throat. "Ariel, I got a letter from your friend Nikki. She said Lance beat you up."

"Nikki?"

My mother nodded. "I decided to come here to kill him, but they wouldn't let me through airport security with the gun."

I sighed for so many different reasons. "God, Mom. It only happened once."

She set down her menu. "Well, maybe it won't happen

again. But that would be unusual. And maybe he won't hit the baby." She unzipped her green LeSportsac bag, reached inside and produced a small packet of papers. She unfolded them, spread them out across the table. "This," she said, pointing to a circular diagram, "is the cycle of violence." She traced the line with a manicured index finger. "There's a tension-building phase: criticism, yelling, angry gestures, threats. Then come the physical attacks. These are followed by a seduction or honeymoon phase: apologies, blaming, promises to change, gifts. It's very difficult to end a violent relationship. Love, hope and fear all conspire to keep the cycle in motion. Somewhere, maybe, you love him. Somewhere, you hope he'll change. And maybe you're afraid of what he'll do if you end it. If you say you're going to leave, often the batterer will threaten to kill you—or himself."

I clenched my teeth, swallowed hard. "Where'd you get all this?"

"From Roberta. She's working at a battered women's shelter now." My mother fixed her night-dark eyes on me. "Ariel, this situation you're in is just *medieval*."

I held her gaze. "I'm starving," I said. "Can we order?"

Love, hope, and fear. I guess my mother didn't know about the fourth conspirator. My love had been fading for a long time, and my hope and fear paled in comparison now to my pride. I mean, how embarrassing. After all these months on the road—months stacked like boxcars on a steep and winding track—my mother was just going to show up and save me? My face had flushed when she said it: "Why don't you just come home, Ariel? You could have the baby at Kaiser."

Like surrender.

My mother in her green Patagonia snowsuit.

I clenched my teeth when I thought of her words now, kneeling at my hearth-altar in the ruined part of the city.

Journal entry #433
42°41′N 11°43′E
Winter, 1989

> *what i wouldn't have given*
> *to have shown her a nursery,*
> *to have been able to say "i already have a layette"*
> *to have introduced lance to her with nervous expectation,*
> *like her new son*
> *i wouldn't have had to kick him under the table*
> *he would have jumped up, offered to carry her fucking bags*
> *i could have laughed and said,*
> *"nikki wrote you? nikki's a liar"*
>
> *what i wouldn't give*
> *to be able to pack my things now*
> *say, "thanks for coming" and "let's go home"*
>
> *my mother has come to save me*
> *my mother has come to save me,*
> *but what she doesn't know*
> *is that i can save myself*
> *i can save myself*
> *can save myself*
> *save myself*
> *myself*

I counted the lire hidden in my journal pages. Nearly half a million now. I held my hand against my belly, whispered, "It'll be OK."

My mother must have had a word with Lance, too, because when I snuggled into our fold-out bed that night, he set down the bottle of wine he was drinking from, said, "Ariel, I think I'm an alcoholic. Admitting that I have a problem is the first step toward recovery. I'm not going to drink anymore. Starting tomorrow."

In the morning he poured the last of the wine down the shower drain.

I said, "My mom wants to take me to Rome. Shopping. Do you still have my passport?"

His laughter might have pissed me off if it didn't make the hair on my neck stand on end. He said, "You're not even going to give me a chance to quit drinking? You're just running home to California with mummy?"

I said, "We're just going to Rome, Lance. I need to carry my passport for identification."

He didn't answer me, didn't make a move toward any secret hiding place. I wondered if he still had it.

On the bus, my mother and I spoke in hushed tones: *Wasn't it cold this time of year?* Yes. *Wasn't the thin-crusted pizza divine?* Yes. *When was the baby due, again? February?* Yes. *Had I been reading about natural childbirth?* Yes. *Had there been any complications with the pregnancy?* No.

In Porta Portese market, we bought mittens and booties, tiny cotton T-shirts and hand-knit hats, cloth diapers and terry-cloth long johns, blankets and bottles, a breast pump and bras, a green and white striped front-pack baby carrier.

We stayed in a blue-carpeted hotel near Campo dei Fiori, ate tortellini with broth at an outside café.

My mother said, "Do I look Italian?"

And I said, "Sure, a lot more Italian than most of these people."

I tried to imagine what our lives would be like now if her grandfather had never left Corleto for the Tex-Mex border. Maybe I'd still be living like an old Italian woman in the South who has no possibilities.

My mother wanted to go see the Pope's Mass, so we crowded into the chapel with all the Catholics and the tourists. I stared up at the golden ceiling while the old man blessed us in Latin. And *Ave Maria Ave Maria Ave Maria*.

She wanted to see the Christian Catacombs, so we toured underground labyrinthian corridors of skulls stacked into pyramids.

At Leonardo da Vinci Airport, I clutched the white plastic shopping bags filled with my new layette. My mother set down her carry-on LeSportsac luggage and counted out two hundred dollars U.S. for me. "If this is where you want to be, there's nothing I can do about it. But you can come home anytime you want. Do you know that?"

I pocketed the money, inhaled quickly. *Did I know that?* I said: "Thanks for everything, Mom." And I gave her a quick hug.

Lance was waiting for me at the bus stop in the piazza. He jumped to his feet when he saw me, tears streamed down his face. "I reckoned you'd left me," he sobbed. And then, composing himself, "Let's go to the bar. I haven't had a drink in three days."

Stateless

aternity meant nothing to the ancients. They attributed conception to inadvertently swallowing insects, to eating beans or to the wind.

In the beginning, there was darkness. From darkness sprang chaos. From chaos rose the wide wandering goddess of all things. She separated the ocean from the sky, danced alone among the salty waves. As she danced, her movement stirred a wind, and when she caught it—*behold*! She was pregnant.

I'd been feeling strange all day, like I was just coming on to a drug trip. The volcanic rock around me seemed to breathe and bubble. My skin tingled under the Chinese army pants I had to fasten with a cord now.

As I headed up Via Roma, Donatella rushed out from her shop, grabbed my sleeve. "Do you want to have that baby in the piazza?"

I laughed. "It's not time yet."

My due date was only a day away, but somehow it didn't feel like a reality yet. I could feel the baby's heartbeat in my belly, could feel her kicks like she was wearing Doc Martens. But I wanted to keep her safe inside. I was scared. Quick prayer to the maternal void: *Sweet Mary, mother of God, please tell me you wouldn't have let me get knocked up if you weren't planning to help me through the birth.*

Donatella pulled me into her shop. From the shelf behind the cash register, she offered me two silver and coral charms. "One for you, one for the baby," she said. "To keep you from the evil eye."

At home, I sautéed mushrooms with peppers, boiled myself a cup of raspberry tea. A tightening pressure, dull weight in my belly. I couldn't decide if it was hunger or saturation. Would eating make it better or worse?

Signore Fiori stopped by with flowers and a bassinet. "For your baby," he said. He studied the posters on my walls. "Are you a Catholic?"

"Sure," I said. "God is food. And I'm not finicky."

He thought about that. "But the Catholics say you are living in sin. The people here, they call you 'whore' behind your back."

I shrugged. "And the Buddhists say my desires cause me suffering. I can still pray to all the faces of god."

"Don't tell them in the piazza," Signore Fiori sighed, "but I don't believe in a god one shit." And then he headed back up to the bar.

"I feel funny," I told Lance when he got home.

"Are you going to have the baby tonight?" He smelled of turpentine. I didn't think I could stand to be near him, near the smell.

"No. Not tonight."

"Good, because there's a party up at the Orsini Castle. You want to come?"

I shook my head, poured two glasses of wine, piled spaghetti onto blue plates. I'd shoved the table back up against the wall to make room for the wicker bassinet. We ate on the sofa bed I hadn't bothered to fold up.

"God," Lance said, knocking back his wine. "You used to like parties. You're bloody boring now."

I apologized, ate my pasta and mushrooms. Vinegar resentment.

"You're feeling all right, then?"

The unnerving thing about Lance was that he could say something totally fucked up like that, like "You're bloody boring now," or call me a cow, kick me in the ribs, and a moment later it was as if nothing had happened. "You're feeling all right, then?" he'd ask. As if he cared.

"I'm feeling great," I snapped.

"Good, then." He threw on his biker jacket and headed out into the night.

I washed the dishes, muttered to myself over the sink: "You're feeling all right, then? You're feeling all right, then? Oh, yeah, I'm feeling great. Never been better. Fuck you. You're feeling all right, then?"

I sat down on the floor, painted my fingernails red. I wanted to paint my toenails, too, but I couldn't reach them. I missed Nikki, could have killed her for writing to my mother. I thought of Djuna, and Peggy Day. I wished I had a Dylan tape, settled for Zucchero. "Overdose d'Amore." I'd been trying not to smoke, but I suddenly had to have a cigarette, a fierce craving from the back of my lungs. I found a good-sized butt in Lance's ashtray, lit it.

Outside, my sweatshirt and leather jacket were no match for the cold. The wintry air stung my cheeks and belly as I climbed down the stone stairs to the ruined part of the city, down the dirt path, dark now, and into my three-walled ruin. I lit four candles in the hearth. The flames sputtered, but there was enough light to count my lire. I rolled them up and put them in my pocket.

JOURNAL ENTRY #467
42°41′N 11°43′E
WINTER, 1990

everything seems surreal
the walls and the roads don't feel dense enough
like i could put my hand through the volcanic stone
my body doesn't feel dense enough
i want to hold the baby inside
i'm not ready
but the moon is almost full

I closed the book, breathed in the icy air. The moon hung bright over the hills. I thought of the vagabond girl, dead in her ditch. I'd outlived her. Dull pain in my belly. I slipped my hands under my sweatshirt and felt it tighten. I inhaled.

One.

Two.

Three.

On my way back up to Via Roma, I spotted tiny Giovanna with her mop of black hair, sitting silently in another ruined house on the hillside. I stared at her for a long time, not sure if she was real. "Listen," I finally said. "I don't think I can work tomorrow."

And she nodded. "It's all right."

At home, I lay down on top of the blankets, counted my breaths. My whole belly tightened, then relaxed. I felt slightly nauseous, closed my eyes. "Just let me sleep this one last night," I begged no one in particular.

It was nearly midnight when Lance crawled into bed next to me. "Are you all right?"

"I don't know," I admitted. "Maybe you should go and get Norma."

Sitting in the passenger's seat of the little silver hatchback, the winding-road journey to Acquapendente felt interminable.

Each turn of the road brought on a contraction. *Or was it a contraction?* My belly tightened. A dull cramp. I wanted to throw up, go back to bed. When the wave passed, I wondered if this was it, for real. I'd feel like such an idiot, dragging Norma out in the middle of the night for nothing. "Will you hate me if this is a false alarm?"

But Norma just laughed.

From the back seat, Lance kept putting his hand on my shoulder.

"Don't touch me," I seethed. Another wave.

In the birthing room, I could smell grappa on Lance's breath, cigarette smoke on Norma's sweats. I wanted to be alone, shooed them away.

Lance retreated to the waiting room.

Norma said she'd come back in the morning. "I have told all the nurses you want natural birth, do not let them drug you."

I paced between the two single beds. I didn't crave drugs. I wished I hadn't eaten. A bleach-blond nurse hurried in to mop the floor with the strongest *disinfettante* I'd ever smelled. I cursed at her in English. "Shit head—"

She called me a Gypsy.

I wanted to go back to sleep, but every time I closed my eyes, a wave of dull pain pressed up and down simultaneously. I watched the clock. The hands didn't move. Instead, the face of the clock grew bigger until all the numbers were blurred and unreadable. I was underwater, breathing somehow magically through the blue.

From the next room, I could hear the unrhythmic beeping sound of a fetal monitor. The muffled weeping of another woman in labor. Medical staff rushed in and out of her room, but they left me alone.

I'd read that after childbirth, some kind of amnesia caused mothers to forget the pain, so I jotted a note to myself in my journal: *Never do this again.*

I wanted to climb out the window, escape into the medieval night.

I was crawling across the cold floor when I heard Lance's voice: "Jesus, Ariel, are you all right?"

Are you all right? I said, "Get the fuck away from me," then rested my forehead on the floor. I took a deep breath, tried to hold it in. I didn't want to give the pain anything to feed off of. I wished I'd stayed in my ruined half-house. I could have had the baby by myself. Lance held my arm as I stood up. "Go away," I managed before I felt the gush of water between my legs. I thought I was peeing, turned to cross the hallway into the bathroom. Just then, a nurse I hadn't seen before rushed in, shrieked something, shoved me into a wheelchair. "Can I go home now?"

I was tied to a metal delivery table with cold stirrups and a leather belt when someone finally placed the little space alien, still glistening with the ocean waters of the womb, on my chest. Her little fingernails, semitransparent. She suckled at my tit, didn't cry until the bleach-blond nurse grabbed her from me and slapped her hard across the butt. *Welcome to the world. Suckle your endless desires, but watch out for the assholes.*

We stayed in the hospital for over a week, me exaggerating the pain from a bad episiotomy because I didn't want to go home, didn't want to cook, didn't want to clean.

Lance visited every day, brought yogurt and new baby clothes, told me Gitana had run away. Sometimes Norma gave him a ride, other times he hitchhiked the thirty miles.

On the eighth morning, the blond nurse told me we couldn't stay much longer. There was nothing wrong with me.

When she leaned over the little metal crib, I heard her whisper, *"Povera zingarella."* Poor little Gypsy baby.

I said, "Her name is Maia."

From the waiting room pay phone, I called the American Consulate in Rome. I'd lost my passport, I told the woman on the other end. And now I needed two.

"Replacing yours will be a cinch," she chirped. "But are you sure the baby is eligible?"

"What do you mean?"

"Eligible. For citizenship. Are both parents American?"

"I'm American," I said.

"How long did you live in the States?"

"Until I was sixteen."

"Continuously?"

"Um."

"Did you ever leave the U.S. before you were sixteen?"

"Yes."

She sighed into the phone. "Ma'am, you'll have to fill out an application to establish the baby's citizenship. You'll have to document that you spent at least fifteen years of your life in the United States. Citizenship is not automatically granted to every offspring of an American."

She said it like I was asking this huge favor. It had never crossed my mind, the possibility my baby wouldn't get an American passport. "But I'm only nineteen," I tried, as if she'd care.

"Ma'am, if you can't document fifteen years—"

I hung up the phone, bummed a cigarette from a nervous father.

Norma had already done the Italian research: If neither parent was a citizen, birth alone wouldn't make a baby Italian.

And since Lance and I weren't married, the baby's chances of becoming a Brit were next to none.

On a scrap of paper, I added up the years of my life:

U.S.	**ABROAD**
1/2 year in California	*2 years in Europe*
12 years in California	*1/4 year in Africa*
3/4 year in California	*1/4 year in Europe*
1/4 year in California	*1 1/2 years in Asia*
	1 1/2 year in Europe
13 1/2 years	5 1/2 years

I closed my eyes. *Holy shit.* And now we were going to be trapped in Italy for all time, unable to cross a single border. Me and my passportless baby in our uninhabitable town.

She slept soundly as I packed our things, then lifted her from her little metal crib and zipped her into the green and white striped front-pack carrier. We headed out of the hospital into the clear winter day.

I guess it was because I had a newborn, but the first man who stopped for me at the side of the road in Acquapendente drove me all the way to the American Consulate in Rome, cursing traffic all the way.

Silent in the passenger's seat, I tried to come up with a game plan. I could lie about how many years I'd spent in the States. But maybe they'd know. How closely did the American government track its citizens? And if I got caught lying? Then what? No. I'd just have to plead my case. I needed a new passport. I needed two. I must have dozed off in the traffic jam outside the city, because all at once Italy dissolved around me. I was in a barren land. A single mountain of quartz monzonite rose up out of the nothingness. I was Sisyphus, pushing my boulder of tumbled granite—up, up, up.

"What's in the bag?" the armed guard outside the consulate wanted to know.

I peeled back the cotton cloth, showed him my sleeping girl. He laughed, waved us through the metal detector.

Behind bulletproof glass, a bird-eyed official shuffled papers. She didn't look at me when I spoke, just shoved a few forms under the glass. I filled them out, brought them back to the window.

She glanced through them, lowered her glasses onto her nose, peered out at me. "We can replace your passport, ma'am," she said in a nasally voice. "But the baby isn't an American unless you can document fourteen years of residence."

Fourteen years? I thought to tell her that they'd said fifteen on the phone, like maybe it was flexible. But I didn't want to push my luck. I was only six months short of fourteen. "Um. Maybe I should recount those months?"

"The baby isn't an American," she said again.

Tears welled up in my eyes. "But she isn't anything else, either."

The bird-woman frowned. "Just get her an Italian passport, ma'am. She isn't a boy. She won't have to do military service."

Tears streamed down my face now. "But you have to have at least one parent from here to be Italian," I sobbed.

"Where's the father from?"

I swallowed hard. "She doesn't have a father."

The bird-woman raised both eyebrows now. She gathered up my paperwork. "Just a moment, ma'am."

I wanted her to stop calling me "ma'am."

When she returned, I thought I detected a hint of compassion behind her bird-eyes. "Please enter the white door," she said, pointing.

In the fluorescent-lit room, I sat on a metal chair. A white table separated me from the bird-woman.

"Now," she said, pulling off her glasses and letting them dangle from the gray cord around her neck. "Are you saying that if the child is not granted American citizenship, she will be stateless?"

"Stateless." I'd never heard the word before, didn't like the sound of it. "Yes. She'll be stateless."

The baby readjusted her position in my front-pack, but didn't wake.

"Do you consider yourself an American, ma'am?"

Did I consider myself an American? I bit my lip. Too quiet, maybe. But what else was I? I never thought I'd have to *consider* myself an American. *What was it Martine used to say? We're all citizens of this earth.*

The bird-woman cleared her throat. "Do you consider yourself an American, ma'am? Do you hold any other passports?"

"No. I mean—yes. I'm an American. I don't have any other passports."

"And do you consider the United States to be your primary place of residence?" She leaned forward across the table.

"Yes," I nodded.

"And in applying for these passports, I take it you intend to return to the United States to raise your child as an American?"

I didn't know what that meant, *to raise your child as an American.* I pictured my girl-child as she grew up monolingual, reciting the pledge of allegiance in a stark city schoolroom. "Uh huh."

"But you are a resident of Italy?" She pointed to the Via Roma address on my application.

"No—I'm American—I mean, I'm just, well, I'm just *here.*"

"Either you are residing in Italy or you're on vacation, ma'am." The bird-woman was getting annoyed.

"Oh. Vacation," I said. But it sounded like a lie.

From the other side of the white table, the bird-woman looked me up and down. "Miss Gore," she said. "Do you have the means to return to the United States?"

In the pocket of my Chinese army pants, I fingered my coil of ten-thousand lire notes. "Yes I do."

She tapped the table. "Well," she said, then picked up her black pen and wrote "Otherwise stateless" across the top of the application form. "All right. You'll have your passports in a few weeks—unless you need them expedited."

I shook my head. "A few weeks will be perfect."

And then the bird-woman smiled for the first time. "Sorry about all of this. We don't get many teenagers giving birth to American citizens while they're on vacation here."

I laughed uneasily. But once she'd stamped the forms, I knew the bird-woman couldn't take it back. My baby had a passport. Even if we didn't go home just yet, she had a passport. I don't know why I started crying just then.

Italo Calvino in unassigned reading (Marco Polo to Kublai Khan on the inferno where we live every day): *There are two ways to escape suffering from it. The first is easy for many: accept the inferno and become such a part of it that you can no longer see it. The second is risky and demands constant vigilance and apprehension: seek and learn to recognize who and what, in the midst of the inferno, are not inferno, then make them endure, give them space.*

Another through-ride all the way back to our uninhabitable town under a sky the color of watered milk. Our grandfatherly driver was not inferno. His eyes filled with tears when he looked at the baby. I offered to buy him a glass of wine in the piazza, but he just waved his callused hand. *"Auguri,"* he said. Congratulations. And he buzzed off in his battered Fiat.

I'd hardly had a chance to wave goodbye when Norma lunged toward us from her table outside the bar. She wore all black, had a fresh black eye.

I said, "What the fuck happened to you?"

She grabbed my shoulder. "Forget me. Where have *you* been? The hospital called my house when you disappeared—Lance has been calling me all day about driving him out there. I thought you had taken off for good."

"He doesn't know we were gone?"

She shook her head, lit a cigarette.

"Thanks, Norma. But what happened to you?"

She waved her hand dismissively. "My husband thinks I am running around."

I reached out to touch the side of her face, but she pulled back.

The baby started to fuss, so Norma took her from me, cooed, *"Bellissima."* Then she said: "Lance is meeting me here in one quarter of an hour. I was not going to be able to put him off any longer—"

"I'm sorry—"

Just then Signore Fiori shouted from his table. *"La bimba!"*

And a great cheer came up from the cluster of old men.

The berry-mouthed barmaid skipped towards us, grinning.

The butcher rushed out from her shop, still wearing her bloody apron.

Donatella stood by, hands on her hips.

"La bambina!"

"Che bella!"

"Bellissima!"

I wondered why no one looked twice at Norma. Maybe darkly bruised women were just another thing to get used to.

I sat down at a round red table, started to cry.

The leathersmith wandered out from his shop, approached us shyly. He placed a hand on my shoulder, smiled down at the baby as she was being passed around the table. "The first three months are the much difficult," he whispered. "If you survive this time, you survive anything."

Norma ordered a round of dark beer. "It will help your milk come in," she promised.

When the drinks appeared, so did Lance—proud and surprised in his trashed biker jacket. He pulled up a chair, put his arm around me. "Shit, honey, you didn't hitchhike back here with the baby, did you? I've been trying to get Norma here to take me all day," he complained. But when he glanced up at her, his face flushed. "What the fuck? Did that bastard hit you? I'll fucking smash his face in—"

Norma shook her head, glanced down. "I fell out of an olive tree."

Lance nodded. "You have to be careful climbing trees." He ordered a grappa to go with his beer.

That night, I nursed the baby to sleep, set her in her bassinet. I rinsed cloth diapers in the bathroom sink, then set them to boil on the camping stove.

"Any sign of Gitana?"

Lance shook his head, offered me a Guinness.

I gripped the glass bottle, said, "I want to go home."

He took a step back, sat down on the floral sofa bed, whispered, "This is our home."

I felt like crying, but I didn't have any tears left. I looked up at the world map on the wall behind the couch, traced the path from the Bay Area, across the Pacific and through Asia, across Russia and down the European subcontinent, back over the Atlantic and the United States to the far western coast. California. "No. I want to go back *home*. Me and the baby."

Silence.

My beer tasted like dread.

Lanced laughed, shook his head. "Can't imagine you'll get very far without your passport." He cleared his throat and his expression changed to something like sad. He looked down at his boots, then up at me. "I love you, Ariel," he said irrele-vantly, then dropped his cigarette onto the floor and crushed it with his boot. A tightening in the jaw. His cheeks reddened. I thought he would cry, but he suddenly leapt from the couch.

I jumped back to shield the bassinet with my body, but mercifully, he dove for the door, not the baby.

He hurled himself out onto Via Roma, then turned around to face me in the doorway. "If you fucking leave me, I'll kill myself." He turned again, away this time, stumbled-ran into the dark.

The strange sound of leather against stone—I could hear his body tumble down the tunnel of stairs that led to the ruined part of the city. Footfalls on dirt, falling stones, then a great thundering howl, a distant thud. I just stood there in the doorway for a long time, stunned and cold. He'd thrown him-self off the cliff, down into the milky ravine. I closed the door.

Sitting on the pull-out bed, I tossed three pennies, opened my *I Ching*. The yellow cover barely clung to the pages now. I counted the lines to find my fortune: *Return (The Turning Point). It furthers one to have somewhere to go. After a time of decay comes the turning point. The powerful light that has been banished returns. The idea of return is based on the course of nature. The movement is cyclic and the course completes itself.*

It was a good half an hour before Lance crawled back inside, mud-covered and moaning. He passed out on the tile floor. And in the morning, he wanted to know why his body ached so.

Because the World Tips

U nder a pewter sky on the Pagan New Year, I wrapped Maia in cotton sweaters and headed up Via Roma, under the stone archway, across the piazza to the little post office.

Waiting for me behind the counter: two midnight blue American passports in a manila envelope and a translucent airmail letter from my bio-dad. I flipped through the empty pages of our crisp new passports. No visas. No histories. I whispered 'Thank you' to whatever gods still had our backs. I opened the letter:

Dear Ariel,

Having a baby is a monstrous project requiring millions of dollars. However, working together with the limited facilities we have we can only do what we can do with what we have to work with. I myself plan to expand my computer infinitely in all directions, but I need more hardware and more soft-ware and above all more knowledge to know what to do and how to do it when I have the money.

IT's spring in Japan. Spring in China.

Spring in Paris and London and at home in Rome, but when it's winter in the north, it's summer in the south, so when it's spring in the north, it's fall in the south, and when it's summer in the north, it's winter in the south.

IT's because the world tips.

> *By spring we don't mean hopping and skipping and*
> *bouncing across the grass such as springing and bouncing*
> *around town with the sound of a clown.*

> *IT's spring at the small community college*
> *where Polly and Molly and Dolly are gathering*
> *knowledge,*
> > *warbling in their books,*
> *mulling through the lull in their dull*
> > *studies in the library*
> > > *while outside the flowers are blooming*
> > > > *springs the delicious*
> > > > > *x-plodding*
> > > > > > *vixen!*
> *blowing the top off the one sun in the sky*
> *and knocking a hole in the spring equinox—*
> > > > > > *Love, Dad*

It's amazing, when you think about it, that so few people go mad.

Back in our converted wine cellar, I slipped a Joan Arma-
trading tape into the boom box, packed up the baby's blankets, bottles and booties, packed up my *I Ching*.

Norma appeared in the doorway, cried smiling. She said, "I
have news." She placed both hands on her round little beer
gut. "I am going to have a baby."

I hugged her, whispered, "Why don't you leave him,
Norma? Just leave."

But she didn't answer me.

"You could come to California with us," I offered.

But she shook her head. "Will you go to university?"

"I will," I promised.

From the pay phone in the piazza, next to a fountain without any water in it, I called my mother to tell her we'd be coming home for the summer.

She said, "All your old stuffed animals are waiting for our granddaughter." And then sighed into the phone. "Honestly, Ariel, if I had it all to do over, I'd do everything differently."

In the familiar rattle and hum of the airplane lifting off the runway, I nursed the baby. Up, up, up. We both fell asleep.

Somewhere over France, I dreamed of the vagabond girl in her ditch. The dream-camera panned over her, zoomed in. Her pale pale face. Her unwashed curls. Deep wine-red stains on her clothes. Then I noticed her chest: a slow rise and fall. She was breathing. I placed my hand over her heart. A cold but rhythmic beat. I took her hand, felt a pulse. I said, *Are you a ghost?* And her cracked lips parted. *No*, she whispered. *I'm just tired.*

I woke up, the flight attendant's face too close to mine: "Chicken or beef?"

"Chicken."

A pretty woman with a thousand braids smiled from the seat next to us. "Your baby's so good," she said. "When I had my son, I just couldn't believe it. The way I could love someone so much."

And it was true. All the immense landscapes and chanced-upon streets in me led to this tiny someone. She didn't look like a space alien anymore. Fat and beautiful, she gurgled something like a smile, held my whole heart.

A girl with bleached and pink hair sat in the aisle seat drawing labyrinths in a leather journal.

"Where are you going?" the woman with a thousand braids wanted to know.

The girl smiled, shy-excited. "Everywhere!"

I closed my eyes, tried to count my breaths, tried to count

back through the boxcars of months, all the lost and eager faces, mindlessly enthusiastic, passionately sad. There is geography. And there is circumstance. And then there we all were. Changing. And roughly the same. I imagined Guy organizing a protest in Washington, D.C., Jack lip-syncing to Madonna in a New York City club, Vincent getting his degree from the university in Shanghai, Kuan eternally rushing back to the square, Martine holed up in a cave somewhere on the Tibetan Plateau, Krishna fast-talking some whitey as mystic shards of sunlight battle a monsoon, Violette screening her tacky little movie at an independent film festival in Milan, Djuna blaring "Tangled Up in Blue" from a council flat in London, Nikki camping on a moonlit beach, Norma throwing up in her terra-cotta-tiled bathroom, Signore Fiori crying in the bar. And Lance. I'd left him in our converted wine cellar, but he'd pledged to follow me, saying, "Don't think you'll be rid of me just like that. You can run, but I'll find you. When we first met, you said you wouldn't remember me. I think you'll remember me now."

Dread-tinged hope for a whole new life.

No fixed plans, but I imagined we'd stay with my parents in their narrow Spanish house for the summer. I'd nurse Maia under the Australian tea tree, eat bitter herbs to keep my heart flow contained. We'd head out of the city then, find a little house with white walls and huge picture windows. I'd go to university. Four years. Time enough for me to get a degree, time enough for Maia's legs to grow strong for the road. All the poems of our lives not yet made.

The alchemists understood: the within is as without, and without as within. The heart is a globe, based on the curve of the diaphragm, its axis inclined at a twenty-three degree angle like the axis of the earth against the path of the sun. The world tips. But the heart tips, too. Twenty-three-degrees. The below is as the above, and the above as below.

Quarter moon rising over eastern hills, I watched out the window as we circled the bay and the Golden Gate. The plane flew so low over the Pacific, I could almost taste the salty blue, the ropes of seaweed, the spindrift foam.

Maia whimpered through immigration. Maybe she already knew that borders were bullshit.

A sleepy-eyed official stamped our new passports red.

Then a SamTrans bus from the airport. Red tracks of cars through tunnels. The freeway lined with yellow glowing McDonalds arches and dull neon hotel signs.

As darkness fell, we stepped onto a commuter train. The percussion heartbeat of iron wheels on iron tracks lulled the baby back to sleep as we barreled south through Redwood City, Menlo Park, up over the San Francisquito Creek bridge— *ch clack ch clack ch clack*. I glanced toward the window, but no familiar scenery spun past—just the mirror-clear image of my own face, Maia in my arms. I wanted to stay there, just like that forever. But moments don't last, do they? Time divides itself into seconds.

Onward.

Bonus Track

Maybe it's time for the happy ending now, because we've all seen an American movie. Me and my girl-child riding into the sunset. I went to university. I became, am becoming, quickening away and toward. Four years, and then some. Maia's legs grew strong for the road.

Or maybe it's time to emphasize the price now, because pity is power and we all know how to process. Me and my girl-child waiting in line for our food stamps. I got a restraining order. I ran, am running, my underground city still full and rich. Twelve years, and then some. There are still things I am afraid of.

Which do you want? Both stories are true enough, and common as pennies.

"Are we there yet?" my girl-child asks on the plane, on the train, in the car.

"What town are we in?" I used to ask my stepdad as we drove out of the city, across the state, up into the Sierras.

"We are in no town," he'd say.

And that seemed so strange to me, the way we could be in no town.

I want to take a night train to a city at the edge of a jungle, hike trails I am too tired to hike. I want to be everywhere at once, show my girl-child everything before all the places become one place, before all the tastes are one taste. And how is it that downtown Bangkok looks more and more like Los Angeles to me?

Acknowledgments

An Oregon Literary Arts residency teaching creative writing at Benson High School in Portland got me flashing back to my own teen years. So, in the spring of 2001, I signed up for a memoir workshop at the Attic and started working on the first dozen chapters. Good thing Attic-master David Biespiel liked what he read, because taking his class was also my passive-aggressive way of asking for a job. I took over teaching the memoir workshop and kept hammering away at what would become *Atlas of the Human Heart*. Other writers at the Attic—Lani Jo Leigh, Kathleen Hildenbrand, K. P. Raphael and Emily Whitman—read early chapters and offered most excellent advice.

Meanwhile, Maria Fabulosa moved in, bringing with her the annoying habit of asking, nightly, "Honey, did you finish your novel yet?" This grated on my nerves so much that I locked myself in my room with thirty-three bottles of $4.29 Barefoot Merlot and typed madly until I had 300 pages of the "novel."

Maria subsequently read and edited every draft.

My sister Leslie read it and offered, "Why don't you just admit that it's true?"

Novel or memoir?

With Bee Lavender and the Dolly Ranchers, I performed an excerpt from the work-in-progress at the Nye Beach Writers' Series. Folks seemed entertained, so I stuck with the project. By the summer of 2002, I was nearly finished, so I sent it to Leslie Miller, my editor at Seal Press. While I waited to hear back, Maria taped together a '69 VW bus she'd won in a bet over whether or not Debra Winger was the voice for E.T. and we headed down to the Bay Area. With my mom in the audience and my daughter off surfing, I read another excerpt at Ladyfest San Francisco. Mom didn't seem too annoyed, called it an "art piece."

It was time to enlist fisherwoman Moe Bowstern of *Xtra Tuf* zine and the mighty Inga Muscio. They read the manuscript, promised me it didn't suck and helped me fine-tune. Maria Fabulosa helped me out with the Spanish bits. My sister helped with the Italian.

Then Leslie Miller said yes! She set to work editing.

While I sat at the computer fixing linguistic problems and shuffling scenes, Maria Fabulosa drew all the maps and illustrations.

Jennie Goode proofread and fact-checked in mind-boggling detail.

How can you tell when a book is done? my students sometimes ask me.

It's done the day before your deadline when the FedEx guy shows up and pries the manuscript from your hands.

If it's January 7, 2003, it must be done. Thanks for reading.

ARIEL GORE is Maia's mom, editor-publisher of the award-winning parenting zine, *Hip Mama*, author of *The Mother Trip* and *The Hip Mama Survival Guide*, and co-editor of the anthology, *Breeder: Real-Life Stories from the New Generation of Mothers*. Raised in northern California by a small guerrilla army of hippies, artists, and rebel Catholics, she spent the years she was supposed to be in high school as an international bag lady traveling through Asia and Europe. Following her misspent youth, she earned degrees from Mills College and the University of California at Berkeley. She lives with her family in Portland, Oregon.

Selected Titles from Seal Press

The Mother Trip: Hip Mama's Guide to Staying Sane in the Chaos of Motherhood by Ariel Gore. $14.95, 1-58005-029-8. In a book that is part self-help, part critique of the mommy myth, and part hip-mama handbook, Ariel Gore offers support to mothers who break the mold.

Breeder: Real-Life Stories from the New Generation of Mothers edited by Ariel Gore and Bee Lavender, foreword by Dan Savage. $16.00, 1-58005-051-4. From the editors of Hip Mama, this hilarious and heartrending compilation creates a space where Gen-X moms can dish, cry, scream, and laugh.

Chelsea Whistle by Michelle Tea. $14.95, 1-58005-073-5. In this gritty, confessional memoir, Michelle Tea takes the reader back to the city of her childhood: Chelsea, Massachusetts—Boston's ugly, scrappy little sister and a place where time and hope are spent on things not getting any worse.

Valencia by Michelle Tea. $13.00, 1-58005-035-2. The fast-paced account of one girl's search for love and high times in the dyke world of San Francisco.

The Boxer's Heart: Lessons from the Ring by Kate Sekules. $14.95, 1-58005-077-8. A brilliantly candid memoir and first-ever guide to the world of women's boxing.

East Toward Dawn: A Woman's Solo Journey Around the World by Nan Watkins. $14.95, 1-58005-064-6. After the loss of her son and the end of a marriage, the author sets out in search of joy and renewal in travel.

The Big Rumpus: A Mother's Tale from the Trenches by Ayun Halliday. $15.95, 1-58005-071-9. Halliday celebrates the stranger-than-fiction, real-life existence of one American family.

Give Me the World by Leila Hadley. $14.95, 1-58005-091-3. One young woman's account of her world travels aboard a schooner with her six-year-old son, Kippy.

Dream of a Thousand Lives by Karen Connelly. $14.95, 1-58005-062-X. The award-winning account of a young woman immersed in the heart of Thailand.

Seal Press publishes many books of fiction and nonfiction by women writers. Please visit our Web site at www.sealpress.com.

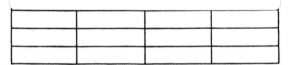